Lindley Murray, Sarah Grubb

Some Account of the Life and Religious Labours of Sarah Grubb

Lindley Murray, Sarah Grubb

Some Account of the Life and Religious Labours of Sarah Grubb

ISBN/EAN: 9783337225803

Printed in Europe, USA, Canada, Australia, Japan

Cover: Foto ©Lupo / pixelio.de

More available books at **www.hansebooks.com**

SOME

ACCOUNT

OF THE

LIFE

AND

RELIGIOUS LABOURS

OF

SARAH GRUBB.

WITH AN

APPENDIX,

CONTAINING AN ACCOUNT OF THE

SCHOOLS AT ACKWORTH AND YORK,

Obfervations on CHRISTIAN DISCIPLINE, and EXTRACTS from many of her

LETTERS.

JOHN vi. 12.
——Gather up the Fragments that remain, that Nothing be loft.

TRENTON:
PRINTED BY ISAAC COLLINS.
M.DCC.XCV.

CHAP. I.

Her Education.—Divine Visitations.—Conflict arising from her natural Vivacity, &c.—Solid State of her Mind in the early Part of Life.—Exercises about the Time of her first Appearance in the Ministry.— Visit to Part of the Counties of Westmoreland and Cumberland.—Visit to the Meetings of Cheshire and a Part of those in Lancashire, &c.

CHAP. II.

Her Marriage—and Journey into Scotland, Cumberland, &c.

CHAP. III.

Visit to her Husband's Relations in Ireland.—Journey into Norfolk, &c.—Visit to the Meetings of Friends in Ireland.

CHAP. IV.

Visit to some of the Western Counties of England.

CHAP. V.

Family Visit at Sheffield.—Illness there.—Consideration of removing into Ireland.—Journey into Lincolnshire.—Removal to Ireland.—Journey into Holland, Germany, and France.

CHAP. VI.

Her Concern respecting a Boarding School for Female Youth.—Visit to Friends Families in Cork.—Journey to London.—Visit to Dunkirk, Holland, Pyrmont, &c.—Her Return—and Decease.—Testimonies concerning her.

INTRODUCTION.

AS few lives have exhibited a more pure example of piety and virtue, than that which is set forth in the enſuing pages, it has been thought right to bring it forward to general notice; under a hope, that an account of this humble, ſelf-denying, and dedicated ſervant, will prove the means of inſtructing others; and of ſtrengthening their faith in the efficacy of that Divine Principle, "which wrought all her works in her."

It will be proper to inform the reader, that the materials from which this work is compoſed, conſiſt of journals written by herſelf of her travels through Scotland, Ireland, and ſome of the weſtern counties in England, and of a conſiderable number of letters to ſome of her intimate friends. From theſe laſt have been extracted ſuch parts, as were deſcriptive of her other labours and travels, or likely to be of publick uſe. A connexion of the different events and circumſtances, has been made throughout, by ſhort narratives or explanations; but great care has been taken to preſerve, as much as could be, her own words and arrangements.

Thoſe extracts of letters which do not appear to have a peculiar connexion with the narrative, and which could not have been regularly introduced there, have been collected together, and are, nearly in the order of time, inſerted in the Appendix.

INTRODUCTION.

The importance of their fubjects, and their inftructive tendency, it is apprehended, will render them an acceptable addition to the other part of the work. Although, from the time of her engagement in the miniftry, fhe was greatly dedicated, and much employed in various religious fervices during the remainder of her days; yet, for want of materials left by herfelf, an account of many of thefe is omitted in the following work; which it feemed proper to confine, almoft throughout, to fuch part of her life and labours as could be collected from her own writings. It may not be improper to obferve alfo, that this mode of compofing a narrative, by extracts from letters, will fometimes be, unavoidably, attended with a want of clofe connexion, and with a degree of repetition: but as this was the only way by which a material part of her labours could be brought into view, it is hoped that thefe circumftances will not be deemed of much confequence; and that the deeply inftructive nature of her literary correfpondence, will fufficiently warrant its publication.

THE

L I F E.

OF

SARAH GRUBB.

CHAP. I.

Her Education.—Divine Visitations.—Conflict arising from her natural Vivacity, &c.—Solid State of her Mind in the early Part of Life.—Exercises about the Time of her first Appearance in the Ministry.—Visit to Part of the Counties of Westmoreland and Cumberland.—Visit to the Meetings of Cheshire, and a Part of those in Lancashire, &c.

SARAH GRUBB, daughter of William and Elizabeth Tuke, was born at York in Great Britain, 20th of 6th month, in the year 1756.

In her tender years she was deprived of her mother, who was removed from her by death, before she was five years old : but her father marrying again about the tenth year of her age, this loss was, from that time, abundantly compensated by the maternal care and regard of a second mother ; of whose tenderness, and solicitude for her best welfare, she has left many grateful and affectionate testimonials.

The watchful and religious education with which she was favoured, proved as a hedge round about her, and, under divine care, preserved her during that dangerous season of life, from the many corruptions and follies, that abound in the world, and to which unguarded young people are sorrowfully exposed. In the days of her youth, she was often made sensible of the goodness of her heavenly Father, and her eyes anointed to see the emptiness and delusion of all worldly enjoyments, and to behold the beauty which there is in the truth ; and strong desires were often raised in her mind, that she might be thoroughly refined, and, even at the loss of every thing else, be made to possess the pearl of great price.

These gracious extensions of divine regard met with great opposition from the liveliness of her disposition, and the strength of her natural powers ; which occasioned the self-denying meekness and simplicity of the christian life, to be to her an hard attainment ; and many painful struggles she experienced, before she was made willing to yield up every sacrifice, and to follow her Lord whithersoever he might be pleased to lead.

During

During the laſt illneſs of that eminent miniſter, John Woolman, ſhe was, at times favoured to wait upon and aſſiſt him. His faith and patience, with the ſweet favour of his pure ſpirit, made a deep and profitable impreſſion on her mind; exemplifying the power and goodneſs of that divine hand, which ſhe felt ſecretly at work in her own heart, calling her to newneſs of life, and holineſs before the Lord. It was to her that this valuable friend, when near the cloſe of life, addreſſed thoſe comfortable expreſſions, which, indeed, may be called a bleſſing: "My child, thou ſeems very kind to me, a poor creature; the Lord will reward thee for it."

A deep ſenſe of the purity of the divine life, and a lively feeling of her own frailties, joined to an earneſt concern that ſhe might become fully purified in heart and life, cauſed great circumſpection and fear, and made her often go mourning on her way. This appears from the following extracts of divers letters to her friends, written in early life, which, in ſome meaſure, ſhew the exerciſe, and ſtate of her mind, at that period; and which may be acceptable, as they ſerve to exhibit the beginnings and gradations of that work, which conſpicuouſly marked the future periods of her life.

1772.——" I feel thy bearing with my weakneſſes, and thy candor in judging of them, which makes me the more ready to communicate what I feel. Oh could I tell thee, it would be comfortable! But that which is felt and not underſtood, cannot be deſcribed; and, indeed, I begin to think a ſtate of inſenſibility to what is good is approaching.

ing. I may truly fay I dread it. May I, by that fear, guard the more; yet my infirmities feem fo juft a caufe, that they are numerous enough to deprefs the little life that is left."

1772.———" Thine has excited in me the warmeft wifhes for the extendings of divine bounty, to be enabled, with refignation and fortitude, to do, bear, or fuffer, whatever it may pleafe the Father of fpirits to inflict upon me. Yet I cannot but, with confcious forrow, own the truth of thy remark, concerning a too great anxiety for a larger portion of the defcendings of the Father's love, than is fuitable in the fight of an omnifcient Deity."

1773.———" I feem recovering from my late illnefs, and have favourable fymptoms for life; but for what kind of a one I know not. I am at a lofs to fay whether it is a pleafing, or a painful profpect. I feel the effects of both, and am ready to countenance the latter, knowing there is fomething in my nature, which is loth to be fubjected under that power, which ought to actuate every part of our demeanour; and there is nothing, that I know of, fo contrary to my natural will, as that patiently waiting, and quietly hoping, which thou mentions; it being, certainly, preparatory to the work of reformation in us; and if this be rightly performed, no mundane enjoyment would be adequate to the foretafte of that confummate felicity, which I believe is the refult of fo defirable a work: and, indeed, without fome degree of that bleffing, even in my unworthy ftate, this life, would be little fuperior to that for which I fhould look. But O this glimpfe of hope, how

how ready are we to catch, though the twig be ever
fo flender, and the profpect ever fo faint! yet there
is a danger of being deluded, as the Adverfary is
ever ready to attack the weak part, and that is one
which is generally expofed, there being room in
the human breaft for fuch prepoffeffions. I ac-
quiefce with thee, that it is in filence we enjoy
advantage, and in folitude we mufe the wonders of unfearchable wifdom. Could we but partake of a larger fhare of retirement, I am fenfible
the works of an almighty hand would have a greater influence, and the mind would not be fo alienated from this fource, this pleafing fource of
every joy."

1773.———" Surely the commemoration of the
goodnefs of infinite wifdom, in favouring a large
fhare of the youth of our fociety with a virtuous and
fober education, ought to infpire us with a willingnefs to imitate the bright examples we have, rather
than thofe, whofe lofs we fhould compaffionate; for
many are the irreligious principles, that the Adverfary is endeavouring to fuggeft in the minds of
youth, more efpecially when they are expofed to the
tempeftuous billows of an unftable world; but happy
is it for thofe that refift the temptations, and fur-
mount the difficulties : if any may look to the
recompenfe of reward, 'tis certainly they. But for
my part, I am often afraid left I fhould grow like
the heath in the defert, that knoweth not when
good cometh ; or that the manifold favours fhould
prove, as water fpilt upon a ftone ; for I am fure
there is a hardnefs in the natural heart, not eafily
penetrated ; and though I experimentally confefs it,

yet

yet I hope there are many, on the other hand, who can say, they witness the returning from their gatherings with friends, as arising from the washing pool."

1774.——" We certainly reap the greatest advantages from a friend, when the mind and natural flow of spirits are most depressed. It is at these seasons we hear the intelligible language of sympathy, in its pleasing notes, and look upon friendship in its exalted station. A view of these enjoyments excited me to taste their fruits, (which are the disclosure of our minds) by opening the fountain of sorrows, and unlocking the spring of painful feelings. That they may overflow the banks of my pleasures, and bring down the tall cedars of Lebanon, laying waste the hills and the mountains, and establishing in the room, that Rock whereon the church must be built, is the swaying inclination of my heart. But how apt are we to turn our feet from the path which is narrow; being unwilling to make straight steps, a thing most repugnant to our unregenerate wills! We therefore cull out every discouragement, and stumble at the smallest stone; each prospect appearing in its gloomiest colours, or rather, our eyes being dimmed by the glitter of worldly objects, and inexperienced in the joys accruing from faithfulness, we see them not."

1775.——" Though trials and conflicts are allotted to the faithful followers, yet they rise, as with stones of memorial, from the bottom of Jordan; when alas! I, and such like, instead of being benefitted by these baptisms, find them unpleasing and
contrary

contrary to our natural propenfities, and fo fhun them, for a more eafy way to peace; but cannot fuch be met with in a ftraight place, where neither the devices of the creature, nor the pleafures of the world, can refcue them from the pains of a wounded confcience? When I look at thefe things, and confider how intricate the path to our real happinefs is, it makes me frequently fay in my heart, " bleffed are the dead that have died in the Lord."

1775.———" My mind was often with you yefterday, though I could not thereby partake of the valuable company of our dear friends; but I hope many that are more worthy did: for certainly the fociety of thofe labourers in the great vineyard, muft be pleafing and inftructive; yet, at times, we feel a mortification in their abfence, which, if fuffered to have its proper effect, might be a means of exciting us to feek after an inward communion with the fource of all good, the fpirit of truth, which is pure and unmixed with human propenfities. But I am afraid that I am fpeaking more from hearing the experiences of others, than from my own; for I know the language of this internal monitor is not intelligible, without the mind be prepared by the fubjection of its will, and all its powers yield to the Supreme: and this ftate I am fo often deprived of, by the predominance of felf, that it feems hard to fay, whether I ever rightly enjoy this divine privilege."

1777.———" When we are favoured to feel an internal communion, an intercourfe incomprehenfible, 'tis indeed attended with rejoicing of heart. A ftate state which I can impute to no good cause, frequently accompanies me, in which it would be hard for me to say, I love my friends; but perhaps it is a constitutional stupidity, which nothing but the immediate operations of truth can divest of; and it is only during the overshadowings thereof, that the useful faculties of my mind are applied to good purposes; for the spring of thy S. T.'s machinery is indeed weak, and daily requires a supernatural aid; but when wisdom utters her voice, when the gentle movings of uncreated purity have gained our ear, what obduracy does it require to resist its energetic language, and lightly esteem the offers of permanent peace! My heart glows with an earnest solicitude, that we, my dear friend, may never faint in our pursuit after celestial treasure, but resignedly surrender our whole affections to the gracious disposer, and preserver of his people; then, I doubt not, our union will increase, in the increase of purity, and our joy and rejoicing in the fruition of reward, will be of that nature with which the stranger doth not intermeddle."

In the twenty third year of her age, she appeared in the ministry. For this awful service she had been prepared, by the great head of the church, with deep and humbling baptisms of spirit. But as she continued patient and faithful, under this proving dispensation, she experienced divine support, was graciously brought through all, and enabled to stand acceptably for the cause of truth and righteousness on earth.

The clofe trials and humiliations of her fpirit about this time, are, in fome degree teftified, by the following felections from her letters, to fome of her near, fympathizing friends. And though thefe extracts are of confiderable extent, it is hoped their inftructive tendency will warrant the infertion of them thus at large.

1778.———" I don't know but a little love for my friends, and fenfibility of their favours, are the only virtues I poffefs, and, confequently, all that I can derive any good from: for to my dear friend, to whom my heart hath ever been open, I may confefs, that whatever has heretofore felt like life, or been a participation of eternal fubftance, (though always fmall, and no doubt the food convenient for me) is now entirely extinguifhed; and the law, the teftimony, and the effufions of fome little fecret devotion, are all as fprings fhut up, and fountains fealed. Thou art experienced, and tried with many deep baptifms, with wants and with aboundings; but perhaps fuch a ftate of infenfibility to, and defertion of, all that feems good and valuable, was never feen meet for thee; thy refignednefs rather bringing thee its rewards, thofe of true obedience, which have built up and compacted as a Jerufalem, the foundations whereof are fure. But if thou knew the different fituation of my poor toffed mind, it would, I believe, excite a degree of thy fympathy, and fear that the Tempter will wholly overcome: for now, in this time of deep poverty, the world has indeed occupied much room, and what may be called the enjoyments of it, are as clay fettering that part appointed for immortality."——" I often wonder

der when better times will come; when, in truth, we can adopt the language of the juſt to their ancient ſource: " ſpring up, O well, ſing ye unto it!" But how can my humiliation be deep enough, when I confeſs that this fountain appears to be to me, neither ancient nor new?"

1778.———" There is, I believe, an holy intercourſe and communion experienced by thoſe whoſe language is ſimilar and pure, whoſe feet are eſtabliſhed upon the immovable Rock, and whoſe teacher and ſtrength is the ſovereign Lord. This is, I doubt not, one of their rewards; but its ſanctity, its refined and exalted nature, ſeems to exclude me from the participation thereof; for I may confeſs, the painful experience of my mind is often under ſuch a ſtate of deſertion from infinite goodneſs, that I ſcarce dare look towards his holy temple, or addreſs him, but in ſighs unutterable."

1778.———" Let us travel, unitedly travel forward in the path of humble obedience, which though tribulated, and thoſe that walk in it have often to experience a ſhare of this legacy, " In the world ye ſhall have trouble," yet the annexed peace, the bread that is handed in ſecret, and the joy with which a ſtranger doth not intermeddle, are ſurely ſufficient rewards in this life, and an earneſt of that which is to come, that glorious reſerve of immortal bliſs. I feel a greater ſolicitude than words can deſcribe, that we may, unitedly, be entitled to it, and partake thereof, and that we may feel this certain mark, that we love one another, even with that love which will ſubſiſt beyond the grave. But I wonder

wonder how arofe thefe fenfations, for I daily conclude myfelf deftitute of any that are good; and in the abfence of him whom I wifh to be to me the chief of ten thoufand, I implore the path of obfcurity, and, with the mournful prophet, exclaim in my lonefome habitation, the fecret of my heart, "Oh that I had in the wildernefs a lodging place! but alas! this will not do, this is not the will of him who defires, not to take us out of the world, but to preferve us from the evil that is therein. It is the path of fuffering, it is the crofs and the fhame that we recoil at; and for want of true dedication of heart, many deep and hidden forrows are ours."

1779.———"To inform thee, my dear friend, of the fecret path I have trod of late, is a thing which I know thy good fenfe, and experience in the myfteries of godlinefs, will prevent thy requiring. In the facred union, we fee the neceffity of the leaven being hid, which cements together and brings our nature into a onenefs, till the whole lump is fanctified. Under this apprehenfion, I have of late been led to endure many new and fevere conflicts, without daring to feek confolation, fave from that fountain, which iffues in the right time, an inexhauftible ftream; but to which I am ready to conclude, I am not entitled to approach."

1779.———"I lately thought the bleffing that was craved for us, was abundantly fhed, and our walking feemed, a little, as if it was by the pillar and the cloud; but now, the fun and the moon, even thofe heavenly bodies which are univerfally diffufed, have, from our eye, withdrawn their light. For my part,

I have several times concluded the work is done; and if it be sufficiently, I am glad; but when it feels like the description of meat and drink, there wants, not only patience, but resignation; an attainment which appears to me to be a degree harder than the other. Oh may we walk in the way cast up for us, and may we, now our Moses is withdrawn, be preserved from making a likeness!"——
" A south land" will, I hope, yield thee " springs of water :" they require hard digging for here; but the fountain is found to be so deep when come at, that we need not be afraid of the labour. But I have nothing to boast of, for the refreshing influence of the waters of this fountain, has, I doubt not, been wisely withheld from me; and to have a channel ready for their return, is, what I endeavour, though feebly, to preserve."

1779.——" My mind has been, for some time, incapable of deriving any satisfaction, from either the intercourse with, or consolation of a friend. And not having any desire to seek comfort, or have any, but from the fountain of it, silence was not only most consistent with my judgment, but most easy to myself, if I found any thing that could bear that character. Floods of distress have indeed nearly overwhelmed me, and I know not where to turn, or where to look; I abhorred myself, and beheld not the power that could purify. " When I looked for good, then evil came; and for light, behold there was darkness."

1779.——" I went to meeting yesterday morning, with, I thought, some degree of devotedness, and

and for some time sat in darkness; but after a deep labour of mind, there felt something to gather about me; and with it came my deep rooted dislike to the work; which so strove with the other, that for a time, enduring a state of agony, the meeting broke up. On going in the afternoon, I concluded myself given up, and little expected to feel any thing again at that time: but after sitting a while, the matter again returned, and would, I believe, have terminated the same way, had not a friend stood up with the passage, "He that knew his Lord's will and prepared not himself, neither did according to his will, shall be beaten with many stripes." This did indeed come home, and so operated with what was already kindled, that after such a conflict as I have cause ever to remember, I ventured upon my knees, and, in a manner I believe scarcely intelligible, poured out a few petitions. Now I feel in such a state of humiliation and fear, as I never before experienced; and my strength, both natural and spiritual, so low, that the floods are ready to come upon me again."

1780.———" I often keep silence, and find myself a subject copious enough for meditation, which is not always of the pleasing kind; but I endeavour to pass along as quietly as I can; it being seldom my lot to experience much sympathy or fellowship with my friends, and, consequently, I cannot expect to derive much from theirs. And yet for all this, I do not mean to complain, but am abundantly convinced, that I lived upon this pleasant fruit, this sensible union, long enough; and to know the want of it, is, I doubt not, sometimes as

necessary

neceſſary as its free circulation, which may perhaps return in its feaſon, when it may prove like the dew of Hermon."

1780.————." I cannot but fear thy apprehenſions of my alliance to a ſtate of properly attained peace, ariſe more from thy good wiſhes to me, as an individual, and from that univerſal love, which is impreſt with a ſenſe of the benevolent extendings of divine regard, that defires all may partake as at the river of life freely, than from a juſt ſenſe of the real ſituation of my mind; which has not yet caſt its ſackcloth covering, nor received a garment of praiſe. And as this change cannot be effected, but by the miraculous power of the divine arm, I wiſh only to ſeek for it from this ſource of ſtrength; and if it be my lot to go ſoftly all the days of my life, in the bitterneſs of my ſoul, I wiſh to ſubmit to this allotment, and endure the neceſſary turnings of the divine hand: but Oh! that I had in the wildernefs a lodging place, that no eye might fee, nor ear hear, the imperfect ſtate of a heart, the depths of whofe diſtreſs, omnipotence only can fathom."

1780.————" When thy letter, before this laſt reached me, it was my full intention to have replied to it very ſoon; but in this, as in the moſt important and neceſſary purſuits the human mind can have, the ſpirit of procraſtination prevailed; which I generally find is the caſe, when the firſt ability the mind poſſeſſes to do good, is not accepted. This is a reflection I have often painfully to make, becauſe its ſubject never fails to impart a feeling
ſenſe

sense of weakness; and when we consider it properly, that our being here is uncertain, and that the time, wherein we can acquire durable riches, is, though sufficient for the work designed us, short and fleeting, we can scarce quench an impulse to vigilance, or view ourselves in any other light, than sojourners in a land of exile, where the spirit that is pure, and the light which is the life of men, is oppressed and rejected, because to the natural eye, it hath neither form nor comeliness. I may, to my dear friend, confess, that my travel hath long been through a waste howling wilderness, where, (though surrounded with innumerable blessings) my mind hath been led mostly to feel itself like a pelican, and to wish for an outward situation similarly obscure, that I might for ever be hid from the eyes of men, of whom I often feel a fear that baffles description; but as this allotment has not fallen out for me, there seems no way, but simply to attend to that impulse which I have apprehended to be divine, and at the same time am thoroughly willing to be convinced, is not. Thy wish, that faith may be equal to the trials of my day, was peculiarly applicable; for could I give thee an idea, how often I am ready to sink in the depths of distress, when the weeds are indeed wrapped about my head, and all supports are either refused or withdrawn, thou would readily conclude me short of faith and patience too. But no language is able to set forth that situation of mind, when the wisdom which is from above, and that which is from beneath are struggling for victory. It is truly a fiery trial, but one which I fear will never in me consume all the reprobate silver. I have stumbled on a subject, which I had no thoughts of even hinting at,

when

when I began; but in confidence and freedom I have often been led to open my mind to thee, and I truſt That, wherein we were heretofore united, will not fail to ſtrengthen our bond, and open to us a channel of converſe, more hidden and pure than we have yet altogether experienced; and a fellowſhip which is only underſtood, when the myſteries of the true church are opened. Tell me, my beloved friend! art thou paſſing through this wilderneſs, and often ready to faint for want of water? If ſo, allow me to ſay, prolong not thy journey there, through a fearfulneſs of taking thy poſſeſſions in the promiſed land, nor of the inhabitants which are to be ſubdued before it can be enjoyed; for I truſt no tranſient, fading joy, can yield thy mind that peace it deſires: wherefore let not thy hands hang down, but rather put on ſtrength, in the name of him who is able to help, and in whom is the fulneſs of power, and be ſtrong and work; for I believe it is a day, in which this command is gone forth to thoſe whoſe hands are not polluted, and whoſe language is not that of confuſion. Deep are the baptiſms of ſuch, or how could they be fitted to ſtand in that day of trial which is, with a gradual and ſteady pace, approaching, if not rooted and eſtabliſhed upon that Rock, againſt which the gates of hell can never prevail. And though theſe, for the preſent, have to drink of that cup of adverſity, whereof our holy pattern firſt taſted, and have to be baptized with the baptiſm he was baptized with, yet, in the immediate revival of his promiſes, from that comforter which he has ſent, there remains to be conſolation."

In the 4th month 1780, with the approbation of the monthly meeting, and in company with her mother, she was engaged in a religious visit to friends in the counties of Westmoreland and Cumberland.

The following extracts contain the material parts of what are collected, from her own account of her concern in this visit.

―――" The meeting at Bowes was trying, though I believe satisfactory to my mother. For my part, I had deep heart-felt mortification, (which I have been very little free from since) and went very much fatigued to bed, it being ten at night when the meeting broke up, and we had a hard day's work in travelling. Next morning, we sat a little with a schoolmaster and his wife, to whom there was much openness to communicate close counsel, as well as encouragement. Next day we went to Penrith, where we staid over First-day, and had two suffering meetings; in both which I felt a greater unwillingness to submit to a necessary wading of spirit, than I can describe; for really, the spring of life requires such digging for, in places where the substance of religion is departed from, and only the image retained, that, in this exercise, I frequently felt ready to faint, and always engage with it in great dread ; because it opposes that natural part, which would keep the house in peace, and be free from all these troubles. However, I felt more ease of mind in the evening than I could have expected, having drank tea at the house of a widow friend, and had an open, favoured opportunity amongst her daughters, several

ral of whom appear to be under a frefh vifitation. We were at the monthly meeting at———and a moft painful, trying time it was : but after much labour, and deep fuffering, the right thing got uppermoft, and though the other was not flain, it was a favour that it did not altogether rule. Oh the untempered mortar there is in that place, and the unfoundnefs almoft from the crown of the head, to the fole of the foot! I ventured to ftammer out what appeared, though in a manner fcarcely intelligible, and in great fear, having previoufly had fpecimens of offerings, which carried not the evidence of having been prepared at the altar, and which indeed often create the query, " who fhall ftand ?"

———" Longtown * was, as I expected, a place of fome fuffering to me; but I could not have expected to have felt myfelf fuch a fpeckled bird as I did, though I kept myfelf much to myfelf : but it was impoffible to keep as retired as was defirable, nor were my motives for it juftifiable, being only to fhun the appearance of a fool, amongft a fet of wife and fine folks, whom we had at our inn. Indeed, a ftate of deep heart-felt mortification has been my lot, moftly, fince I faw you ; but as the caufe, without doubt, originates in the impurity of my own mind, I ought to be thankful for difpenfations fo neceffary, though hard to bear ; for furely there never was any, to whom the fimplicity of truth was fo irkfome, and who caufed themfelves fuch deep and hidden conflicts as myfelf. When one is got over, and another approaches, that difpofition, which loves not forrow, but would walk eafily

through

through life, is ready, in the remembrance of what it has suffered, to say, like the king appointed for destruction, I thought the bitterness of death was past; but Oh! how many strokes do I need to accomplish this death! It has been hard for me to have my mind bent under any degree of that weight and suffering, which are generally necessary to feel, before the spring is found to be opened, or any circulation of divine life experienced: because flesh and blood cannot aid in this labour, and, its strength being set at nought, it wars with the spirit: in the feeling whereof, I am often ready to faint. Oh! that my feet may stand fast in the bottom of Jordan; that I may neither flinch from a necessary wading of spirit, nor be overpowered with the floods of the mighty deep; and, above all, that I may be preserved from uttering words without life, for truly, " I am a child!"

———" When I wrote you last, my mind was indeed in a sad spot; the billows seemed to go over my head, and life felt almost to be a burden; for I could not at that time, look at our going to Whitehaven without the view of visiting the families, and that work appeared so ungrateful to me, that I could not bear the thoughts of having any thing to do in it. However, I endeavoured to forget it, and to consider that if the thing was right, it would be got through, and that somebody, better able and better skilled than myself, would have the burden to bear, and the work to do; and that if I got mortified with having something to do, now and then, the visit might be of as much benefit to me as to the whole meeting besides. Thus I endeavoured to rest it, it, when my mind would submit to think coolly on the subject; and indeed I had almost lost the painful impression when we got to Whitehaven, till we both felt it in the forenoon meeting on 1st day, with this conclusion, that to yield was the only way to leave the place in peace. My mother having previous to her view of this visit, concluded to have a meeting at Maryport on 3d day, found herself most easy to pursue that plan, and acordingly we went on 2d day afternoon. We found that the right time was fixed on for Maryport, and a favoured meeting it was, there being much openness to labour, indeed far more than in some places where a greater appearance is retained; but where, it is sorrowfully to be felt, the mighty are fallen, and tribes are lacking amongst them. There are many such places in this county, as well as in ours; and under a sense thereof, we have known a going bowed down all the day long. After this meeting, we returned to, and proceeded in, the work at Whitehaven. The labours in this visit were of the mortifying kind, and required a continual exercise of both faith and patience : because we had generally to sit where the people sat, which was often in dismal places; but being, I trust, in the right line, it will be made more profitable than could then be seen. It got finished on 6th day, and in the evening there was a meeting appointed to begin at 5 o'clock; which was, like all the visit before, a suffering meeting; but I hope the rightly concerned in that place, will reap the benefit of it, for it was, though painful, a remarkable time. It is with a degree of thankfulness I may acknowledge, that I felt in this visit, a greater resignation to what I apprehended

prehended was the divine will, than I ever experienced before; and I can, now it is over, cheerfully submit to the belief, that I was of no use, (if even preserved from doing harm) but that the thing was made useful to me, in subjecting my own mind, and teaching me, by a little more experience, the true way to wisdom, which is first becoming a fool. This state of preparation I expect to be in, all my life long; but I wish, (with a fear) that it may be so abode in, as to obtain the prize at last. Well, this trial is over, with being refused, reviled, and fought with as by beasts at Ephesus; yet these are small troubles indeed, when compared with the enemies of our own houses, that host of opposition which is often hard to press through. This wo is past, and I pray in my heart that another of the same kind may not soon come; for though I was favoured to feel it made much easier to me than I could have expected, yet the work of visiting families has always, since I was led seriously to consider it, appeared to be so awful, and to require the royal signet to be so evidently affixed, that the fear is great, of either moving without it, or being concerned in so momentous a work, when there is not strength enough to support, and wisdom to teach."

On their way home, they felt a concern to visit the families of friends at Kendal; near the conclusion of which, she says, "The spirits and body seem both ready to fail under the present exercise; but we have no reason to repent engaging with it; for, thus far, we have experienced strength sufficient for the day." Soon after her return from this journey, she writes concerning it as follows: "After many close exercises and deep trials, mine chiefly of my own making, we are now enjoying a good degree of peaceful ferenity, and though (I think) fufficiently ftripped, yet we feem pretty clear of any painful reflections on the paft allotment.

Towards the latter end of the year 1780, fhe came under a religious concern to join her friend and relative T. Hoyland, in a vifit to the meetings of Chefhire, and a part of thofe in Lancafhire. And having the concurrence of the monthly meeting, and a certificate thereof, fhe fet forward to engage in this fervice, in the 12th month. The enfuing parts of her letters on the fubject, afford fome account of this journey, and fhew the fituation of her mind, under the profpect of the work before her, and in the profecution and completion thereof.

———" Chefhire has long attracted my mind, and of late more than ufual; and on my coufin T. H. laying a fimilar concern before me, thofe feelings revived with fome weight; and not without a great fear left, (though the impulfe might be right) the time and companion might not be in the fame appointment : and hence appeared the neceffity of having it hewed and fquared.

———" It is only in a little faith that I look towards the journey in profpect, and at the rectitude of it ; and though I fear it is not equal to a grain of muftard feed, yet I think I am thankful for this little : and fince it has been received, and the affair mentioned, a degree of peacefulnefs and quietude hath attended my mind, which is all the light I find upon it ; and which requires fometimes, all my vigilance

gilance to retain, left the floods from the mouth of the dragon should overwhelm, and cast away that little strength that is at present afforded; and instead of adding thereto by devotedness, to be any thing or nothing, leave me tossed upon the unstable element, where neither rock nor shore can sometimes be perceived."

―――" It was not indeed the least of my concern, or rather dislike, to submit to the thoughts of going to some places in Lancashire, which I had in view; for, indeed, that seemed not much less than giving up my life; and this proceeded from considerations which I think thou canst hardly share, having surmounted many of the difficulties and mortifications which appear very formidable to me. But when we have suffered for disobedience, and are favoured with a view of the rewards of the faithful, and are likewise convinced of the importance of our duties, though ever so small in appearance; when our nothingness is sufficiently felt, and our minds impressed with the awfulness of the divine requirings; life itself looks but a small sacrifice, and so reasonable, that there is no excuse for withholding it, especially that inward existence which does not co-work with the life of true religion."

―――" From Ackworth, I had a companion who imparted some good and wholesome counsel to me, and more encouragement, than I could have looked for; but my secret sitting was in the dust and much gloom seemed to cover my little views. I reflected on the preceding evening, and found its enjoyment was then like manna two days old, having loft both favour and nourifhment; and inftead of a renewal of the fame, a faft was difpenfed, the caufe of which I muft leave; but it is a painful one, and if I had felt myfelf before I left home, as I have done fince, it is much if the venture had been made. Could I believe that this is any thing like going forth without either fcrip or purfe, I fhould perhaps be more reconciled. I am thankful that, in every ftate I have fome degree of the comfortable impreffion, that unity is good; and though mine is not of the moft expanfive kind, yet in a renewed feeling of my little, I cannot but wifh, that we may be fo willing to fuffer together, and frequently to go down to the potter's houfe, to be there fafhioned and formed either for veffels of honour or difhonour, (as may beft pleafe him who hath power over the clay) that we may alfo experience an humble afcent to the houfe of true prayer, and a rejoicing together. My heart is too full for words to relieve, but being convinced that there is a better and more refined intercourfe than this, a communion which, proportioned to our obedience, is pure and edifying, I wifh in that to remember, and be remembered."

——" We went to Lowlayton on 6th day, and found there but one family of friends, who came in by convincement. It was a comfortable place; for their fimplicity and integrity rendered their cottage an agreeable manfion, in which there was nothing painful to be felt. The meeting there next day, was much larger than we looked for, many people in the neighbourhood coming in, whofe folid, innocent

nocent countenances, were, I thought, as likely to do us good, as we to do them any. It was a satisfactory meeting, and afforded some encouragement to proceed. We went to Stockport on 7th day afternoon; the meeting on firſt day was a painful, trying one, and yet ſtrength was not withheld. From Macclesfield we came to Leek, and have juſt finiſhed (except one family) a viſit to the families here. We have had eight ſittings to-day, beſides the week-day meeting, which has been cloſe work. We are however (and have cauſe to be) thankful, that ſtrength equal to the undertaking has been afforded; and though we have been deeply tried, yet, upon the whole, I believe we may acknowledge, that we have lacked nothing, and have been much united to a few in this place. This work of viſiting families, is the laſt I ſhould chooſe for myſelf, if I might be my own chooſer; but as it is wrong to deſire that indulgence, I ſee I may as well give myſelf up to what appears in the line of duty. —It is with thankfulneſs of heart, that I acknowledge myſelf in a tolerable degree of health, through many different diſpenſations which have fallen to my lot ſince I ſaw you; for there have been experienced a wanting, and a ſufficient abounding; but I wiſh I could add, that in every ſtate I have learned to be content. Great indeed hath been the condeſcenſion of him who is pleaſed to make uſe of poor, weak inſtruments, and by things which not only appear low and contemptible, but are ſo in reality, to bring to nought, and reduce things that are mountains in proſpect; proving to us a preſent help in every needful time, and, by his inviſible power, ſtrengthening us when we are ready to faint in our minds. And still greater, I may acknowledge, hath appeared his wisdom in deeply trying us, or however myself, with the most abject poverty and strippedness of mind; indeed so much so, that I think I never before experienced such humility, in a sense of myself, and, under the convincing proof, that of ourselves we can do nothing. This is a situation wherein we see whence all good comes, and the necessity of casting ourselves so wholly upon the divine arm, as to have no confidence in the flesh. No dispensation, however desirable the enjoyment of good may be, seems so much to drive us to the root of life, if we endeavour sufficiently to profit by it; and consequently, none that we ought to be so thankful for, when our hearts are capable of feeling true gratitude; for he who knows the weakness of our frames, and is touched with a feeling of our infirmities, sees what we can bear, and knows how frail we are. Thus have I, in this little journey, been wisely taught, through many trials, to live by faith; and thus far, in reflecting on the past, to own I have lacked nothing. But we are abundantly convinced, that they who are sent out in this day, to a people who have, in a great measure, forsaken both law and testimony, and what is still worse, see not their states, but are secure in themselves, have not to eat much pleasant bread: for I think I may say, it hath often been our lots to go bowed down all the day long, and to mourn in a deep sense of the great desolation which overspreads the society: insomuch, that we often admire that there should be any sent out to visit them, and that the feet of those that are rightly shod, should not more generally be turned to others: for from these, there are

the

the greatest hopes in this county, which is likely, in many places, to be left defolate of friends who keep their places. We have, however, in a few of the meetings which we have laſt attended, been agreeably difappointed, in finding more preferved or quickened by the life of religion, than we expected; and it hath been our lot to vifit thefe, as well as a very contrary fort, by families. A very trying work it hath been, and it is not yet done. In it I have often lamented, left for want of that fpirit of difcerning, with which the prophet was endued, when he went to anoint one of the fons of Jeffe, there fhould not be a right divifion of the word, and thereby much harm be done. And under this confideration, great abafednefs hath attended my mind, and a defire that the fleece may be tried both wet and dry. We left Namptwich undone, and hoped, nay even refolved, to return to it no more; but now I have to confefs, we are on our way thither. It is however a favour, that, through all, we are led to feel and fympathize one with another; I mean my companion and felf, and that our little fervices have been harmonious; and if we keep near that preferving arm which hath been with us, I doubt not but this ftrength will continue and increafe; for in unity, if it be of the right kind, there is certainly ftrength."——

" We got to Manchefter, after a week of many probations, which ended better than we could have looked for, at the beginning of it, when our hearts were ready to faint, and the billows feemed to run over our heads, in the feeling of what we had already fuffered, in remembering the affliction and diftrefs, the wormwood and the gall. Our minds were humbled in the profpect of an opening field; but I truft it was He who commanded the waves to be ftill, that calmed thefe floods, and renewed a degree of faith and patience to perfevere in the tribulated way. What need there is to keep near to the fountain of life, and to receive our refreſhment folely from it! becaufe from thence only, arife our freſh fprings, and immortal food; which, though the bread of adverfity and the water of affliction, yet coming from this fource, it is no lefs efficacious to the nourifhing, ftrengthening, and building us up, than the fenfible union with divine purity. Our hearts are very incapable of judging, concerning the virtue of the difpenfations of providence; we know not ourfelves, and confequently, cannot prefcribe for ourfelves. How paffive then, and how like little children, fhould we be to him that fearcheth the heart? but I am often afraid, left, by indulging my own ideas of what is good, and not labouring after a total refignation of mind, but wanting to have things in my own way, I fhould fruftrate the divine intention, which may be to humble and reduce felf, more than flefh and blood would point out. The great meetings we meet with, are almoft overmuch for us, and what made it ftill worfe to us at Liverpool, was a funeral in the afternoon, and a vaft number of people. We little thought when we fixed to ftay over 2d day at Manchefter, that we fhould have one to attend there, which is the cafe this afternoon, and how it will be got over, I know not. If we may but be favoured to be rightly quiet, it is all we defire; and if we cannot be that, it is certainly our beft way, as far as we are able, to take up the crofs,

and

and despise the shame; which sometimes feels great, and at others, I may thankfully acknowledge, is in a great measure removed; but then, what need there is of care not to overrun the guide, and work without the power of the word? Dangers surround us on every hand, and our standing often seems as on a sea of glass."

———" With satisfaction and pleasure, I have lately looked towards home; indeed with so much, that a fear sometimes strikes me, lest in wisdom some unforeseen affliction should be sent to moderate it. According to my present feelings, I am returning peaceful and easy; and though we have missed some meetings, which I own I had a view of, yet it was with a full belief, that they will not be laid to my charge. I wish that we may be thankful enough for the favours we have received divers ways, since we left home; and, what appears to me no small one, for the readiness of my beloved connexions, in making every thing as easy as outward means can possibly do, and affording accommodations, for want of which many lie under very great difficulties. The consideration of these things often affects my mind."

Bradford, 19th of 1st month 1781.

———" I thought, when we left Manchester, that it was a strange thing if we did not return to it again; yet I had since lost the impression, further than wondering why such a thought should then have struck me; and even the concern about many meetings, which I thought we had missed, was so much gone off my mind, (where it had

dwelt

dwelt with some weight) that I seemed perfectly easy, under the belief that the concern would devolve on my companion, but little expected it was so soon to be evinced: for after much secret sorrow, which I perceived, but durst not pronounce my apprehensions of the cause, she disclosed last night her uneasiness, and desire to return to the places we passed by, as well as to go to some others in this county. On looking a little seriously at it, (indeed not a little, for we had nearly a sleepless night) I could not see that it was less than my duty to return with her; not only from having had a view of the same places, but as a companion, which, if truly one, cannot leave in the day of trouble. I wish myself better qualified to sympathize with her in this trial, which is a very great one, and requires all the alleviations that are in my power to bestow. I believe her willingness is now so great, that, for the purchase of a little peace, she would return to all the places, to do the things which appeared needful, and were not fully joined in with; but when this great sacrifice of the will is completely made, I trust some ram will be caught in the thicket, or some smaller offering accepted. Home now looks at a great distance, and I find that it will contribute most to my peace, to think as little of it as I well can; and if it had been less in my mind of late, this turn in our affairs, would by me, have been less felt. We find ourselves after the meeting to-day, in a very gloomy situation of mind; as it was a suffering time, and we thought left us with the sentence of death in ourselves; perhaps that we may not trust in ourselves, which I ardently wish we may be preserved from.

from. We intend going to Leeds to-morrow evening; we dread it not a little, and this day's work increafes the apprehenfion of very great fuffering; but it often feems beft to leave, or draw the mind from future trials, and endeavour, as well as we can, to bear thofe of the prefent day, which are generally found to be fufficient."

Manchefter, 4th of 2d month 1781.

———" Our minds are often bowed down, under a fenfe of the awfulnefs of our engagements, and difmayed at the fight; nor need I fay how clofely our time is filled up therewith; for after fitting with feven or eight families, we are generally ready for reft. I have the very great fatisfaction now to fay, that, except one family, we have finifhed in this place; have had four to-day, befides the two meetings, and upwards of forty fince we began, with putting now and then two together. We were at Stockport on 4th day, and had it unexpectedly in our power, to pay off a fmall debt which we contracted when there before. It has been wonderful to us, how we have been, and are likely to be, turned to places, and thrown in the way of doing our firft works; which we cannot but view, as a mark of divine condefcenfion to our infant ftate: Indeed it hath been manifefted to us far beyond what we could have looked for, in the courfe of this journey throughout; and not lefs fo fince we came into this place, where inftruction hath been daily adminiftered from different fources; fome of which have proved deeply trying to flefh and blood; but being, I truft, in the ordering of unerring wifdom, I wifh (perhaps

more

more than I endeavour) to profit patiently thereby, and value the rod as well as the staff. It is indeed high time to number our blessings. They are truly many, and we cannot fail of seeing and feeling them; that of having the parental care and solicitude of several of our much honoured and valued friends, is not small in our estimation."

———" We have now got to Warrington, and are endeavouring to keep ourselves quiet, and, as much as we can, labour to feel what is the divine will concerning us; which, with respect to our coming here, hath been much a mystery. The prospect almost dismays us, attended with a fear, that we may now be in danger of compassing a mountain in the wilderness, and engage in a service, for which our strength is not proportioned; and so, notwithstanding we have been favoured with divine condescension to our states heretofore, bring upon ourselves unnecessary trials, and thereby pierce our minds, in future, with many sorrows. It is no small concern to us to find, with the present view of things, every qualification wanting for such a service; and our minds greatly stripped of strength and clear discerning: and to move without a renewal of these, we dare not. When my companion first proposed our return, the evidence I thought was so strong, that I cheerfully complied: yet feelings very unlike these ensued, even a state of deep distress and mortification, when I found we must turn our backs on home, and return from whence we came, to do our first works. Great was our pain, from, I believe, an unsubjected will; but great likewise and evident, was

was the operation of the divine hand, in judgment upon us for the paſt, and, no doubt, as a preparation for the future; for it never appeared clearer to me, than when under this diſpenſation, that for every freſh ſervice and work in the church, we muſt experience a renewed baptiſm of ſpirit, and purification of the gift; and that the more we have of the droſs, or the reprobate ſilver, the more frequently muſt we paſs through the refining fire. Notwithſtanding I was ſometimes, in the impatience of my heart, ready to query as the children of Iſrael did, " were there not graves enough in Egypt, that we are brought hither to die;" yet there were times, when all that was within me, was proſtrated under the chaſtiſing hand, and ſought that it might not ſpare. How preferable is it to all ſecondary adminiſtrations of judgment, when, with David, we wiſh rather to fall into the Lord's hands, than into the hands of man! and ſurely, the more we ſeek to derive our inſtruction and food from the fountain of good, the leſs we ſhall be ſubject to inſtrumental means."

———" I never felt myſelf under ſuch complicated diſcouragements at any time; and Oh! that we may both be enabled to bear theſe fiery trials, with reſignation to the divine will, and ſeek to profit by them, that the ſtate of a weaned child may become our experience."

———" As I make no doubt it will be acceptable to thee to hear from two poor pilgrims, who are almoſt worn out with things that appear too mighty for them, I juſt embrace a little vacant time, to hint how we have fared; and may in the firſt place ſay, that the preſent engagement hath been the moſt trying of the kind we ever experienced. It hath been frequently our lot, to go down as to the bottom of the mountains, where the earth with her bars, was about us; under this preſſure, our minds have been ſecretly clad with ſackcloth and deep mourning, when it has evidently appeared, that the pure life of religion is in a ſtate of bondage, and that it ſenſibly utters the language, "I am oppreſſed under you, as a cart with ſheaves." To viſit this ſeed of the kingdom, we find to be no light matter, eſpecially when hid under the briers and thorns, and then plumed with human wiſdom; who indeed is ſufficient for theſe things? I often lament, and with reaſon, that my heart is not more bound to the cauſe, and more willing to ſuffer for it; and I fully believe, that until this is more experienced, there will remain to be, as there have already been, many trials and afflictions, which originate not in the divine will; for it is ſtill a truth, that our greateſt enemies are thoſe of our own houſes, and that to endeavour to ſubdue theſe, is our indiſpenſable duty: but oh! what ſtrokes are in wiſdom adminiſtered to us, to deſtroy that life which hath no exiſtence in the divine purity; and except we be faithful unto this death, we can with no probability look for the crown immortal. We have frequently had to recur to the moving cauſe of this journey, and, as an additional trial, found the feeling ſenſe of that withdrawn from us; but all theſe things teach us where to place our preſent dependance; and notwithſtanding diſpenſations thus painful have been our portion, we have

great

great cause, thankfully to commemorate the blessings of the divine and bountiful hand, which hath been strength in our weakness, riches in our poverty, and a present helper in the needful time; and hath refreshed our drooping spirits, insomuch that, with alacrity of heart, we have pursued the path cast up for us, and have been favoured to see the great necessity of passing frequently through the furnace; and oh! faith my heart, that I may be willing to descend again and again, till He whose invincible arm sustaineth us there, is pleased to say, " It is enough."

——" We have now finished, for what we know, our engagement at Warrington. We wound up all in this family last evening; but oh what a day was yesterday! my companion's situation and mine were very different, though both trying; and the more so, because we were not alike led; but still there is a secret trust, that we were both in our places. The meeting was held at Penketh, and being the preparative meeting, was very large. The first meeting was so low and painful in the forepart, that I was glad secretly to offer myself to do any thing, if light might but shine upon my dwelling. In this situation, I soon saw that we had nothing to do in that sitting; but it seemed as if I heard a voice, " visit the men and women when separated, for they require different food." The evidence was, I thought, so strong, that I earnestly desired to be preserved faithful, however hard it might be to the creature, lest a worse state should befal me. When the meetings parted, I just requested my companion to feel if it might not be best

best to go into the men's meeting: her reply was, "she had seen nothing of it, but would go with me." This greatly increased the burden that was upon my mind, but remembering my recent view and request, I durst not, after all the favours I had received at the divine hand, in our late probationary visit, refuse a compliance with this intimation of duty; and finding I had a little strength, was made willing, with that, to become still more a spectacle to angels and to men, than before in this place.—I believe I had my companion's sympathy, but she said she had nothing to do; which I own, so discouraged me, with the painful apprehension that I had been out of my place, led by an unsanctified zeal, or, at least, had so imprudently administered the right thing, that I had already done more harm than good; so that, though there was a covering of good over the women's meeting, and a little ability to relieve my own mind at least, I so lost faith, and gave way so much, to thinking myself quite spent and exhausted, that I managed to bring my load away with me; which, added to the mortifying remembrance of what I had done, nearly sunk me for a time into the deepest distress. But by endeavouring to keep it to myself, (my greatest discouragements however) and to recur to what I apprehended, was the moving cause of my doing and leaving undone, there ensued a little quietness, and a small, but comfortable evidence, that the offering of obedience, as far as it had been made, was acceptable; and that what was omitted, was viewed with divine, compassionate regard to the weakness, and not wilfulness, of my poor depressed mind. And notwithstanding we had three fittings afterwards, and my body almoft as ill as I thought it could be, to bear up, yet there felt to me full as much ftrength and life, as I have found before in this place; and this morning I feel fo refrefhed with the foregoing, and a good night's reft, that I don't know that I have a complaint of any fort; only I could wifh for a little more clearnefs refpecting fome approaching days. Thus I comfortably and thankfully experience, that though forrow has come for a long night in this place, joy fprings in the morning. When the fun of righteoufnefs, in any degree, arifes, and the mind feels its refrefhing influence, how does it encourage to prefs forward, and to think nothing too hard to fubmit to, for this excellent appearance! but how ready, like the difciples, are we to folicit that our tabernacles may be built here, and we not defcend into the lower parts of the earth again, there to be covered with its bars, and feel ourfelves as at the bottom of the mountains; though it is from thence, we are led to look for a better habitation, and to labour that the pure life may arife, and we be favoured to dwell with it, though feldom in a ftate of dominion, remembering for our inftruction, that Aaron the great high prieft, was permitted to enter into the holy of holies but once a year, for his common fervice was in the tabernacle.—I cannot but look upon this morning, which feels pleafanter than many, to be perhaps the opening of another tribulating day; for it does not appear a time for fuch as are, in the fmalleft degree, able to be baptized into the prefent ftate of the church, to eat much pleafant bread: but I wifh I was more preferved

from

from those infirmities of darkening counsel, &c. in times of proving, when a gulf seems to open for present destruction. Oh what a trial, or trials of this sort have we had in this place! but I wish to forget these toils, and rather seek for greater wisdom to bear the future. It is marvellous to me, how things are brought about, that we have had views of, but no probability of being effected; and particularly with respect to this monthly meeting, which I thought I saw, before we set off from home, and often wondered when we were leaving Lancashire, how such things could be? and sometimes, on that account, was ready to call all in question; finding many such causes of discouragement, which now seem gradually removing."

Liverpool, 20th of 2d month, 1781.

————" The fellowship and tenderness of our friends was never more desirable, than in these days of deep probation and instruction. Wonders are indeed yet manifested in the deeps, where, finding the demonstration of the spirit and power, even my strong heart has, to my own admiration, been made willing to receive the bitterest of cups; and all that is within me, has bowed and done obeisance to him, before whom I have had daily and piercingly to abhor myself; under renewed, powerful, evidences, that without the frequent administration of the Holy Ghost and fire, and repeatedly descending to the washing pool, there is no offering an acceptable sacrifice; and that this must be a dispensation for life, if ever any offering is found to be without blemish, which I fear it it never will; but if preserved with spiritual fight, and a necessary jealousy over myself, I shall, I trust, so far deem myself blessed.—How are such as move in this line to be pitied! their standing cannot be better described, than as being on a sea of glass, mingled with fire. But I would not say any thing to discourage, nor would I wish to be like the evil spies; therefore may add, that from what I have seen of the good land, attainable at times in this work, it is well worth our pressing after, and its fruit is so pleasant, that it amply refreshes the weary traveller. I could, yesterday morning, set my seal to the truth of this; but alas! the scene, since then, has changed much. We were at the monthly meeting at Hartshaw to-day, for which we have both cause to be thankful; not because the food was pleasant, but because it was, we trust, wholesome; and this evening we are come to this place, to which we set off in the bitterness of our spirits. It looks indeed often to my mind, as if a singular visitation is renewedly extended to our society; but there is a painful fear, that the day will pass over the heads of many: yet, with it, a hope springs, that there are others who will be purified, tried, and made white."

York, 3d *of* 3d *month* 1781.

——" Many of our late tribulations appear to me, more and more, to have been in the orderings of divine wisdom; and such as have more evidently arisen from our unwillingness to submit to the humbling power of the cross, will surely be profitably remembered by us, and gradually work that patience and pure resignation of heart, which can enable us, in holy confidence, to rejoice, and count it all joy, when we fall into divers temptations and tribulations, for the trial and refinement of our faith in him, who was made perfect through suffering. My mind, has, in general, since my return home, felt a state of deep prostration, and humble gratitude to that all-ruling power, which hath, I fully believe, helped us in our late engagements, and would more eminently have done it, if our minds had borne a greater similarity to the passive clay. Great instruction arises in the commemoration of these things. To feel our minds centred in a quiet submission to the present allotment, now we are returned, and a willingness either to do or suffer, appears the most desirable state for us, and is what I hope thou largely experienceft."

In the twelfth month 1781, with the approbation of the monthly meeting, she was concerned in a religious visit, to a part of the families within the monthly meeting of Owstwick and Cave. Although her steppings along in this service, were attended with close trials, yet she was enabled to perform it with a degree of peace and satisfaction; which appears from her own expressions on this occasion: " We have got along as well as we could have looked for, considering the prevailing declension and weakness of the present day; which in these, as well as in many other places, widely spread themselves. Deep suffering, and a painful exercise of mind, are often our lot; but being, I trust, in a good degree resigned thereto, they are, at times succeeded

with

with a calm, and a little evidence, that the fervant is not wholly difunited from the mafter."

She was engaged, in the 1ft month 1782, in a vifit to fome families, which had not been vifited by the friends who had lately been concerned in a family-vifit in that quarter. At the conclufion of this vifit, fhe remarks as follows, " It was, I think, the moft trying fervice of the kind that I ever had any fenfe of; the general unfeelingnefs and impenetrablenefs of the vifited, rendered the labour almoft without hope. So greatly departed are many amongft us, from the virtue of heavenly dew, that it is now deemed an unneceffary attainment."

CHAP.

CHAP. II.

Her marriage—and Journey into Scotland, Cumberland, &c.

IN the 4th month 1782, she was married to our friend Robert Grubb, of Clonmel in Ireland, who had for some time resided at York; to whom she was a faithful and tender companion, and a sympathizing, strengthening helpmeet, in the various probations of their spiritual pilgrimage. On this subject, the following instructive letter, written some months afterwards, appears to be worthy of insertion.

―――" It was an awful thing to me, to enter into this new sphere. I am now blessed with all, and more than I had any right to ask for in it. I wish to number these blessings, and approve myself worthy of them. This belief ever accompanies my mind, that if we wrest not ourselves out of the divine hand, whose fatherly care and protection is over us, our cup of life will be so blended, as to prevent our sitting down in outward enjoyments. Few and fleeting are the days of our pilgrimage; and every additional experience confirms the sentiment, that our solid satisfaction depends not on our possessing all that the unmortified part in us can desire; for there still remains, in the immortal part, a void, which immortal fubftance only, can fatisfy. To have this fupplied with wholefome food, and every other gratification to ftand fubordinate thereto, is the prefent fecret breathing of my fpirit : that fo the bleffing of prefervation may attend us, and patience have its perfect work, till the burning of the Lord's day hath done its office, and a quiet centre in everlafting repofe, is obtained."

About two weeks after this event, fhe entered on a religious vifit to friends in Scotland, in company with her friend Mary Proud; having previoufly obtained a certificate of concurrence from the monthly meeting. This concern had, for many months, dwelt frequently on her mind, and had now matured fo, that fhe thought it her duty to engage in it, at this time. Her feelings under the view of it, and in the profpect of her marriage, with her refignation to the fervice, and defires for divine prefervation and direction ; are, in fome meafure, fet forth, by the following extracts from fome of her letters, written on thofe occafions.—" I cannot be on the verge of fuch important, and fome new, concerns, without feeling deep anxiety, and many fears; my mind is often fo deeply oppreffed with my prefent load, that I feel continually bowed down under it, and not very fit for this employ. The mind and body feldom fuffer alone, and it is comfortable to believe, that they are not intended to be always, or long companions. I have not been very well of late, which is not to be wondered at, nor is it worth much attention."

—" The

———" The fentiment thou drops refpecting Scotland, is fo exactly fimilar to my own, that it was like a little ftrength handed in the time of need; and I greatly wifh, if the thing be proved to be right, to be enabled to make a facrifice of every felfifh inclination; that my offerings and prayers, in this one ftep, may be pure and acceptable to Him who fees in fecret. But I often feelingly remember a faying of M. Peifley's, that fhe was " torn as between heaven and earth ;" and it many times is matter of doubt, in which I fhall centre. I have as much nature as moft, and as great an aptnefs to cover myfelf with it, and live upon it; and though to be thus drawn from fuch a fource, is caufe of thankfulnefs, yet it feems like the pangs of death, and I fometimes query, whether my natural body will not fall under the operation. Was it not for, now and then, experiencing my ftrength a little renewed, and my mind clothed with the quietnefs of that habitation, which the arrows of the archers cannot penetrate, I muft fall to the oppofition of the enemy in myfelf; but when the arm of power is felt to be near, then it is, that we rejoice in the means of our falvation."

———" There is ftill a fecret belief, that the growth and cultivation of my views refpecting a northern journey, were, by that hand, from which I have apprehended my moft important engagements have proceeded; and though it has, for many months, dwelt frequently upon my mind, yet I cherifhed a belief, that it was very far off; till the profpect of fettling in a new line of life

drew

drew nearer, and then, this diſtant view as faſt approached. It was afreſh revived when I wrote to thee laſt; but I wiſhed to try it ſtill a little longer, if, in the kindneſs of Him, who knows my great unfitneſs for an engagement ſo important, my reſignation to it might be an acceptable ſacrifice. Inſtead of this, the weight increaſed, and I found, on complying with ſome early proceedings in another affair, that my peace materially depended, on having thee informed of what I had in view; that thereby this concern might keep pace with the other, and I attend to what may appear to be my own buſineſs, no further, than reſignation to a ſuperior ſervice was experienced. My dear friend knows the neceſſity of an entire ſurrender of ourſelves, to what appears, in the pointings of duty, to be our proper buſineſs, and of keeping our eye as ſteadily to that as we can; that ſo, by its ſingleneſs, we may have light ſufficient for the work of our day. And as, without this quiet attention, we are often led into doubts, fears, and many reaſonings, ſo we are frequently found to require provings of mind, ſtrippings, and many baptiſms, in order to fit us for the ſtate, in which alone there is ſafety; a truly humble, dependant ſtate, reduced of ourſelves, and ſeeking that honour, which cometh from God only. It is with great awfulneſs I look at the work before us, and under a deep ſenſe, how unable we are of ourſelves, at all to help forward the cauſe, wherein we deſire to be engaged, or to bring honour to that name (either amongſt us as a ſociety, or thoſe who are not of our fold) to which the nations may yet be ſeen to gather. It is deſirable,

sirable, however, that our dwelling may be deep, that the wisdom and instruction we receive, may (though small) be pure; that if we venture to move, the cloud may sensibly be taken off the tabernacle, and we careful to follow the appointed guide, for our days and nights, and be favoured, in this day of deep degeneracy, with an evidence, that we have done what we could."

The following is an account of her journey through Scotland, &c. taken from a short journal written by herself, and found amongst her papers.

————" The twentieth of the fourth month, 1782, I left York, with my friend M. Proud, for the yearly meeting at Edinburgh, intending from thence, to visit the friends in Scotland, Cumberland, &c. We were at Thirsk on first day, the twenty-first, where we sensibly felt the pure life of religion to be at a low ebb, though the professors thereof are numerous; and such as have been anointed for, and employed in, the Lord's work, dwell amongst them. But these being only standard-bearers, whilst they continue exercised in the Lamb's war, and prove their loyalty to the King of kings, by their careful attention to his pointings, and humble walking before him, have need to live under an awful sense of the importance of that service to which they are called: that so, their spirits may be kept favoury, their conversation, likewise, seasoned with the heavenly salt, ministering grace to those that hear. For want of the Lord's servants, or those in the foremost ranks of the people, being thus preserved near that

power,

power, in which their life and their ftrength confift, great declenfion has happened to us, as a people; and thofe, who have been looking for the fubftantial part of religion in them, have, inftead of finding its influence, received, by the lightnefs of the conduct of fuch, a warrant for their own propenfities. Under the confideration of thefe things, I was affected, and feeling the aptnefs of my difpofition to yield to the like infirmities, I was led, renewedly, to beg for ftrength. Notwithftanding we had to fuffer with the feed in this place, and to behold the breaches which are made as in the walls of the royal city, yet, a renewed vifitation was extended to many, and efpecially to the youth; and our minds were a little encouraged to prefs forward in the work before us, under a frefh fenfe of divine regard. The next day, we left Thirfk, and my hufband, who had accompanied us thus far, went with us a few miles further on this day's journey; and after we parted, my mind felt a covering of divine love to replenifh it, with faith and patience; and, from a little fenfible experience, I could thankfully fay, with a difciple formerly, " I have left all to follow thee." And under a renewed fenfe of this holy attachment, and of my own unfitnefs for the fervice before me, without frequent baptifms of fpirit, and the fanctifying power thereof, I was inwardly favoured with fome new inftructions, refpecting the office of a minifter of Chrift, and openings how to fulfil that office: and thus, I was led to acknowledge, that he who had called is faithful, and his grace is fufficient for us, as our dependance is placed thereon, and all confidence in ourfelves removed. We attended a meeting on third day, and had painfully to feel the state of things amongst them; and it appeared clear to my mind, that the work was in the Lord's hands, and that he will, in his own time, make manifest the hidden things of darkness; when those that retain a little life amongst them, will be enabled to renew their strength, and shew themselves on the Lord's side, though their numbers may be few. We were favoured in some degree, to relieve our own minds, and left them that afternoon.

The next day we were at a meeting which, for some time, was a painful sitting, under a sense that the leaders of the people caused them to err, and were crying, " the word of the Lord," when the Lord had not sent them. But after experiencing something of the baptism unto death, with our holy High Priest, we were favoured to feel the resurrection of life; in which, judgment was placed on the head of the transgressing nature, and the minds that were desirous to know something of the work of religion for themselves, were pointed to the means of redemption from sin. From thence we went to Newcastle, and were at their week-day meeting on fifth day, where truth, measurably, prevailed. On sixth and seventh days, being the twenty-sixth and twenty-seventh of the month, we travelled from Newcastle to Kelso, and were at their meetings on first day, which are very small of friends, but many others came in, especially in the afternoon; and though, at first, they appeared rude and ignorant, yet the power of truth, in which the authority is felt, rose so into dominion, that it became a solemn opportunity. And thus we had

had fresh cause to observe, that it is only by divine strength, that we can run through a troop, or leap over the walls of opposition. On second day, we went to Edinburgh, where, on third we rested, and on fourth and fifth attended the yearly meeting, which was but small, there being very few members of society of that nation then present. There were several, who through neglect of christian discipline, think they have a claim to the society, as being the offspring of friends; others were like the Philistines in whose hands the ark of the testimony is fallen, and esteemed by them as a contemptible thing; there were also present a number of students from distant parts, whose parents are not only members of society, but some of them useful therein. On account of all these, our minds were painfully exercised: and notwithstanding the publick meetings were large, and owned with divine favour, in covering these assemblies with a degree of holy awe, and the minds of some of his servants with gospel power and authority, to declare the way of life and salvation: yet through all, the sense of deep, hidden, as well as flagrant corruption, so impressed my mind, that I was led to believe, truth will never prosper in this place, nor the excellency of it appear unveiled, till, not only the branches of the corrupt tree are cut off, but the root so dug up that the remembrance thereof may rot; and then, there is a hope that the present planting may get watered, the ground renewedly cultivated, and fruits appear to the praise of the great Husbandman. Deep discouragement attends the Lord's exercised servants in this day, when labour is added to labour, baptism to baptism

tifm, for thofe that are dead in trefpaffes and fins, and for thofe that are unacquainted, in their own experience, with the glad tidings of the gofpel; fo that, if they were not at times refrefhed with a little bread handed in fecret, and their evidence confirmed, that the foundation of God ftands fure, having this feal that the Lord knows them that are his, they would be ready to faint in the work, and to fhrink in the day of battle, when the arrows of the archers furround, and the fpirits of the people are oppofing found doctrine, and crying " prophefy unto us fmooth things." But I have had frequently of late, under thefe difcouraging views, to remember the prophet when he mournfully exclaimed ; " I have laboured in vain, and fpent my ftrength for nought ;" yet recollecting himfelf in holy confidence in, and intereft with, invifible and divine juftice, he added, " but furely my judgment is with the Lord, and my work with my God." From fome neceffary baptifms of mind, and renewed evidences that this is enough for any true minifter of the gofpel to defire, I have been led awfully and humbly to implore increafing ftrength and ability, to walk before that gracious eye that fees in fecret, without feeking the praife, or regarding the cenfure of men who are not circumcifed in heart and ears, and who cannot difcern, or value, found uncondemnable words, but want their fenfual wifdom and depraved ideas gratified with the divinations of men, and approbation of themfelves. We had an exercifing, clofe, and fearching opportunity on fifth day evening (after the publick meetings were over) with thofe under profeffion with us, and particularly the ftudents ; to whom divine regard was

eminently

eminently manifested, and a powerful call extended, to close in with the present visitation and day of salvation that is offered; whereby they would be redeemed from that wisdom which separates them from the pure fear of God, and the tree of immortal life; and also preserved from going down to the chambers of death, by falling in with those snares and gilded pollutions, with which the unwearied enemy of our souls is seeking to entrap and defile us. Their minds were sensibly affected, at that time, under the power of truth; and he who was pleased thus to influence their spirits, is alone able to prosper the work.* The next morning we went to Kirkaldie, (by Queen's Ferry) where we had a meeting with the town's people, some of whom behaved well, the glad tidings of the gospel were preached; and a satisfactory meeting it was. From hence we went that evening one stage further,

* It is difficult to suppress a remark, respecting young men of our society being sent to complete their education at this place; which is, that the advantages of medical improvement are, beyond all comparison, out-balanced by the pernicious principles of infidelity which are imbibed there. Several young persons, religiously hopeful at the time of commencing their studies, have returned from thence deeply poisoned in their religious principles; and some who have not been altogether slain in the contest, have, it is feared, become so much wounded, as to endanger their going halting all their days. It is of unspeakable importance for parents and guardians solidly to consider, in their disposal of youth, the danger not only of this, but of every other exposed situation in life. No professional advantages, or qualifications whatever, can be put in competition with the loss or injury of that pure faith and principle, which is our unerring guide, our support and comfort through time.

ther, and purposed next day for Montrose, forty-nine miles. The first stage in the morning was to Coupar in Fife, where we felt a considerable openness for a meeting, but having too much, in our own inclination, fixed our work for this day, we put by this simple feeling, and thought that, if way opened, we would give up to it in our return. A few hours convinced us that our plans were frustrated; for when we arrived at Dundee Ferry, we found ourselves about half an hour too late for the tide, so that our horses could not be taken over till about that time in the evening, at which we should have been there, had we staid and had a meeting at Coupar in Fife. From Dundee we went to Aberbrothick, which we left next morning for Montrose, where we had a meeting in the evening with the town's people, who behaved well, and to whom divine regard was powerfully manifested.

From hence we went to Inverbervy, a little seaport between Montrose and Aberdeen. Here we found we could not get away, without a meeting amongst the town's people, which was readily provided for, and a very solid company attended; whose minds seemed like the good ground cultivated by the divine hand, for the reception of the seed of the kingdom. Divine aid was eminently extended to us, and to the people, and we were led, publickly and secretly, to return the gratitude of our hearts to him whose works alone can praise him, and who, in infinite wisdom, after these favoured opportunities, is sometimes pleased to lead his poor, weak, servants, as from the holy mountain, and from tasting the animating wine of the kingdom,

into

into the wildernefs ; and to caufe them, like their Mafter, to experience fomething of the forty days faft, and the power of the Tempter; that fo, their own inability may be proved, their humble confidence renewed in the divine arm, they drawn from having any confidence in the flefh, and taught not to live by bread alone. From hence we proceeded to Stonehaven, and fat with the few friends there, in whom the life of religion is weak. We went to Aberdeen that evening, and next day had a clofe time with the friends there. The fame afternoon we reached Old-meldrum, and next day fat a meeting with them, where we found we could not get away without fitting in the families, and having a publick meeting with the town's people; the firft we fet about the fame day, and had a fatisfactory meeting with the people in the evening. We found things very low amongft the friends, but a comfortable hope, that of the youth would be raifed up fuch as would be qualified to fupport the caufe of truth, which is ready to fall in the ftreets, and the principles thereof almoft forgotten by thofe that profefs them, particularly in departing from the plain language, and lofing the diftinguifhing marks of their profeffion; whereby the crofs is evaded, and the people's minds become like the high-way ground. We finifhed the vifit to the families at Kilmuck, and went from thence on feventh day evening for Aberdeen, and ftaid there the next day. My companion attended the meetings, where fhe had good fervice, and many people of the town came in. I had been unwell for fome time before with pain in my face and teeth, which had now fo increafed upon me, with frefh cold,

that,

that, feeling no particular draft to the friends or people, and scarce being fit to move, I staid in the house that day, in order to use some means for recovery, which were not ineffectual, and next morning we set forward for Urie. Here the friends of Stonehaven met us, but it was a painful opportunity, and little of the divine life to be felt. We reached Montrose in the evening, and next day went to Aberbrothick, where we used some means to obtain a meeting, but they not being effectual, we were easy to leave the place; and went forward, without any other meeting in the way, to Edinburgh, where we arrived on fifth day evening, the fifteenth of the month.* The next evening we reached

---

* From Aberbrothick she writes thus to a friend; " The minds of many of the people in this land seem preparing, like the good ground, to receive, in childlike simplicity, the ingrafted word; and though it may be long before fruits appear, yet if those that come this way, follow the simple openings of truth, in their stoppings at places where there are no friends, and get baptized into the states of the people, it appears clear to us, that such will be instrumental in helping forward the light of the perfect day of the gospel, which has dawned in many of these parts; but it is under present chastisement for neglect of duty, that I acknowledge we have not sufficiently trod this path. One material omission the week before last, has laid a foundation for repentance through this land, if not through time, unless our Master sometime sends us again to pay debt and interest; because, from that one neglect, has proceeded many entanglements, and preventions of doing right. We have great cause to believe and acknowledge, that the divine aid which hath been afforded, particularly in this land, hath been great; and though it may have been chiefly on account of the people, yet gratitude hath covered our minds for it, and it occasions us to feel more deeply any want of faithfulness."

reached Kelfo, and Morpeth on the feventeenth, from whence we went next morning to Newcaftle to breakfaft, and attended both their meetings; in which we had deep, fearching, but honeft labour;

The following letters were written a few days after her getting out of Scotland.

" It is a favour when we are at liberty to feel one another, in the cementing bond of pure love and unchangeable fellowfhip; for, really, in journeys of this kind, our minds are often fo ftripped of fatisfactions like thefe, that inftead of feeling as if we belong to any body, or have any outward fource of comfort, the ftate of the pelican in the wildernefs feems moft fimilar to ours; and, no doubt, for wife ends, our minds are thus clothed with abftractednefs, and feparated from domeftick bleffings; for our eye then being fingle, and we confidering ourfelves fervants that have need to watch every pointing of the Mafter, we are in the greater fitnefs to receive that divine light, in which, and by which only, every fervice in the church can be rightly accomplifhed."

———" We are convinced it is right for thofe who go into Scotland, to go without plans, or fixed times for things, and fimply to attend, day by day, to the openings of truth, giving up their time freely, and confidering themfelves in no refpect their own. Such as thus faithfully vifit Scotland, and get deep enough in their minds to bring up fuch weapons as will penetrate the minds of the people, and reach the divine life, rather than aim merely at convincing the judgment, will have, I am perfuaded, great fervice in that land, and find the free dedication of their time to be an acceptable facrifice."

———" We have now got as into our own camp, where clofe painful labour is often our lot; which being almoft continual, and without apparent effects, we are fometimes ready to fhrink from the work, and turn our faces homeward, confidering ourfelves, in every fenfe of the word, unprofitable fervants. But I have thus far found, that when we have been fo reduced, as hath been the cafe, that we durft not look for great things, divine

bour; and a degree of quietude, refignation, and ferenity of mind, clofed the day. The next day we refted, and on third were at Shields, fourth at Sunderland, fifth at Benfieldfide, fixth at Newbiggin, feventh at Allondale, firft at Aldfton, and fecond at Cornwood: at all which, the effects of an inattention to the unerring fpiritual guide, were deeply felt by us; and, from place to place, our fpirits were pained in viewing the declenfion and defolation which have fpread themfelves, even amongft the foremoft claffes of the people; fo that fome of thofe who have appeared as fhepherds over the flock, have been overtaken therewith, fmitten by the hand of the enemy, and proved their difqualification for fervice; whereby many that knew not

ftrength hath been moft adminiftered, and the bleffings that attend our thus dwelling in the deeps, have been couched under thefe feelings; and the fpirit of difcernment hath fo proceeded therefrom, that we have had humbly to admire the dealings of the divine hand, which, by reducing his fervants, exalteth his own caufe. When felf is moft brought down, there is leaft anxiety about the fruits of our labour; they are left to the great Hufbandman, who caufeth the rain to defcend on the juft, and on the unjuft; and furely it is enough for us to experience our meat and our drink to be an obedience to the will of our heavenly Father: for thereby, we get food that the world knows not of, and feel ourfelves bound to his truth, though many may forfake it. We are reconciled to fuffer therewith, feeing with an eye of faith, that notwithftanding the declenfion amongft us, the fmiting of the fhepherds, fome in being happily removed from the evil to come, and others by the hand of the enemy, and the fcattering of the fheep, yet the promife will be fulfilled, upon the little ones: and thefe keeping to their Judge and Lawgiver, they fhall with the Lamb, experience a victory."

not the sure foundation, but whose eyes were fixed upon man, and whose walking was circumscribed by the appearance of others, have been scattered from the place of true feeding, and thus want an anchor to their souls in the time of trial. This the spirit of truth would have amply supplied, had it been made the object of their researches, instead of the honour, the wisdom, and the complicated gratifications of man in his depraved state. But in the course of these meetings, particularly at Newbiggin, Allondale, and Cornwood, we felt an evidence that the divine promise will be fulfilled upon the little ones, and that there are of this number, who, if they keep faithful under the preparing hand, will be raised up to be standard-bearers in the work and house of their God. But oh the danger of even these, that have been several times dipped as in Jordan, not abiding the day of further trial, wherein nothing but the pure gold will stand; because the fiery baptism of the spirit, is so superior to every thing but what is of its own durable nature, that whatever has been mixed with it must, in this test, be swept away; that the vessel which is formed of the residue, may be so pure as to be entitled to the inscription of, " holiness unto the Lord." As it is for want of this patient dedication of heart to the operation of truth, that many vessels amongst us have been little better than sounding brass or tinkling cymbals to the people, having no authority from that of which they spoke, nor discovering an alliance to the master by following his holy pattern, my heart has been led fervently to implore for myself, and for a number of these, to whom I felt united in our heavenly Father's love,

that

that whatsoever may be the sufferings of the present day, and howsoever one may fall on one hand, and another on another, our eye may be fixed on the Rock of our strength, and our faith so replenished, that though the feet may be placed as in the very bottom of Jordan, we may not flinch therefrom, nor seek an easier path than that which the wrestling seed of Jacob have ever trod; nor have any greater joy than to be united by an exercise of spirit to our holy Head, whether in suffering or in rejoicing. We had, in all these places, the renewed assistance of that spirit which helpeth our infirmities, teacheth how to pray and travail in spirit, and how to minister to the states of the people; whereby some of the hidden things of darkness were searched out, the strayed of the flock invited to the fold, and the little travailing remnant were encouraged to go forward on their way. We had a uniting season at Cornwood, in that pure fellowship of spirit, which supplieth every member in the body with fresh vigour to perform its function.—From hence, with our friends M. J. and J. W. we went to a meeting in Cumberland: it was a time of deep exercise of mind, but in faithfulness thereto, the power of truth rose into dominion, and we had reason to hope it was a profitable time to divers. We left this place, and in the afternoon were at another meeting, which was, for a time, painful beyond description; but by an humble waiting, it was discovered that the people were fed with an unsound ministry, that the ark was taken into the hands of the uncircumcised, and that there was a number who loved to have it so. The power and authority of truth arose, by which

which we were enabled to place judgment on that spirit, which was seeking to support the testimony with unsanctified hands, and to have their honour from men, forgetting that holy anointing and preparation of heart, whereby the Lord becomes sanctified in all those that draw nigh unto him, and the bread that he gives them to break receives a blessing upon it, in that it shall not be void, but prove a visitation of his love to those to whom it is sent, whether they will hear or forbear. Here we had afresh to observe, that where ministers maintain their inward exercise, and keep near to their gifts, the spirit of true discernment, which searcheth all things, is not wanting to prove, from the line in which it leads them, the rectitude of their ministry to the living and wise in heart; who judge not by the sight of the eye, or the hearing of the ear, but by the unerring evidence of truth, which remains to be the favour of life unto life. Our minds were thankful, under the fresh sense of divine favour and strength, in being found worthy to suffer with the suffering seed, and with the little remnant that are thus exercised, and who belong to this meeting: to these, though they are weak, the bread of encouragement was broken.

Next morning we set forward, and on our way, I received an account from my husband who was then in London, of the death of his father, and that he purposed going over with the friends who had attended the yearly meeting, to accompany his sister, and to pay a visit to his mother and friends on this affecting occasion; reasons with
which

which my judgment led me to coincide, though I felt myself deeply affected with so unexpected a circumstance; and having received a letter conveying sorrowful intelligence on various subjects, I was ready, with the additional concern of the important service in which we were engaged, to sink under the general pressure of my mind. But in this situation, I had fresh cause to recur to that divine and invisible arm which drew me out; and in the feeling whereof I could then say, with a degree of holy confidence, " Lord I have left all to follow thee," to that station into which I apprehended myself called, though but a child, and to nothing short of a disciple of the Lamb, to fight under his banner, and to prefer his work to every gratification or concern of my own. I found it was an easy thing to say, I will follow thee wheresoever thou leadest; but when our fidelity is tried with cross occurrences in our natural feelings, united to the fresh painful sense, that the foxes have holes, &c. then are we ready to shrink, and desire that the cup may pass from us, forgetting that all must be left to the great Disposer of all things; that so with holy confidence, our resolutions may be, " though thou slay me, yet will I trust in thee." Under this dispensation, I was afresh stripped, and became a suppliant at wisdom's gate; where, I found, I had nothing to receive for my help, but a patient submission to the divine will, and renewed strength, simply and singly, to wait, not only respecting circumstances relating to my social concerns, but in the line of my religious duty, and in the exercise of the gift; seeing that it is only when the eye is single, that the

the body is full of light. We attended the next meeting, which for a time was inexpreffibly dark and painful; but being engaged fervently to travail for the refurrection of life, we had renewedly to acknowledge, that our labours were bleffed, and ftrength afforded for that time, to awaken a number from a ftate of fpiritual death, and to fhew them the deplorable fituations they were in. We proceeded to another meeting, and on firft day attended both the meetings there; in the firft of which we were enabled to relieve our minds from the weight which, in the forepart, deeply affected us, and it was a time of renewed favour. Numbers will not hear either the Mafter or the fervant when found doctrine is delivered unto them: but the moft fine gold becoming changed, and they remembering fomething of the work of the Refiner, but not keeping under it themfelves, are making fomewhat for the people which is fpecious, and feeds their itching ears, but which at the fame time is putting death into the pot: fo that for want of thofe that hear recurring to the witnefs for God, the true fpirit of prophecy, the feed of the kingdom becomes ftifled, and total infenfibility enfues; a ftate over which, in this county, we had deeply to mourn. The meeting in the afternoon was filent, and our minds preferved in great refignation. On 3d day following we went to Moorhoufe and Kirkbride, on 4th at Wigton and Bolton, on 5th at Berkfoot and at Maryport, and on 6th at Allonby and Broughton. The clofenefs of the exercife in meetings, and in travelling, had by this time fenfibly affected or reduced our ftrength and fpirits; but refting on 7th day with a friend helped to re-
ftore

ftore us a little : yet the wounded and captivated ftate of us as a people, and efpecially in this county, renders a little prefent reft, like the eating of the paffover, with bitter herbs ; for how can the fervant rejoice where the Mafter reigns not ! On 1ft day we fat with the friends at Pardfhaw, where divine regard was renewedly extended to us and to them, in opening the book of His law, and difcovering the tranfgreffions of the profeffors thereof. The fame evening we rode to Whitehaven, and had a meeting there the next day the 10th, which was painful; but a little oppreffed remnant were ftrengthened ; for which thankfulnefs ought to arife, and gratitude cover our fpirits, notwithftanding we, as the poor fervants and offfcouring of all things, are often abafed under the fenfe of our own nothingnefs, and of our omiffions and commiffions ; for on thefe the compaffionate eye of the Mafter condefcends to look, when we feé ourfelves, and are proftrate before him, under the fenfe of how liable we are to fwerve to the right hand or to the left, from the clear and pure openings of truth in our religious fervices, without a clofe attention of mind thereto. This requires a previous ftrippednefs, and baptifm of fpirit, that our own activity may be reduced, and fubjected to the Power that quickeneth and giveth life, and that, likewife, unprofitable timidity and fear of man, may become fo removed, that we can, with finglenefs and refignation, depend folely upon the fimple revelation of the divine will. For though it is needful for our refinement, and fitnefs for fervice, to be clothed with the fenfe of our weaknefs, and the infufficiency

ciency of our wifdom and difcernment in the myfteries of the kingdom, and in performing the leaft work for the fpiritual building; yet on this, when called to labour, our eye fhould not be fixed, but reft, with faith, on the invifible arm of divine power; that being in a fituation ready to receive help from it, we may be therewith content, and favoured with that bleffing which renders acceptable the fmalleft offering, or the bread that may be compared but to the barley loaf. We went to another meeting, where things are very low, fome of the members being fo weak as to let fall fome of the fundamental principles of our profeffion; whereby the few that are faithful are oppreffed with the feed, and are ready to fink under difcouragements, and alfo with fome appearances in the miniftry, concerning which we felt no anfwer of life as unto life. Here we lodged at the houfe of our valuable friends J. and B. D. who next day accompanied us, with fome other friends, to Kefwick, where we had a pretty large and fatisfactory meeting amongft the town's people. On fifth day the thirteenth, we attended the week day meeting, and monthly feleft meeting at Greyfouthen, where gracious condefcenfion was eminently extended to us, and to the members thereof; and we parted with many of our friends on that fide, in much affectionate fellowfhip, and fympathy with each others' tried fituations, arifing from the deep declenfion and defolation which widely fpread over us as a people. Next morning we rode to Ifell meeting, in a very ftormy, tempeftuous day, fo much fo, that the friends belonging to the meeting durft not venture out, except three men, for whom,

whom, in a cold damp meeting-houfe, we waited in our wet clothes three quarters of an hour; having no better accommodations for ourfelves or horfes, than a bare fhelter from the heavy rain that fell here. We fat down with the few that came, and our guides, ready to conclude that, under thefe circumftances, it would be an unavailing attempt to have our minds properly ftayed; but he who mercifully condefcends to vifit the two or three that gather in his name, was pleafed eminently to own us that day. I remembered, and had to open the paffage, " Bleffed is that fervant that watcheth, and keepeth his garment, and who, when his Lord cometh, is found ready." It appeared to my mind that all thofe who have enlifted under the fpiritual, unconquered Captain, have received a mark thereof, a change of heart, an awful covering of fpirit, a loving one another, and means whereby fuch might ftand in readinefs for the word of command; and that therefore the peculiar bleffing of the divine hand refts upon thefe faithful fervants, who when not actually in fervice, fo remember their office, as to be fit, when called thereto, to ftep into it, and move only in that raiment, and with that armour, which the mafter gives them. For want of this watchful, attentive care, in times of withdrawing, many amongft us, when there has been an opening for labour, have not been found ready, nor approved worthy, to advocate the heavenly caufe; and thus the warfare has not been maintained, but the battle is retarded, Ifrael falls before his enemies, and the accurfed thing is in the tribe of Judah. At the clofe of this meeting, where my mind had been led to cen-

tre

tre to a quiet dependance on the smallest evidence of the divine will, after some days of deep probation, and frequent desertion of spirit, the aforesaid passage, "blessed is that servant, &c." powerfully revived and spread before me, and, with a voice intelligible to my spiritual ear, applied it to myself; which introduced such a calm over my mind, and separation from the natural feelings thereof, as I never before experienced. Under this sense, I concluded it was the last meeting I should ever be at; that the dedication of my heart, and some afflictive dispensations that were past, had proved acceptable, and that now there was no obstruction to my final dissolution; nor an attachment in me to any thing below: a situation of mind so different from what I usually felt, when I have feared that the closeness of my connections had the ascendency over my love, and travail of spirit for the cause of truth, that I wondered at the change. I looked towards my friends, saw some of them in their places, and feeling myself in my own, without a cord to break, I apprehended that, in a very little time, I should be gathered to that eternal habitation of rest, whereinto I never before so sensibly entered, and of which I had never such a foretaste. It was nothing that elated me, my natural ideas were dormant, but what I experienced seemed solid substantial truth. After the meeting broke up, and I was making the necessary preparations for proceeding to the next meeting, there was no interruption to my mind, till riding along the road, with a fresh, awful application to the Lord, and breathing that I might not rest too much under this impression, and that if there was any

other

other end to anfwer than what I had feen, it might be difcovered; left by looking too much at an opening fo comfortable to myfelf, I fhould be in danger of neglecting a continued exercife of fpirit, and the fervice I might be called to from place to place; and thereby render that which was intended a bleffing, a block in my way in preffing after fo defirable an end as had opened therein: thus waiting to fee further the way caft up for me, I thought I clearly difcovered, that it was a mark of divine regard at that time extended, in order to fhew me the excellent, ultimate, effect of what I had had to open to others; and the need there was for me to attend to it myfelf, during the courfe of my own pilgrimage; and alfo to remove an idea, that the ties of nature are fo interwoven with my attachment to eternal excellency and purity, that the feparation muft be, like the furnace being heated feven times hotter than it had before been experienced. Inftead of this, I had to behold, in humble admiration, the works of an almighty hand in the deeps, and how, when our hearts are upright before him, he invifibly works our deliverance, by means which the unenlightened underftanding of man cannot comprehend. When the power of truth predominates, we fee, in the vifion of light, its fuperiority to every natural endowment or gratification; fo that the infurmountable difficulties that are beheld by the natural eye, are fubjected, and the mountain of the Lord is exalted on the top of all the hills. In commemoration of this token of divine regard, my mind is bowed, under the fenfe of my own unworthinefs, and how unable I am, notwithftanding this view, to dwell

in

in a state of preservation and acceptance, without wrestling, from time to time, for that faith which overcometh, and that patience whereby we are kept in the hour of temptation: for if the Lord keep not the city, the watchman watcheth but in vain. After the meeting at Isell we went to Coldbeck, where we had a suffering time, but were enabled in a good degree to search out the cause. Next day we attended a meeting at Mosedale, where we had comfortably to observe that the Master's feet had been, though in general things are very low. On first day, the sixteenth, we were at both their meetings at Penrith, where we painfully felt the oppression of the seed, as in many other places. That evening we rode to Terril, and next morning had a meeting there; where the necessity of those who are called to the ministry sitting loose from outward connections and profits, and following the Master whithersoever he leads them, was clearly set forth. From hence we went to Strickland meeting, and on our way, I had a fall from my horse, with which I was hurt, but attended the meeting, which was favoured, and I gradually recovered. From Strickland we went to Hawkshead, and from thence to Swarthmore, where many not of our society attended; and it proved an eminently favoured season. Our next meeting was at Height which was a low time. We then proceeded to another meeting, rested and wrote on 7th day; and on first sat both their meetings, where we had secretly to mourn over, and publickly to discover, the affecting situation of those who, from year to year, have been divinely favoured, and, like the vineyard we read of, dug about, fenced, and visited

D   -   by

by the good Hufbandman: but oh, the falling
fhort! one may plant, and another may water, yet
as the increafe is of the Lord, and He not being
devotedly fought unto, for that dew of heaven
which renders us fruitful, and that pruning hand
which would keep the branches clean, numbers,
after having been planted choice vines, have become
the degenerate plants of a ftrange vine unto the
Lord; and notwithftanding they keep a greennefs,
and an appearance of life, it was clear to the view
of our minds, that if there was not a getting deeper, even to the wafhing pool, and being ftripped of
themfelves, the princes alfo arifing from the duft
of the earth and anointing the fhield, that fpiritual
death will greatly increafe amongft them, and the
judgments of the Lord for difobedience will enfue.
We took the week following, Prefton, Grayrig,
Sedberg, Dent, Garfdale, Ravenftonedale, and Lar-
tington; and alfo had a fatisfactory meeting at
Bowes, where are none of our fociety; and at the
others, we were favoured with ftrength for the
exercife that fell to our lot therein. The firft day
following, we attended the meeting at Staindrop,
and another in the evening at Bifhop Aukland; on
fecond day we went to Durham to their quarterly
meeting, attended the feveral fittings thereof: in
all which we were enabled, far beyond our expectation, to relieve our minds, by honeftly, in the fear
of the Lord, and not of man, expreffing our fenfe
of the ftate of things amongft them; and it was a
time of renewed favour. From thence we went
forward, and at a meeting wherein the uncircum-
cifed fpirit was painfully felt to prevail in the forepart thereof, but our help and fafety depending

upon

upon our going down to the brook, we were engaged patiently to wait for divine clothing, knowing that it would be dangerous to go againſt them in untried armour, notwithſtanding the cauſe might be good: and we may thankfully ſay, that good is the word of the Lord, and efficacious to the ſmiting of the Goliaths of this day."

Her own account of this journey ends here; but it appears that ſhe proceeded from this place, and viſited the meetings at Stockton, and Yarm, back to Benfieldſide, then Ayton, Bilſdale, and Kirby, and returned home about the middle of the ſeventh month.

After ſhe had got out of Scotland, ſhe and her companion felt their minds diſpoſed to ſalute the friends of the monthly meeting of Old Meldrum with an epiſtle; a copy whereof follows.

"Dear Friends!

" As in our travelling along, we have frequently felt our minds covered with an earneſt engagement for your preſervation, and a ſenſe of the love of our heavenly Father towards you, which engaged us to pay you a viſit, we are drawn in the renewed extendings thereof, to ſalute you with a few lines, and according to the ability received, to ſtrengthen the little life that is amongſt you; that the elders may be gathered to the true place of feeding, the middle-aged ariſing may become men and women of valour for God, and the youth having examples ſet before their eyes of a ſteady circumſpect walking, ſeaſoned with divine

D 2   virtue,

virtue, may be engaged, by the efficacy of the same holy principle, to succeed their parents, and the faithful in all ages, in carrying forward the Lord's work, and in His name, which is His power, setting up their banners. But, dear friends, as there are many impediments which have hindered us as a people, both in this land and in yours, from advancing in our spiritual progress, and increasing our strength in the Lord, let us inquire into the cause whence they have come, and to what they will tend; for if we had kept to the sure foundation, and in all things considered ourselves the followers of a crucified Lord, rather than nominal members of a religious society; and been concerned to walk even as He walked; the snares of the enemy would not have prevailed to have led so many captives into a strange land; because, against the Rock of ages, whereon we might have been built, the gates of hell shall never be able to prevail. But for want of keeping an eye open to this preserving Power, a spirit of indifferency hath crept in, and, whilst many have slept, tares have been sown; which as they spring up, have had a tendency to choke the good seed, those tender impressions, and reproofs of instruction, which would have prepared our spirits, and have bound them to the holy law and testimonies of truth. Thus, strength hath been wanting to maintain the discipline of the church, in that purity wherein it was first established; and a door hath opened for increasing liberties. Hence, hath ensued a mixing with the spirit, and customs of the world; so that those who have not been taught the same doctrines, but are looking upon us, may query, " where is your God ?" seeing, that though we profess to be led and guided by the spirit of truth, our fruits differ not from theirs; but the cross is removed out of the way. As one deviation from the path our predecessors walked in, conformable to the precepts of Christ, painfully affected our minds, both when our lot was cast amongst you, and since ; we feel not easy without renewedly observing, that, in the promise of the restoration to Israel, it was said, " I will turn to the people a pure language ;" and knowing that this gospel day is still more glorious than that,. if we did but live in the light thereof, which would clearly discover to us the corrupt source of flattering titles, and seeking to gratify the vain mind of man, how can we, without sacrificing the principle of truth, which leads and guides into all truth, give up that pure language to which our forefathers were turned, and adopt the unsound words of You to a single person ; and calling the days of the week and months by the heathen names ; and those, our masters and mistresses, who are not really so ; forgetting the command to call no man, master. Is not this returning to the night of apostacy, and in our dealings and converse with men, crucifying afresh the Son of God, and putting him to open shame, by thus denying, or refusing to bear his cross and testimony to the world ?

" We believe there is a number amongst you, who, by example, have been trained in a deviation from our holy profession ; and these we tenderly address, and exhort to feel for themselves after the influence of that holy spirit, which leads its followers in the same path, however remote from outward help their situations in life may be; for the peculiar privilege of these is, they need not that any man teach them, but as this same divine anointing teacheth them all things. Though you may have but few to strengthen your hands, by their example and sympathy with you in your honest endeavours to break down the partition walls, which the enemy has raised to prevent your advancement to the perfect day of God; yet be not dismayed in your labours; but remember the fervent zeal of our predecessors in the truth; how they endured the persecutions of that day, and how, with unconquerable fortitude and resignation to the Lord's will, they steadily pursued the path of true self-denial, and fought the good fight of faith. And if we, in this day of deep declension, look to the Rock of our strength, we cannot fail to find that it is a day which calls for diligence; and that whatever pointings of duty we are favoured with, our preservation depends upon a faithfulness thereto. And therefore, beloved friends, be ye engaged to see what it is that keeps you in a state of weakness, and prevents your feeling the strengthening and consolating influence of the spirit of Christ; that so, you may be enabled to remove the impediment out of the way, be faithful to the Lord, and stand in the authority of his truth; that endeavouring to rule your own houses well, and to have your children in subjection with all gravity, you may know his baptizing power upon your spirits, in your assembling together; and your secret prostration and fervent breathings, will be acceptable to his holy eye, and blessed by his bountiful hand;

hand; and in your meetings for difcipline, you will likewife be feafoned with the falt of the covenant, and by your honeft endeavours to keep the camp clean from all diforderly walkers, you will grow ftronger and ftronger, and your minds become united together in the bond of true peace. Thus, may it pleafe the Lord to operate upon your fpirits, and to influence the youth amongft you to a watchful attention to their thoughts, their words, and actions; that being preferved from mixing with thofe, who would draw away their minds from the difcoveries of truth, and centre them in the corrupt language, and changeable cuftoms of the world, they may prefer a religious awfulnefs upon their fpirits, and feek for that pure fear of the Lord which is a fountain of life, preferving from the fnares of death, and fecuring a fafe hiding-place in the day of trouble. With fatisfaction we acknowledge, that we felt, whilft with you, that the hand of the Lord has been at work upon the minds of the youth, and that fome of thefe have fubmitted thereto; to whom our fpirits were, and are led into near fympathy, and filled with an earneft defire for their prefervation and progrefs in that good work which is begun in their hearts. Be encouraged, beloved friends, to hold on your way, and more fully to fubmit your necks to the holy yoke; that thereby you may be made willing to fuffer for the caufe of truth; and though you may not have many examples and helpers in the Lord, yet being engaged to dwell near the Root of divine life, and feeking for ftrength therefrom, you will feel the progreffive difpenfation of the heavenly Vifitant, and grow in ftature, from the ftate of children, to young men in the Lord; let fituations be what they may, and outward advantages ever fo great, we are abundantly convinced, that whoever experience an inheritance in the truth, and an eftablifhment therein, muft purchafe it for themfelves, learn to live on manna of their own gathering, and know from whence all their frefh fprings proceed. And now, dear friends, the fervent defire of our fpirits is, that you may be ftirred up to a renewed fenfe of the declenfion of the prefent day, and under it, be engaged to feek for ftrength to ftablifh you in every good word and work; that being clothed with a zeal according to knowledge, for the profperity of Zion, and the enlargement of her borders, you may become eftablifhed as a city fet upon a hill, having the light of the gofpel day upon your dwellings.

"*Benfieldfide, 7th month 7th,* 1782."

C H A P.

CHAP. III.

Visit to her Husband's Relations in Ireland.—Journey into Norfolk, &c.—Visit to the Meetings of Friends in Ireland.

IN the 11th month 1782, she felt an inclination and freedom of mind, to accompany her husband into Ireland, on a visit to their relations. The deeply instructive exercises which she met with previous to her landing in Ireland; with her humble, watchful state of mind and engagements there, may in part be collected from the following letters, which, except the first, she wrote in that land.

———" This place (Holyhead) is uncomfortable to stay at, amongst a great deal of company, and no woman but myself; and though it is made easier by their great civility, yet the journey altogether is an awful thing. On surveying my inducements for coming and impartially examining myself, I have not yet found any uneasiness, though I am low, and our present situation is a trial of both faith and patience. Indeed the many rocks and shoals attending us in our religious and civil concerns through this trying pilgrimage, will, I apprehend, ever prove a trial of these; and therefore, by the direction of the Best of Pilots, to guard against them, and to steer wisely through life, is the work of our day; and will open most clearly the prospect of the haven of durable rest."

———" I was greatly pleased when we got to Holy-

Holyhead, hoping foon to be in Dublin, and dreading the water but little. Here our difappointments began. We went out to fea next day, were toffed about for fourteen hours, and I then returned extremely ill; fo much fo, that it became a matter of doubt to my hufband whether he fhould not have to bury me there. I thought as foon as my head was laid after our return, that I perceived a cup bitterer than death; for that death, except on R. G.'s account, I fhould not have regretted, fo fhaded are all the domeftick enjoyments and temporal bleffings of life, when, abftracted from them, we are called upon, faithfully and with finglenefs of heart, to do the will of our heavenly Father. To have a meeting at Holyhead prefented with great weight, and at the fame time the appearance of things told me that, on various accounts, (my own bodily weaknefs not the leaft) it was an impoffibility. I was afraid, but I think I was not rebellious. In the depth of diftrefs, I offered myfelf as one unable to anfwer the requiring, hoping the offering would be accepted, and that fome ram would be caught in the thicket; here the call feemed renewed to obedience, and not facrifice; and I faw that if any thing fhort of the demand was offered, though I even exerted myfelf in faithfulnefs in Ireland, as I promifed to do, I might be fuffered to fall into a fnare, and return from thence, inftead of the reward of peace, with the query, Who hath required this at thy hands? Prefent obedience, and fubfervience to the operation of truth on our minds, is no doubt what will preferve us on this fea of glafs mingled with fire; for if we keep with the life,

and

and move therein, it will keep us humble, reduce our confidence in the flefh, and draw us down into fuffering with it. When our dwelling is as amongft the pots, and no goodlinefs remaineth in us, then we know in whom is eternal help, and the travail of our fpirits is for ability to look towards his holy habitation. Our firft failing was on fourth day, and by fixth day I was got fomething better, when the captain, and a great number of paffengers were difpofed to fail, and none of them more fo than ourfelves, if the wind would take us, which, according to the feelings of my mind, I believed would not; but I have no caufe to think it was unacceptable to try the fleece again; which we did, and after getting out of the harbour, the wind turned againft us, and grew very rough. The veffel was violently toffed, and at one time we were in great danger of foundering. I lay quietly as I could, beholding the wonders of an almighty hand concerning us; and in the deeps, both fpiritually and temporally, I felt myfelf a Jonah, when the people were crying, that there was one on board; and all was tremendous about me. The danger we were in was evident, but my hope never failed me; which I efteemed an unfpeakable favour, and which led me to a greater willingnefs than I had before felt, to give up to the meeting, or any thing elfe that was required. We were out this time but about four hours, and after we landed, a large merchant fhip was wrecked in our fight, but no lives loft. My fituation now became awful; there feemed no way but refignednefs to the meeting, and that I could not fee was to be till firft day. My hufband

I perceived was afraid, for he confidered us accountable for whatever the caufe fuffered by us, efpecially as there never was a meeting there before. On firſt day morning we were tried again, for the wind being fair, we prepared for failing, and when all was ready for going on board, a ſtorm came on, and the captain durſt not venture to loofe the ſhip in the harbour, believing that if he did it would be foon wrecked. We then returned again, and the time came on for the people to go to fome place of worſhip; when finding an empty houfe near the inn, we engaged it, and felt moſt eafy to give notice to but a few, that we were going to fit in our ufual manner to worſhip, and that if they, or any others, chofe to accompany us, we had no objection. Before we got to the place, many were there, and more followed; and to our humble admiration, divine affiſtance was near, and wonderfully helped us over that fitting. At the concluſion, the people were defirous of another in the evening, which, when we had confidered it, we confented to; and if I may venture to fay, it was crowned with good, and the melting operation of truth appeared to be experienced by many of the people, who behaved with great folidity. The next evening tide fuited for our paſſage, and with peaceful minds we embarked, and were but nine hours from bay to bay. Thus have we caufe to turn back to this page of our lives, with humble gratitude of mind, and to acknowledge that a fimple pointing of duty, and a fimple difcharge thereof, is productive of folid fatisfaction, when, on the other hand, no exertion or anxiety of our own, can furniſh us with one

grain

grain of it, nor can we, by taking thought, add one cubit to our stature!"

———" Often, very often, since I saw your faces, has my mind visited you in affectionate nearness; but I have seldom felt greater inability, than since I came into this land, thus to converse with my friends; for as our coming was sudden, it has occasioned deep searchings of heart, for preservation, and direction how to move in the line of wisdom.

" We met with a very cordial reception in Ireland; the hospitality and affection of our friends were not unacceptable to a poor stranger like me; nevertheless my mind has not seemed at liberty, as I could have wished, to enjoy that society which is gratifying to self. It is good for us renewedly to feel ourselves not our own, to stand resigned to the divine will, and to know it to be our meat and drink to do it. Every little additional experience tends to convince us, that herein consists our most solid and permanent satisfaction; and were our disposition of resistance to the painful preparation for devotedness removed, we should more often have feelingly to acknowledge, that with the divine blessings, there is added no sorrow; but we make sorrows for ourselves, we add that which our gracious Benefactor hath not in store for us. A path exempt from trials is what I have no right to expect, and what I hope I am learning not to desire. A patient submission to every divine dispensation, is what I wish for an increase of; that so, the mingled cup of life may prove a profitable draught, and impress me, more

and

and more, with an humble fenfe of the multiplied
bleflings beftowed upon me: for by this means I
believe we fhall increafe in knowledge how to
move and conduct ourfelves, amidft the various
temptations, befetments, and crofs occurrences,
incident to this probationary ftate.

"We went pretty directly from Dublin for Clonmel, after the half-year's meeting, and fpent two
days very much to my inftruction, at Ballitore.
We ftaid about ten days amongft our relations,
who are valuable and kind, and then went for
Carlow quarterly meeting, where were Robert
Valentine and his companion, &c. I think, upon
the whole, it was a very favoured gathering, though
here, as in our land, the world and its fpirit has
made great devaftation and fcattering amongft the
gathered tribes."

———" We look with a degree of fatisfaction
at our return. A little reft to body and mind will
be truly acceptable, as our vifit to our relations
feems now completed. Our paffage through this
land has been encumbered with many thorns, and
attended with many trials unforefeen by us. It is
a day of deep humiliation, and it fometimes looks
as if our judgment was taken away. I want not
to make complaints; I wifh rather to profit by
what I have fuffered, and reap inftruction from
every renewed difpenfation of infinite kindnefs;
feeling myfelf unworthy of the leaft of His benefits, and that, without His peculiar care, I fhall
be overwhelmed, and warped afide from the ftability of the truth: but by being baptized into a

deep

deep fenfe of my own weaknefs and frailty, I have been led to acknowledge, that even the bitter things are fweet; feeing, that in infinite wifdom, they are ordered for the ftrengthening of our fpiritual appetite, and bringing down that part in us which is at enmity with the crofs, and loves not its government in the mind."

Her home for feveral years after her marriage, was at Fofton, a village ten miles from York. This was to her a comfortable retirement, when not engaged abroad in the fervice of truth. But though gratifying to nature, and a defirable refting place, her concern for the advancement of her great Mafter's caufe, which was her moft defired meat and drink, often called her from this abode, fo that fhe feldom refided there for a month together. It appeared, indeed, that fhe was unwearied in promoting the caufe of truth and righteoufnefs, and willing to fpend and be fpent for the great Name's fake.

In the fpring of the year 1784, fhe appears to have been engaged in a vifit to the meetings and fome families of friends, in Norfolk, and to divers other meetings, as fhe proceeded to the yearly meeting at London. Of this religious engagement, no regular accounts of her own, have been difcovered; the following are the material parts of all that have been collected from her letters.

———" We had nine meetings laft week, at eight different places, befides private opportunities
in

in families, which we durst not avoid; finding the declension to be so great in almost every one, where we have come, and so few who seem to know it, that we are ready to say, For Zion's sake we cannot rest nor hold our peace, till at least they are informed of their state."———" We attended their week day meeting at this place, with which we were well satisfied, it being a time of much instruction, however to my mind; finding by a degree of living experience, that there is indeed a Minister of ministers, on whom we have great cause to wait to be instructed ourselves, in our private, as well as publick duty; that, in all things, we may approve ourselves obedient servants, and good examples to the flock. It was my lot to sit in silence, viewing the great and almost general insensibility to true religion."

———" We have not only travelled hard, but found much work at places where we have come, finding it rather more than usual in the line of our duty, to bear a testimony, not only to the truth, but against the numerous evils and inconsistencies, which have generally overspread the professors in these parts; and as our peace much depends, in our passing along, in being honest, and speaking the truth without parables, we have been enabled, pretty tolerably, to discharge our duty, and to shew them how far they are from what they pretend to be; though it is hard work, and we find that the more abundantly we manifest our love in this way, the less we are loved by many who have been used to smooth things, and have sought to make the truth conform to them, instead
of

of this conduct being brought to, and regulated by the truth. So that indeed many are blind in error, and those that see, will not exert themselves to search their own houses, and remove the inconsistencies that are in them. A mournful prospect appears in these, as well as many other parts; no likelihood of a succession in the truth, and even the present standard-bearers ready to faint. Under these impressions, we seek not great things for ourselves, but rather are disposed to consider it a favour, (great enough for us to expect) if we have our lives for a prey, from one place to another.

" We have little expectation, that in any sittings, our minds will get above the spirits of this people; and till that strength arises which puts the armies of aliens to flight, I trust our lips will be sealed, and we content therewith; for indeed, it is not an easy task to minister to this degenerate age, who think they know all things, and, like the magicians in Egypt, can account for all the works of the divine hand: but what a favour it is, that there is still extended to us as a people, that power which confounds the wisdom of these, and brings to nought their great understanding."

———" We have been much engaged the few days we have staid at Norwich. It has been to our minds a suffering time, during our stay in that place; but though we have mourned, and perhaps rather murmured at times, yet we have great cause to be thankful for the help wherewith, in infinite kindness, we have been helped. It is a day of great

great difcouragement, and I think I was never more ready to lay down my armour, than in filence this day at meeting. The fituation of mind I was in, I found tended to humble and reduce the creature; and as my foul was hungry, even the bitter food I partook of, became fweet, and I faw the profit of thefe feafons."

———" We left Norwich on feventh day, were at Yarmouth on firft, Pakefield on fecond, Becles on third, Leifton fourth, and Woodbridge to-day, where, as at fome other places, we fat in mournful, but I truft inftructive filence. What falls at times to our lots in meetings, and fometimes in converfations out of them, feems much like pulling down old houfes, and we are often afraid of being choked in the duft; for indeed moft of the buildings we fee are painfully fuperficial, and our little labour has been deeply diftreffing; fo that the language of my heart often is, "Who hath believed our report?" but I am thankful in feeling the burden decreafing, as our work feems clofing."

In the year following fhe felt a religious concern to join her friend Rebecca Jones, on a vifit to the meetings of friends in Ireland, &c. and having laid the fame before the monthly meeting, with the approbation thereof, and the concurrence of the quarterly meeting, fhe fet forward on this journey in the 7th month, 1785. Of this vifit there is preferved a fhort journal written by herfelf, which is as follows.

" I

"I left home the 13th of 7th month 1785, and spent two nights at York, in order to allow a comfortable opportunity of taking a solid and affectionate leave of my connections there; and on the 15th, went with my husband to Bradford, where, next day I parted with him, he returning to York, and I proceeding with my cousin W. M. (who was to accompany me to Ireland) for Manchester.

"We staid there the next day, being the first of the week, and I was at both their meetings; which favoured to my mind of that righteousness and wisdom of man, which never can work the righteousness of God nor favour the things that pertain to His kingdom.

"But there is a precious suffering seed in that place, to which my spirit was renewedly united in the covenant of light and life. On second day we went, with many friends, down the water to Warrington, where, on the 19th was held their monthly meeting, which I felt most easy to attend, though I might thereby miss an opportunity of crossing the water, so early as I otherwise might choose; and I was comfortably satisfied with this little dedication by the way. I went that evening to Liverpool, and waited till 6th day for a suitable wind for sailing. During this time, was their week day meeting and my spirit was there deeply exercised, on account of some who were substituting their own righteousness for the righteousness of God, which is inherited in pure faith, in the virtue and power of that creative Word, by which all things were made, that were made

made in the spiritual creation, and by which, through the reduction of the natural will and wisdom of men, they can no more worship the work of their own hands: and in the strength with which my spirit was renewedly supplied, I attempted to express somewhat on this subject, for which I felt peace. We next day embarked for Dublin, in the Hawke packet, and had a very tedious and distressing voyage, being uncomfortably detained, in part for want of wind, and in part by its being contrary; the latter occasioning us to put into the Isle of Man, where we staid two nights, and found a very courteous and hospitable reception from the inhabitants. My mind was attached to them, in the secret effusion of gospel love, but feeling abundant weakness in myself, and wanting that united exercise which is received by fellow labourers, I did not perceive it to be my wo if I preached not the gospel; and therefore, in an humble trust that the great Shepherd of Israel would send more suitable servants for that work in that isle, and not put my omission in the balance against me, I embarked again with the rest of our company, save one, whom we left dead on the island. Being out longer than we expected, by two days, our provisions were exhausted; and though through divine protection we did not suffer much from want, yet it was a favour gratefully to be commemorated, that we were enabled through some difficulty to land when we did; which, with the instruction conveyed to my mind, under deep discouragement, and close searching of heart, when all human consolations stood afar off, afforded humble cause to believe, that this trying dispensation was intended as a

necessary

necessary baptism of my spirit into the service before me.* On our landing, I soon met with our honourable

* A more particular account of this voyage, with several additional instructive remarks, are contained in the following selections from her letters.——" It is very unexpected to me to write from this port; but so little do we know what, in the course of divine wisdom, shall fall to our lot, that every increase of experience convinces us, there is no safer or easier situation of mind, than a daily dependance on, and quiet resignation to, Him who knows what is best for us, and what will tend most to His own honour. We sailed last sixth day from Liverpool, having got there on third, but the wind not being very fair when we set out, and turning more against us afterwards, occasioned a troublesome and wearisome passage thus far, not only by contrary winds, and severe sickness, but by the almost intolerable stench and suffocating closeness of our cabin and lodgings, and the continual wicked, obscene, conversation of our passengers, who are seventy in number. Sometimes, I was afraid it would overcome me, both in body and mind; when recalling to my remembrance the poor Negroes (who, added to what I have mentioned, in a far worse degree, are chained together, under the load of that anguish naturally attendant on a forced separation from the nearest connections in life, and with the prospect of perpetual bondage under cruel taskmasters) my small trials in this line, and indeed in every other, diminished in my view; and the multitude of blessings, in infinite mercy, showered down, so crouded in their place, that at times, instead of repining, I saw abundant cause to inquire, " what am I, that thou art thus mindful of me, and what shall I render unto thee?" We put in at the Isle of Man, and were hospitably received by the inhabitants, whose engaging simplicity, and religious zeal, have attached my mind to them. I am sincerely desirous that if I do nothing for the truth, I may do nothing against it; and when I look thus, I feel a comfortable belief, that even this care shall tend to the furtherance of the gospel, and that it will somewhat open the way for future service in this place; for if the sense that attends my mind be right, when the feet of the messengers are more eminently turned

nourable friend Samuel Emlen, whose animating company and fatherly kindness, greatly revived me, and into the way of the Gentiles, to Pul and Lud, &c. and to the Isles afar off, this little place will not be forgot, but offerings will be brought here to the mountain of the Lord's holiness, and His glory shall break forth."

——" I am safe arrived in this land, and have humbly to commemorate divine protection, and secret supporting goodness in my passage hither. The ways of the Most High remain to be ways of wonders, and his acts are past finding out; nevertheless, he still revealeth secrets, as he did unto Abraham, when a degree of the same faithfulness is, through His humbling power, attained to; and without it, how little do we know, even when we think we know most? Never did I so sensibly enjoy the bosom of the church, which, I may humbly acknowledge, was cordial to receive me; but how much more excellent is that pure faith, which reveals itself when all human consolations stand afar off, and by centring our spirits therein, wonderfully convinces us, that it is the " substance of things hoped for, the evidence of things not seen."

——" I feel myself much recovered from fatigue, and have gratefully to commemorate divine protection, and secret sustaining help, when the feeble efforts of bodily strength and natural fortitude, seemed unequal to render me that support, which one grain of living faith affords. Oh! what abundant reason we have, not to trust in ourselves, but in Him who died for us, to whose death, if we are not conformable, we cannot fully experience the prevailing power of eternal life."

——" I trust the probation my spirit experienced in our passage here, will not prove altogether an unprofitable dispensation, on entering a service, the right performance whereof depends on our being baptized enough, and weaned enough; so that whatever is brought forth may be of the new creation, unconnected with all old heavens, and old earth. And indeed I may say that, before I left home, though my mind was much stripped and tried, I often suspected whether I had fully partaken of the necessary cup of suffering, preparatory to such an undertaking as the present; and believed I should have a trying baptism to

and helped me to leave the things that are behind, and to prefs forward in profpect to a degree of humble dedication to the renewed pointings of duty. My beloved friend R. J. with G. Dillwyn and wife, having performed a family vifit to friends in Dublin, were gone to Ballitore, where they found a fimilar engagement to that in which they had been employed; and when I reached them, they had nearly finifhed, and were almoft ready to proceed. In a few days we accordingly fet forward together, viz. G. D. R. J. and myfelf; our profpects comfortably correfponding one with another, we cheerfully concurred therewith, to travel in company. On the 4th day following we went to Chriftians Town, and in the evening vifited a family of young people, one of whom was in a declining ftate of health; to whom, with the reft, inftruction and encouragement were handed, to prefer the humbling difpenfations of infinite wifdom, to all temporal gratifications. We then returned to our lodgings, and fat with the family; where my beloved companion was enabled, in awful fupplication, to breathe for continued fupport, and prefervation in the path of obedience; which comfortably cemented our fpirits together. Next day we went to Rathangan, where we had to travail for the arifings of pure life, under the difcouraging apprehenfion of its being very low in that place; but infinite kindnefs vouchfafed to own the deep exercife, and gracioufly fent forth His light and truth, whereby the way pafs through before I entered upon it; though I now have no doubt but my movings this way, were in the right time. It is an unfpeakable bleffing to meet with the crucifying power of truth by the way; and the defire of my heart often is, to be more and more in love therewith."

way to his holy hill was opened in the demonstration of the spirit and power, and the meeting ended under an humbling commemoration of his goodness. In the evening we went to New Park, and next morning to the meeting at Timahoa, which was small, and the publick service rather laborious, because of the unfitness of many of the professors to receive spiritual things. In the afternoon we went to Prosperous, a new settled town where there are no members of our religious society. We had a meeting there much to the satisfaction of visitors and visited; the people behaved well, and we had reason to believe, by the ownings of truth, that there is a precious seed there. We went to New Park again to lodge, and in the morning sat with the family and others then present, and some profitable counsel opened. From thence we went to Edenderry; and next day, being the first of the week, we staid, and were at their own meeting, their preparative meeting, a publick meeting in the afternoon, and in the evening sat with their ministers and elders; at all which, merciful help was near in the needful time, and enabled to discharge our several duties in simplicity, for which the reward of peace and quietude was not withheld. On second day the 8th of 8th month, we came to Oldcastle, and were at their meeting next day, where many people not of our society attended; amongst whom there was openness to labour. After meeting we staid with those few in profession with us, when their low estate was felt, sympathized with, and counsel flowed thereto.

On 4th day we went to Cootehill, where are very few

few friends; they are in a poor shattered situation as to the life of religion, and scarce able to keep up their meetings. Many of the town's people came to the meeting, and it was a solid favoured opportunity; and a comfortable belief attended our minds that there is a precious seed in that place; but the professors of truth are stumbling blocks. We sat down with them select at the conclusion of the meeting, and found it exercising work to visit the seed in them, but were enabled honestly to discharge our several duties.* From thence we went to Castleshane, a place very like Cootehill; and in the evening after the meeting there, reached Grange, near Charlemount, and lodged at the house of ——— a visited young man, who, with two others in his family, afford a comfortable prospect of a revival of ancient simplicity, and right zeal in that place. Our spirits were nearly united to them, and the streams of encouraging counsel flowed freely for their refreshment and strength. We were at their meeting next day, being the first of the week, which was a suffering time; and in the evening, had a very large and satisfactory meeting of the country people not in profession with us, who behaved well, and in many of whom the witness of truth was raised. Next day we proceeded to go round Lough-Neagh by taking Toberhead, Colerain,

---

* In a letter dated the next day, she writes: "Through divine support, mercifully vouchsafed from day to day, we have been enabled to discharge the missions committed, so as to leave each place with a good degree of peace. Indeed it is a relieving consideration, under the discouragements that poor travellers often meet with, that the work is not ours, and that an instrument has only to be passive in the hand of him that useth it, leaving its prosperity, and the honour of the cause, to the all-sufficiency of the divine arm, which can work with us or without us."

Colerain, Ballynacree, Ballimena, Grange, and Antrim; at all which places, we had deeply to lament the low declined ſtate of the profeſſors of truth, not only as to numbers, but in a departure from the precious, preſerving, principle of light and life; whereby the living members of the church are kept in their lots and enabled to ſtand with firmneſs, as a city ſet on a hill, to the praiſe of His grace who hath called them out of the world, into His marvellous light. The country people coming in at the aforeſaid places, tended to the more free circulation of life, wherein the ſpring of goſpel miniſtry was ſometimes opened; but it was my lot to paſs along in gloomy ſuffering, and, at times, inſtructive ſilence. After meeting at Antrim, the 21ſt of 8th month, being met by a friend and his wife, we returned home with them, and reſted next day; on the evening of which my dear huſband came to us from England, and after ſtaying in the neighbourhood where we were, and falling in at divers meetings for diſcipline with us, he went to Clonmel, and ſtaid till we came near that place before we ſaw him again. On the 23d we went to Newtown, and next day had a meeting with the few friends there. The knowledge and virtue of true religion ſeemed very low amongſt them, and it was hard work, by deep and ſecret exerciſe, to miniſter to the pure life. From hence we returned to Liſburn, and attended their monthly meeting, wherein a little ſtrength ſeemed given me for ſome publick labour; but my dear companions were ſilently baptized under a concern to viſit the families of friends in that place, though the time did not appear to be then come. After being at Hillſborough, Lurgan, Ballyhagan, Moyallen, and Ballinderry meetings, we returned to

Liſburn,

Lisburn, and in about a week performed the service; the Minister of ministers being near to hand forth in the needful time (often after long suffering silence) suitable instruction and consolation to the visited. Great indifference and insensibility, as to the knowledge of the Lord's dealings with His people, prevail in that place, though a little tried remnant dwell amongst them.* At the close of this visit, came on the quarterly meeting at Ballinderry for the province of Ulster, which was rather a low suffering time. Here we met with our friend Zachariah Dicks from North Carolina, who was come over on a religious visit to this land, and who was in some expectation of our companion G. D—— joining him; but not feeling released one from another in the service wherein we were joined, it was judged most prudent to wait for the openings of truth, as much in our separation, as we had endeavoured to attend to them in joining. We left this

* The following is extracted from a letter bearing date the 1st of 9th month, 1785. "Such is the state of our society in these parts, as well as in divers places in our land, that it is hard dragging along for poor travellers; the prevailing death is ready to swallow them up, and so put a stop to all circulation of life. Well! drooping as our spirits often are, we have no where else to go but to the fountain, which is, at times, when faith and patience are at the lowest ebb, unexpectedly opened for our renewed refreshment, and encouragement to trust a little longer. Here are, notwithstanding, in the North of this nation where we have been, a few beautiful plants amongst the young and younger men, whose roots are, I trust, deepening in the heavenly soil; but in the prospect of their future trials, if they are faithful, I am almost ready to tremble, there is such a host of opposition for them to press through, in reviving the purity of the gospel. We are nearly united to them, and to find them was like meeting with near kindred.

this province pretty directly after the quarterly meeting, and set off towards Dublin, taking Rathfriland meeting in our way, to which many town's people came, and it was a large and favoured meeting. We reached Dublin the 15th of 9th month, where we staid near a week, and sat several meetings, under great oppression and discouragement of mind, and without much relief saw an opening to leave the place and go to Timahoe. Here we visited their families and had peace therein. From thence we set off for Edenderry; and going by way of Rathangan, an opening which had been put by when we were there before, of having a publick meeting amongst the town's people, presented again; and we had cause to admire, how providentially we were cast in the way of performing such pointings of duty, as had been, more from diffidence than a rebellious mind, passed over. Here we staid over first day, and had a large crowded meeting in the evening, which was considerably disturbed by some rude people in liquor, but divers were very solid, and it ended well. From Rathangan we pursued our journey to Edenderry, Tullamore, Moat, Ballimurry, Birr,* Killconnenmore, and Roscrea; in all which a degree of painful exercise was our lot, under the feeling sense of the general departure of the professors of truth, from that ancient, righteous zeal and primitive simplicity, which the people

---

* From this place, she writes as follows : " Gloomy is the prospect that opens in many places, and yet, by getting low enough, we sometimes find to our refreshment, that there is in most places, a hidden suffering seed, with which we have sympathized, and in the extendings of renewed strength, been led to visit, though it is but little known or valued by the easy carnally minded professors ; and I have sometimes thought, that if our coming answers no other

people of God who walked faithfully before Him, were, in all ages, conspicuous for. But He who never said to the wrestling seed of Jacob, " seek ye my face in vain," graciously condescended to reward the travail of our spirits, by arising for His own name's sake, and giving strength to lift the standard of righteousness, and furnishing with an invitation to the youth to repair to it, and so inherit the blessed effects thereof.

We went to Limerick from Roscrea, and staid there over first and second days. The publick meetings were low, distressing opportunities, and little ability to labour amongst that people, who seem much under the influence of the god of this world: but on first day evening, a number of youth being present at T. M's and a few honest-hearted friends more advanced in years, we had a very favoured season of retirement, and the streams of love and life, through instructive, consolating ministry, ran freely. On third day we left Limerick for Youghall; my mind was dipped into a sense of my own weakness, and great discouragement and dismay surrounded me. I saw the necessity of an increasing labour to dwell near the pure gift in myself, which I have ever found to be the most effectual preservation, in the conflicting work of purification and faithfulness in more publick service; for when it reduces the mind, and brings it down as into the bottom of Jordan, it likewise stays the billows thereof by pure faith, and succours by the incomes

end than to strengthen a few, weak hands, and be instrumental in reviving the hope of the humble, tried children in the family, it will be enough, though the reward to ourselves may be but small."

of patience, whereby every divine difpenfation is rendered profitable, and every bitter thing fweet; centring us out of the reach of flefhy confidence, in that ftate of abafednefs to which divine compaffion is moft eminently extended. We lodged one night at an inn, and on fourth day reached Youghall, where, on fifth, we had two large and favoured meetings. Next day we got to Springmount near Cork, to the houfe of our dear and honourable friend S. N. Here I heard of the deceafe of our beloved friend Robert Walker, who departed this life at Tottenham, near London, after having paid an acceptable religious vifit to friends of that city and its neighbourhood. He was a man who having paffed through deep baptifms of fpirit, in preparation for the work of the miniftry, became eminent therein. The multitude could not judge, neither did they know, his frequent, fuffering defcendings with the feed, when crucified in the hearts of the people, as in the ftreets of fpiritual Sodom and Egypt; and confidering himfelf as an unworthy minifter thereto, he was clothed with refignation to the difpenfation of the day. Great was his induftry, and yet many were the trials of his faith for the fupply of temporal things. Though unadorned with human literature, he was inftructed in the fchool of Chrift, as a good Scribe to whom was committed the knowledge of the myfteries of the kingdom, wherein all neceffary accomplifhments where acquired, and difplayed in gofpel fimplicity.

Since my coming into this Province, the fubject which has for fome time been under my confideration, of fettling in thefe parts, has often prefented ed to my mind; with an anxious defire, that the moft endeared companion of my life, may, with myfelf, be kept fingle in all our views, and refigned in our fpirits to whatever infinite wifdom fees meet to do with us; that the way before us, though it be ftrait and narrow, may not be made more difficult, by any willings and runnings of our own. I am often afraid of myfelf in this refpect; I feel, when unfupported by beft help, a partial attachment to my native land; and to part with my connections, and fome to whom I am clofely united in fpirit, at times appears hard: but even on this footing, I find a counterpoifing weight on my hufband's fide, who has alfo valuable relations, and many friends in the beft fenfe, with temporal concerns and conveniencies more fuitable than elfewhere. Oh then, may divine counfel influence our fpirits, in the confideration, and determination of this important ftep! Thou knoweft, O Lord! the fervency and exercife of my fpirit herein; thou knoweft, that, above all things I wifh to ferve thee, with the dedication of all that I have, when thou calleft for it; and as by thy power only, an holy compliance is wrought; O withhold it not in the needful time! Suffer not our feet to flide from the ancient foundation, but with the right arm of thy ftrength, enable us to make war in righteoufnefs, in the lot thou affigneft! O fhew us the lot! Suffer us not to wander in the dark, but be thou gracioufly pleafed fpiritually to lead us, by the cloud and pillar of fire, certain tokens of thy holy approbation of the way that we take!

At Cork we ftaid, (except going one day to Bandon, and returning the next) eleven days, and attended nine meetings, and many private opportunities in friend's families, where counfel and encouragement often unexpectedly opened; which were miniftered under the precious influence of divine love and life; wherein the fpirits of a remnant were cemented together, in a degree of holy fellowfhip, and an exercife generally prevailed to help one another forward in the new and living way; which in many places lies much unoccupied, the travellers having got into paths fo widely different, that it is fometimes difficult to find it; and when found, fo to believe in its rectitude, as to make ftraight fteps therein.

During my ftay in and about Cork, I had frequent occafions humbly to commemorate the wifdom, mercy, and power, of our gracious Helper, who, in a time of deep humiliation and adverfity, fuftained my poor toffed foul; and, by a portion of that holy faith, which I knew to be his own immediate gift, gave me to fee his all-fufficiency, and my own nothingnefs; and after melting all that was within me, by his humbling difpenfations, faw meet again to renew his image upon my heart, and to caufe me to experience more largely the work of the new creation, and the neceffity of ever abiding in lowlinefs of mind, and treading the courts of the Lord with holinefs and fear. O! faid my foul, withhold not from me whatever hath this tendency; let the voice of the Holy One go forth, which faith, " cut down the tree," rather than it fhould overfpread, and bring forth fruit, to difhonour the great and ex-

excellent

cellent Name: neverthelefs, may that which is pure be faftened, as with a band of iron in the tender grafs of the field, that fo, humility and fimplicity may fpring, and more loudly acknowledge, that the Moft High reigns in the kingdoms of men, and giveth of his own precious gifts and favours to whomfoever he will.

We went from Cork to the houfe of a friend who, for fome months paft, has been in a low dejected ftate of mind; and in the evening my dear companion R. J. was dipped into his fituation, and her mouth was opened in living counfel and encouragement, which for a time feemed to revive him. Here I met with my dear hufband, to our mutual confolation; and from hence, after attending a meeting next day at Garryroan, which was rather a low time, we went to Clonmel to our mother's there, and refted one day before the quarterly meeting for Munfter province came on. Our minds were meafurably baptized for the approaching folemnity, particularly that of my beloved friend R. J. who with dear G. D. had good fervice; and the meetings, though laborious, were eminently owned with the extenfion of divine good, and friends were renewedly encouraged to faithfulnefs in their refpective lots. I fat all the meetings filently, not without a fellow-feeling and travail with thofe engaged in turning the battle to the gate; but my fpirit was fo clothed with the garment of mourning, and the fenfe of my own infufficiency, that I was ready to fay, with the Prophet, " I will fpeak no more in Thy Name." Yet to be preferved in a ftate of patient exercife, and in refignation to what might be the allotted portion of fuffering in this day of trial, was the fervent defire of my mind. In this frame, I have often known the moft fenfible incomes of holy help, and been more enabled from thence to bring up ftones of memorial, than when the travail of my foul has been more fhallow, and the ftreams of the miniftry have lain nearer the furface of the people's fpirits ; and O ! that, in all feafons of proving, I may never fhrink from under that mournful covering, till the fenfe of what I am, and a degree of living faith in the immediate teachings of divine wifdom, are not only raifed, but prevail in my heart; that fo, the creature, its wifdom and activity, may die daily, under that Power which crucifies all that is of the flefh, and fanctifies throughout. After the quarterly meeting was over, we were moft eafy to fit with the friends of that particular meeting ; where I felt an opennefs for fome religious communication ; and it was a clofe, but favoured time ; neverthelefs a degree of fadnefs remained with me. After this meeting was over, and partaking of a cup of heavenly confolation in the family of a relation, we went down to Anner Mills that night, and next day fet off for Dublin, in order to attend the half year's meeting, held in the eleventh month. It was rather a low time, but holy help was near (according to ancient declaration) to the Poor in Spirit, the exercifed wreftling feed, of which, through preferving goodnefs, there is a remnant in this land ; with whofe tribulated path I have often been dipped into near fympathy, and was renewedly fo at this time : neverthelefs, we had unitedly to believe, that if fome of thefe perfifted in unfaithfulnefs to the manifeftations of duty, concerning their religious fervices, they were in danger of occafioning

cafioning to themfelves fuch a wildernefs travel, as might prove very difficult for them to be delivered from. Thefe were fervently and honeftly laboured with, " to offer to the Lord the facrifice of thankfgiving, and to pay all their vows;" that fo, a generation might be raifed up more zealous for the honour and promulgation of the great Name, than many of later times have been. My mind was greatly depreffed in this city, and I found it conduce to my fafety, to weigh well what I apprehended to be the motions of truth. The meetings were large, and my beloved companions being not only better qualified for fervice therein, but coming from fo diftant a part of the world as Pennfylvania in America, and there being little or no profpect of their ever having another opportunity, of fo fully relieving their minds to friends in this land, I fought for obfcurity: which is always moft defirable to my own mind, knowing that fafety attends it; and that it requires deep baptifms, and a clofe dwelling with the gift, rightly to minifter life, and vifit the feed in large mixed congregations. Without an extraordinary degree of thefe, it feldom happens that the appearances of thofe who are young in experience, afford fatisfaction to the true church of Chrift, or that they reap the reward of folid inftructive peace in their own minds; and often feeling that I am one of thefe, the prayer of my fpirit has been, that I may be kept under the humbling fenfe thereof, and be preferved from burdening the living by being too fhallow in my fpirit, or fpreading too much into fruitlefs branches; that fo, the great and excellent caufe of truth may never be difhonoured by or through me. Infinite wifdom is, neverthelefs, to direct

direct and go before us, in the line of His own appointment: and under an apprehension of the puttings forth of the heavenly Shepherd, I ventured to step forward in two large meetings; and through his sustaining goodness, I was enabled to relieve my own mind in a good degree; for which with many gracious assistances, from time to time dispensed, may my soul bow in humble gratitude and awful fear, through the continued stages of my tried pilgrimage. My dear friends R. J. and G. D. had great and good service in the course of these meetings; and R. J. feeling an engagement to have a meeting with the women friends, (none being held for discipline for them at that season of the year) after laying it before friends, it was cheerfully complied with, and a solid profitable meeting it proved. R. J. and myself, feeling something more than a freedom to sit with a committee of men friends, appointed by the national meeting to consider the state of society, and complying with it, we were enabled to feel with friends thereon, and to lay down our respective burdens. The evening preceding our leaving the city, and after the meetings were over, many friends being collected at our lodgings, we had a refreshing, instructive, opportunity of retirement; wherein counsel and encouragement were ministered, and friends parted under a living sense of the extension of divine favour to His church and family. Next day we went to Baltiboys, a very poor small meeting; after which we procceded about five miles further, intending next morning to set off for Mountmellick; but when all was ready for our departure, a hesitation sprang, and spread, respecting the propriety of our pursuing the intended plan;

plan; and the more it was looked at, the more clearly it appeared beft to fit with the few friends felect, there having been many not of our profeffion at meeting the day before. One of our guides, therefore, kindly undertook to collect the members of that meeting together; which was done, and we had no caufe to repent our ftay, but were rather encouraged to truft in future to the turnings of the fpiritual guide, who requires that we fhould be followers, and not leaders, if we purfue the path of true peace. Inftead of going to Mountmellick from Baltiboys, we went to Ballitore that night, and next day to Athy meeting; then to Mountmellick, Montrath, Knockballymaher, Ballynakill, and to Carlow to the quarterly meeting for Leinfter Province held there. It was a remarkably low time, and the minds of many were baptized into a feeling fenfe of the coolnefs and indifferency, that prevails amongft the profeffors of truth in thefe parts, and filent fadnefs was much our lot. Intending from hence for Waterford, and the counties of Wexford and Wicklow, we firft paid a vifit to the little meeting at Caftledermot; it was fmall, but divine goodnefs was near. My mind, in time of filence, was comfortably gathered from fome buffetings, doubtings and difmay; and the language of the apoftle fweetly paffed through, and fettled me in an humble confidence and calm; be patient, eftablifh your hearts, for the day of the Lord draweth nigh. We returned to Carlow and next day attended their week-day meeting; after which we went to Ballydarton belonging to Kilconner meeting, which I was prevented from attending by a pain in my head and teeth; but was enabled to proceed with my companions to Rofs next day, where growing worfe, they were under the neceffity of leaving me, after they had fat with the few friends there, in order to attend the firft day meetings at Waterford; where my hufband and divers of our relations from Clonmel came to meet us. My R. G. came to me, and was a truly acceptable gueft, my mind having funk, and my ftrength feeming to be exhaufted with the pain. I was fo much relieved as to be able to go next day to Waterford, to rejoin my beloved friends R. J. and G. D. whofe company and fervices have been, through the courfe of this journey, inftructive and ftrengthening to my often doubting mind. When through the defcending of heavenly virtue, my fpirit has been cemented with theirs, and in the unity and covenant of life, an harmonious exercife has prevailed in me, either in publick or in fecret, I have had renewedly to admire the gracious condefcenfion of our holy Head and High Prieft, in anointing, in any degree, for a work fo great and awful, and leading into this excellent fellowfhip. At Waterford we ftaid their week day meeting on third day, which was a favoured time; and after having likewife divers comfortable religious opportunities with friends of that place, (there being a quickened remnant growing in the fpiritual life) we took leave of them under a precious fenfe of divine fuperintending care, and went to Foreft, Cooladine, Randal's Mills, Ballinclay, Ballicane and Wicklow; and found an honeft-hearted fet of friends, who are preferved in a good degree of confiftency with the principles we profefs: yet there are others who widely differ in this refpect. Our kind friend J. W. having met us at Ballicane, we went in company

pany with him to Dublin on the feventh day of
the week, and next day attended their meetings
in Meath-ftreet and Sycamore-alley; at both which
my companions were filent. My mind was deeply
exercifed in them, and as I perceived fome little
opening for publick labour, I gave up thereto under many difcouraging impreffions; in part the
effects of a reafoning difpofition, and unprofitably
ruminating on the repeated labours of more qualified inftruments, and the unfuccefsfulnefs of many
of them; and in part, I truft, of a right and neceffary jealoufy over myfelf, left I fhould be the
means of conveying a lifelefs multiplicity of words,
or be found feeding the people, when the divine
word might proclaim a faft. But it awfully fprang
in my mind, that if ever fo fmall a warning was
given me to deliver, and I concealed it, the blood
of thofe for whom it was intended might, according to the declaration of the Moft High to
the Prophet, be required at my hands. As this
vifit to the nation was clofing, a fecret prayer
was begotten in me, that we might be enabled,
as faithfully and willingly to finifh the work,
as, through humbling operations, we were refigned to begin it; which, to the praife of His grace
who puts forth and goes before His own fheep,
we were ftrengthened to do, and had afrefh to
difcover that His ways are not as our ways, nor
His thoughts as our thoughts. When we apprehended ourfelves at liberty to fail from that city,
and had agreed with a captain bound for Whitehaven for our paffage there, the wind proved
contrary, and we found it fafe to look around
us, that if any little fervice was omitted, it might
then be performed. This we were ready to think

was

was not much the case, having attended their men's and women's meetings on third day, where, through divine ability graciously afforded, we had a close, searching, and humbling season: but now standing in the resignation, not being detained of ourselves, divers opportunities for publick and private labour unexpectedly opened, generally tending to invite the ignorant, and to encourage the sincere and drooping minds to a faith in the sufficiency of the gift of God in themselves, for the sanctification of the soul, and the necessary supply of every spiritual enjoyment, and qualification acceptably to worship; which must now, as formerly, be sought for, in the beauty of holiness, and in newness of life. The wind proving contrary, we staid over another first day, when my companions G. D. and R. J. were enabled to bring up living stones of memorial, to the sealing I trust of their testimony on the spirits of many; and my cup of affectionate fellowship seemed to overflow in secret. The next day a gale rose in our favour, which we thankfully accepted, and were gently wafted over by it in twenty-five hours, having had as pleasant a voyage as we could wish for, sickness excepted; and for the holy directing and protecting power of immortal goodness, we were gratefully humbled. We staid one night at Whitehaven after our landing, and next day attended their week day meeting, which was a low time. Soon after it closed, we set off for Greysouthen, where R. J. and I staid that night. Our much loved friend and companion G. D. and his wife (who had been with us ever since we were at Cooladine) finding it conduce most to their peace to stay the quarterly meeting for Cumberland, to be

held

held the week after ; and we having a profpect of attending the quarterly meeting for the county of York, to be held at Leeds ; we found the time for our feparation was come ; and had to commemorate the kindnefs of infinite wifdom, in fo cafting us together, and cementing us, according to our meafures, in the hidden life. Here we took an affecting and affectionate farewell of each other.

We ftopped at Cockermouth in our way to Kendal, and fpent a few hours very agreeably with our friends J. and B. D. and their children ; and before we left them, the fpring of heavenly confolation arofe, and refrefhed both vifitors and vifited ; and with grateful hearts we fet off, and reached Kefwick that night ; and next day, having a pleafant ride among the mountains, we were favoured in good time to get to Kendal, where my dear companion had an opportunity of vifiting J. and R. W.'s children, who, fince fhe was there before, had loft their honourable father, and it was a humbling favoured opportunity. Finding ourfelves at liberty to leave that place, and R. J. having paffed by Wray and Bentham meetings when fhe was that way before, and now feeling a draft towards them, we went next day, the twenty-fourth of the twelfth month, to Wray, and in the evening had a good meeting with the few friends there, and fome others who came in. Next morning we went to Bentham meeting, which was an exercifing time, but ended in awful fupplication, wherein my beloved companion was publickly engaged. Having an evening meeting appointed at Settle, we reached there in time, and it proved a folid, inftructive, feafon.

From

From thence on fecond day, the twenty-fixth, we got to Leeds, and there met with my dear father and mother, to our mutual fatisfaction. The quarterly meeting came on next day, and held till the evening of the twenty-ninth. Through the feveral fittings thereof, I had undoubtedly to believe that my companion was in her right place; and was thankful, under the confideration that we were there in better wifdom than our own, and were found worthy to bear a fhare in the weight of fufferings, which generally attend thefe large affemblies. Rebecca Jones being difpofed to fpend a little time in reft with our mutual friend C. H. we parted after our quarterly meeting, and I came homewards, with a defire rightly to feel my way, whether to continue a while longer with this my endeared friend, in her religious fervice, or to give up and furrender my certificate: for though I had a profpect, when I left home, of vifiting the weftern part of this nation, to which my certificate was alfo addreffed, yet if the commiffion fhould clofe fooner than I looked for, my compliance therewith appears as neceffary, as it would be if it fhould extend further; feeing that the virtue of all our religious movements confifts in the divine putting forth, and the continuation of holy anointing; which we have abundant caufe to acknowledge, is not at our command.

C H A P.

CHAP. IV.

Account of her Visit to some of the western Counties of England.

A FEW months after her return from Ireland, she felt a renewed engagement to accompany her friend R. Jones, on a visit to some parts of the western counties in England. Of the principal parts of this visit, she has left the following journal.

After my return from Ireland, my beloved companion R. J. being detained in Yorkshire, on divers accounts, for three months, I was thereby set at liberty to adjust some family concerns at home, and pay some visits to neighbouring meetings, as truth appeared to open the way; especially to Whitby, Scarborough, Bridlington, Hornsea, and Hull; in the course of which my mind was, in the needful time, mercifully supported with renewed supplies of holy help, though, in general, in a low and stripped state; fearing lest, in the exercise of the gift, a zeal which is not according to true knowledge, nor originating in that baptism of spirit wherein the creature is humbled, should so mix with the divine openings, as to carry away the feet of the mind from that safe standing in the deeps, which is justly compared to the bottom of Jordan. Here, it is necessary for true gospel ministers, steadily to abide, with the weight of the service they are engaged in upon their shoulders, till the spirits of the assembled are, in some degree, attracted to the promised land, the new heaven and the new earth, wherein dwelleth the righteousness of faith, and where spiritual

ritual worſhip is rightly performed, in the beauty of holineſs and newneſs of life. To be inſtrumental in the divine hand of thus, in any meaſure, converting the ſpirits of thoſe to whom we may be led to miniſter, requires an unction altogether unmixed; but when revolt, backſliding, and a ſuperficial ſpirit, have been neceſſarily unveiled, I have, ſometimes, diſtreſſingly found, that ſome of my armour was carnal; and O! how hath all that was within me been humbled at the diſcovery, that the Lord's righteous controverſy with the works of darkneſs, had not been righteouſly upheld, nor the door of eſcape therefrom wiſely opened. An increaſe of experience convinces me, that preaching is a myſtery which every one exerciſed therein, has need to be often induſtriouſly, and impartially learning, as far as concerns themſelves; and where this is the caſe, I am abundantly perſuaded, that our dependance muſt be drawn from the ſentiments of thoſe friends to whoſe judgment we are moſt attached, in order rightly to diſtinguiſh betwixt the unity of the one infallible ſpirit, and their partiality to us, and to be weighed in the juſt balance of the ſanctuary, where we are ſometimes found defective, even when all around us ſpeak peace.

" My dear huſband accompanied me in this little round: his ſympathizing mind, and care for my preſervation every way, was truly ſtrengthening, and afforded frequent occaſions of humble thankfulneſs to the Author of all good, who had ſo bountifully provided for me, both in ſpiritual and temporal things. After our return home we gave up houſekeeping, not with a concluſion that we ſhould remove from England, but under an apprehenſion that

that it was right to take that ſtep, as the way opened for my being again united in ſervice with my beloved companion R. J. and my huſband had no proſpect of being ſettled during my abſence. We therefore removed our furniture, and ourſelves to York, the quarterly meeting there being at hand; after which, the 1ſt of 4th month, 1786, I went to Ackworth to meet my companion, who had gone there the day before. We ſtaid there on firſt day, and found ſome cloſe and neceſſary labour, not only in publick, but in private opportunities, amongſt the maſters, miſtreſſes, and ſervants, ſeverally; for the Enemy of all good hath proved himſelf buſy, in endeavouring to ſow his tares amongſt the good ſeed in that inſtitution and family; and unleſs thoſe on whom the weight and care of it moſt devolves, keep in view the neceſſity of attending more to the holy Oracle in their movements, than to the ſtrength of their own wiſdom and underſtanding, it will loſe the luſtre that truth would put upon it, and become the nurſery of a worldly ſpirit, though diſguiſed with an appearance of religious form. There is in that family a ſuffering, wreſtling ſeed, an exerciſed remnant, which though ſmall, is a means, under the divine bleſſing, of keeping open the ſpring of life; and if ſuch keep their places, there is reaſon to hope that more will be added to their number, and, through the influence of their example, the truth, in its own ſimplicity, gain ground, inſtead of the diſguiſed ſpirit of error. A ſalutation of love flowed to ſuch, under a ſenſe whereof we left them, ſave our worthy friend W. S. who went with us to Wakefield, where divers are under convincement, and ſome of them appear to be rightly ſo. Here we had an open, inſtructive opportunity;

and

and from thence went to Bradford, and next day proceeded to Manchester, where we attended their week-day meeting; in which my companion was greatly favoured to dip into the state of the seed, and profitably to visit it, and silence was I believe rightly my lot. From Manchester we went to Stockport, Macclesfield, Morley, and so to Warrington, to the monthly meeting there; where again I thought my companion had eminent service, and close searching labour, wherewith I felt a spiritual travail, and sympathetic mourning over the great carnality, and departure from the way of peace, which greatly prevail in that, and the neighbouring places. Though there is a peculiar people, and a royal priesthood, in that monthly meeting, yet as the number in a very different spirit, is great, the pure life is prevented from circulating, and purifying the temple. So that the prospect, amongst the youth especially, is exceedingly discouraging; dissipation, or the gilded corruptions of human nature, having possession, and, like the strong man armed, keeping the house and all the goods thereof in peace: and until a stronger than he, by the spirit of judgment and of burning, dislodges him of his hold, casts him out, and spoils all his goods, there is but little room to expect such to demonstrate unto others, by the liveliness of their spirits, the circumspection of their conduct, and a rightly seasoned conversation, that they are acquainted with the efficacious virtue of true religion. From Warrington, my husband returned to Yorkshire, in company with William Rotch of Nantucket, and we back into Cheshire. It was rather a gloomy parting to me, being very unwell with a rheumatic complaint in my head, and more depressed

fed in mind than I was free to exprefs to any;
which is often the cafe with me, when under a
fenfe of the awfulnefs of the work I am embarked
in, of the little effect it has on the minds of many,
and of my own exceeding great weaknefs, and apparent unfitnefs for engaging with facred things;
fo that my way oft feems to lie by the valley and
fhadow of death; where I feel myfelf fubject to
fearful apprehenfions, and a deep and gloomy
exercife. Neverthelefs, to the praife of the divine
grace, my foul can thankfully and humbly acknowledge that, through what appeared the
fmalleft grain of faith, prefervation hath been
experienced, and ftrength to afcend, in the
Lord's time, that holy mountain where nothing
can hurt or deftroy; becaufe the creature, and
its attendant evils are fubjected, and accefs to
the feaft of fat things, and of wine well refined,
is gracioufly afforded, to the renewed fupport
of the drooping mind, which was ready, but a little
before, to caft away its confidence, and fay, " the
Lord hath forgotten me." Thus, as by a tender
father, are we dealt with, under thofe proving difpenfations, which are effentially neceffary for carrying forward the work of fanctification in the foul,
and a preparation to receive the infcription of,
" Holinefs unto the Lord." When I confider the
neceffity hereof, a fear, on the other hand, often
arifes left it fhould be partially or fuperficially effected ; and a fervent craving of fpirit, that the refining operations of the Holy Ghoft and Fire, may fo
perform their affigned office, as that every fpecious
appearance of felf-love may be confumed, and the
fpring of action, in the performance of both religious and moral duties, rendered pure. Thus vari-
oufly,

oufly, is the attention of the travailing foul turned; and if the pure difcoveries of truth are but the object fingly fought for, He who created light out of darknefs, and hath fown it for the righteous, doth, in times of our greateft extremity reveal himfelf to be the Lord Almighty. From Warrington we went to Sutton, Franley, Newton, Chefter, Nantwich, and Middlewich, when our vifit to Chefhire feemed ended, where, as in other places, we had to view, and mourn over, the defolation which hath prevailed amongft the profeffors of truth; fo that the Heathen may query, "Where is their God?"

Our next ftage was to Leek, and fo to Colebrook Dale; we had meetings both at the New and Old Dale, which were favoured, ftrengthening feafons; by ability being gracioufly afforded and accepted, to fink down deep into fuffering with the precious feed; and a little exercifed remnant were found wreftling in fpirit for the divine blefling, who were vifited in the renewings of life, and inftructive counfel flowed towards them. Divers of the younger fort amongft them, have been vifited by affliction; the day of the Lord hath come upon all that was lifted up, and the projects, like the fhips of Tarfhifh, which were intended to go to fetch gold, have been broken early in their fetting out, as at Eziongeber, and all their pleafant pictures fpoiled; which have evidently been permitted in mercy, that their affections might be loofened from things tranfient and perifhing; and, inftead thereof, durable riches and righteoufnefs become their inheritance. But as this work is great and glorious, and cannot be effected, fave by the humbling proceffes of the work of fanctification in the foul, a deep

engagement

engagement dwelt upon my mind, that thofe in whom this work is begun, may be preferved from flinching under it, or taking themfelves, or one another, as out of the furnace, before it effect the great end for which it was prepared; and, that being redeemed from the fuperficies of religious experience, to an entire dependance on the holy purifying fpring of immortal life, they may approve themfelves the humble followers of Chrift; and, through the efficacy of his own fpirit, be qualified to advocate the caufe of truth and righteoufnefs. From hence we went to Shrewfbury, and were at two meetings there on firft day, which were favoured opportunities; the latter was publick, and a great many of the town's people attended. There are fome vifited young people in this place, and a profpect of a revival comfortably affected our minds. It was here to be determined whether we fhould turn towards Worcefterfhire, Herefordfhire, &c. or into Wales, which was occafion of deep inquiry to find out the good and acceptable way; and as our minds were fingle herein, we were favoured to unite in the conclufion, that it was better now to turn into Wales, a ftep we had no reafon to repent on any account, finding a peaceful ferenity attending our minds through the courfe of a folitary travel therein; and fuch a fupply of ftrength to dip into, and vifit the feed in thofe parts, as was caufe of humble thankfulnefs to the Author of every good and fpiritual gift. His eye perceives the moft obfcure parts of his own creation, and gracioufly compaffionates His humble fuppliant children, who, under a fenfe of their own wants, are cafting all their care upon him, and looking fingly to his bountiful hand for food convenient for them, both spiritual and temporal, in preference to the luxurious enjoyment of transitory things; desiring that blessing which makes truly rich, and whereunto no deadly sorrow is added. We were comforted in finding a number of this sort in Wales, particularly at Tuthynigarrig and Llanidloes; though, at the former, among divers of their members, a worldly spirit and lukewarmness about the best things prevail. We were also at Eskergoch, a very poor desolate place every way; but some solid people not professing with us, attending the meeting, were a help to it; and my beloved companion was drawn in the language of consolation to visit some of these, who were as sheep wandering upon the mountains, and panting after a shepherd. It was from this place we went to Llanidloes, where we had a large publick meeting, and from thence to Rayadar, a place where there are no friends, but where we had unsatisfactory meeting among the town's people, in one of the rooms of the inn; and after it went to Pales, and were at meeting there next day, which was a laborious, searching opportunity, many disorderly walkers being there. We then stept out of Wales, and visited the few friends at Almilly and Leominster, in Herefordshire. The first is very small, having scarce any weight to support a meeting; but many solid neighbours attending, it was a precious lively opportunity, and my spirit was humbled, and awfully reverenced the condescending goodness of our Almighty Helper, whose loving kindness is better than life, and the lifting up of the light of his countenance, than great riches. The meeting at Leominster was low and trying.

trying. We went from hence to Troy near Monmouth in South Wales: here we lodged one night, and next morning set off for Pontipool to the quarterly meeting, which was to be held there the first day following. Our dear and much valued friends, T. Corbyn, H. Wilkins and T. H. overtook us upon the road; we were mutually glad to see each other, and also to feel each others spirits in the meetings we attended together at Pontipool and Cardiff, whither we went (after the quarterly meeting was ended) to attend the Welch yearly meeting there. My mind, on drawing near to that place, was awfully affected, in a renewed sense of the important station of a gospel minister, which, the more my understanding is opened, the more I perceive it to call for a watchful care to keep in the station, and to preserve it unblameable, by endeavouring to dwell low enough with the gift, so as rightly to distinguish between a silent union with the seed in meetings, (wherein we sometimes sympathize with the concerns of others,) and our own publick service for the cause. And I was thankful in feeling my spirit humbly contrited, under a sense of my own weakness, and the commemoration of infinite kindness in times past; and I secretly supplicated that the approaching solemnity might be graciously owned with the virtue of divine life, immediately imparted from the great Minister of ministers; whereby I felt, in a good degree, strengthened for my own measure of exercise, which proved altogether in silence. But this was not the case with some others; with a few of whom a sense of near unity attended my spirit, both in a secret travail of spirit, and in the exercise of their gifts;

gifts; never that I remember, being so sensible of the purity of that life which, and which only, quickens services in the church, and qualifies the centred mind, to judge righteously concerning publick offerings in meetings. Whatever has a tendency to close up the spring of this life, by casting rubbish thereinto, instead of industriously removing it, such as the shallow, superficial judgment of the natural mind, its old experiences and wisdom, which are held out of the life, can never availingly invite the wrestling soul, that is panting after the pure milk of the divine word, to the fountain of spiritual consolation, or refresh the christian pilgrim in his journey heaven-wards. O the purity of that life which is hid with Christ in God! It cannot be supported but by the flesh and blood, the virtue or divine nature of the Son; nor can it unite with that which is not congenial to itself. There is a ministry which, like the whirlwind, the earthquake, and the fire, makes apparent effects upon nature, shakes it, throws it into confusion, and kindles it with untempered zeal; but proves very deficient in settling it upon the sure foundation; or introducing it into that rest which is prepared for the people of God, who cease from all their own works; or teaching it to distinguish between the voice of the Shepherd, and the voice of the stranger. Hence, many, otherwise well disposed minds, have got bewildered, their attention diverted from the one great Object, and fixed upon sacrifices of their own; which, in time, are so depended upon for righteousness, that the hunger which was once begotten decreases, and the state of the church of Laodicea becomes theirs; growing rich and full,

increasing

increasing with goods and in need of nothing; when alas! though specious their appearance, their situation is most wretched, and, in the light of truth, they are discovered to stand in need of every thing. Under these considerations, my mind is often instructed in the necessity of confiding only in the Spring of life itself, and approving nothing as religious, but what comes from it, or is under its preparing, sanctifying power: and for this end, it is necessary to be very watchful over the activity of self, that the spirits may be tried, and my faith proved, whether it is grounded and established upon the right foundation, or is of that sort that wavers and floats upon any imaginary presentation, whereby I may be rendered of those who are not to expect any thing at the hand of God, James, i. 6, 7. There are so many ways for the mind, when it is off its guard, to be ensnared either into sensible darkness, or a righteousness of its own, which is worst of all, that, when clothed with a sense of my infirmity and weakness, I mourn in spirit; and am thankful when, in a grain of unadulterated faith, I can say, "if thou wilt, thou canst "make me clean," and breathe for the blessing of preservation. From a fear of being instrumental in settling down young people especially, in the form of godliness without the power; and urging them to an appearance which might create self-complacence, and reconcile them to an apprehension, that they are further advanced in the work of religion than is really the case; I have often forborne to drop such advice upon the subject of dress, among those who were inconsistent in their appearance, as, sometimes, I felt the testimony of truth to dictate; a departure

departure from true simplicity herein being generally obvious. At large meetings particularly, where friends from distant parts are collected, there is a considerable appearance of inconsistency in clothing and demeanour, which, with many other things, indicate a love of the world, and a fellowship with its spirit; but though a regulation herein is only a small part of the fruit of the good Tree, yet it is as assuredly a part, as the more striking constituents of a christian. " Whatsoever is not of faith is sin," is a comprehensive truth, which neither approves an inconsistent, nor a plausible appearance and conduct, merely as such; but wholly condemns every part of our lives which is not governed by the redeeming Spirit of truth, wherein our faith should stand: so that, to attain this state, to live under the righteous control of divine monition, is I apprehend to be a follower of Christ, under whose spiritual baptism the precious is separated from the vile, and by whose fan, the chaff, to which the vanities of this life may be compared, will flee, and leave the wheat, for divine protection, in the heavenly garner. Feeling my mind drawn to a little solid conversation with a young woman, to whom I had felt near unity, and whom I believed to be under the preparing hand for service, but diffident in spirit, and a suitable opportunity offering, I accepted it; wherein I dropped a little matter by way of encouragement to her, in her silent steppings and hidden exercises; taking occasion to observe, that as she had hitherto been preserved, in a good measure, independant of human consolations, so I wished her to continue, believing that the arm of omnipotence was most eminently revealed to us in this state of singleness, under such

spiritual

spiritual provings and conflicts as are essentially necessary for sanctification. It was a time of mutual comfort, and I was thankful that I gave up to it.

At Cardiff we met again our beloved brother G. D. which both he and we rejoiced at. He was much favoured in several of the meetings especially the publick ones, which were large; but my dear companion had not much openness for publick labour, till the last opportunity with friends select; when she was strengthened to visit the members of our society in a memorable manner; which with some, will I trust be as a nail fastened in a sure place. In our way from Cardiff to Bristol, to which we were bound, we stopped at Newport to breakfast, where my companion and G. D. felt an inclination to have a publick meeting, which was readily complied with, and held in a room in the inn; many came to it, and it was a favoured opportunity. We then proceeded on our journey, crossed what is called the new passage, and reached Bristol late that night. We met with a hospitable reception from Lydia Hawksworth, with whom we sojourned, and next day I went with my companion and Lydia, to see our beloved, honoured friend C. Phillips, then at J. Hipsley's at Congersbury. She was in a languid state of health, which in some degree occasioned a depression of spirits, but her best life was strong, though hid from herself with Christ in God. She hath been a faithful, laborious servant in the church, especially under the exercise of her gift, which was eminent for its purity, its copiousness, and clearness; distinguishing the good and evil trees by representing their fruits in their true light. Her miniſtry had a tendency, to raiſe into dominion the pure life, and in ſupplication ſhe hath been often wonderfully favoured with near acceſs, and enabled to caſt down every crown, and to aſcribe worſhip and praiſe, ſalvation and ſtrength, to the Lord God and the Lamb. Since my mind has been graciouſly viſited with a ſenſe of truth, ſuch hath been my ſentiment concerning this great and good woman: but about two years ago, to my humble admiration, in a ſeaſon of great proving of ſpirit, it was ſo renewed and ſealed to me, the inward attraction ſo ſtrong, and the evidence that ſhe was a faithful follower of the Lamb, ſo undoubted, (a language ſweetly flowing through my mind, "I have choſen her and ſhe is mine") that I not only rejoiced, and was ſtrengthened, but ſaw the abundant ſuperiority of the unfoldings of truth, to all the prepoſſeſſion we can receive from the experience of others; my want of an outward acquaintance with her being thus amply ſupplied by the gracious condeſcenſion of the Head of the church, who wiſely and myſteriouſly unites together the large and ſmall members of His body, and, by ſuch connection, makes them more uſeful to each other than they know or can of themſelves conceive. Where this union and ſenſe is thus received, I am of the belief that nothing but a departure from the divine life, wherein a chriſtian fellowſhip ſtands, can ever alter our inward feelings towards the Lord's anointed. Though I am often diſmayed at the ſight of things within and without, and ſince the time alluded to, have been ready to ſay in mine haſte, "all men are liars;" yet it was matter of renewed conſolation

and

and abasement of mind, that on being in company with our beloved friend, C. Phillips, my feelings respecting her were revived, with sweetness and rejoicing. But these were mixed with an inexpressible sympathy, and sense of the buffetings and floods of the dragon, yea, and of his temptations as in the wilderness; where, though she hungered, yet, with unconquered fortitude, nobly resisted every importunity, to command the stones to be made bread. Having suffered with her Lord and Master, and been preserved through many temptations, my secret belief was that life will again arise abundantly in her, and her garments, even in this state of mutability, be washed and made white in the blood of the suffering, yet victorious Lamb. And oh! how did all that was within me bow under this persuasion, and under a sense that the disciples of Jesus have, in proportion to their strength and gifts, a measure of afflictions to fill for their own, and the body's sake, which is His church. Here my reflections on myself were exceedingly awful; I considered that I was just entering the field, unskilled in war, with the armour but newly put on, and exceedingly uncertain whether I shall not fall a prey to mine enemy. But O Lord! teach, I pray thee, mine hands to war, and my fingers to fight, even the good fight of faith, in the sufficiency of thy power, and against every intrusion of my own; that thou, in all things mayst be glorified, and if I perish, it may be at thy footstool!

The yearly meeting at Bristol came on, and lasted three days. It afforded many opportunities for suffering, and deep gloomy exercise, to those who travailed.

travailed in spirit for the arisings of life, which, nevertheless, for a short season, in divers of them, sensibly circulated; but it seems as if, for want of vessels rightly prepared, the current was often turned backward, and retired again into obscurity, where a baptized number endeavoured patiently to dwell; among whom was my beloved companion, who found but little liberty to relieve her burdened mind. The first day after the yearly meeting we were at Claverham meeting, which was a favoured instructive opportunity, and returned to Bristol to their evening meeting; at the conclusion of which, my companion had to revive the message sent to Hezekiah, and, with evident strength and clearness, to apply it to some there. A young man who was then in the vigour of life, was soon seized with an epidemick fever, and in a few weeks removed from this stage of mortality; and several others who took the disorder, narrowly escaped with their lives; to whom the previous admonition, to set their houses in order, was likewise seasonable. Next day we went to Sudbury, to the quarterly meeting for Gloucester and Wilts. Here we found a great want of true zeal, and love to the cause of truth, wherein living members are united in harmonious labour, and cemented together in the covenant of life; which preserves from a disposition that would look only to selfish things, and enlarges the heart in an upright care for the prosperity of others. From Sudbury we took meetings at Bath, Westbury, Lavington, Devizes, Marlborough, and Uxbridge, in our way to London, being favoured to get safe there the thirty first of fifth month, which afforded us a few days to rest, before the yearly meeting began. This

meeting

meeting opened, to thofe whofe fpiritual faculties were alive in the truth, a field of exerciſing labour; wherein a fteady, watchful care was neceſſary for all to keep to their own ftations and vocations, with an attentive eye to the great Mafter; as a bufy indifcreet interference of His fervants, ever interrupts the beautiful order and profperity of His work. The felect meetings were to me, as they generally are at our yearly meetings, (though not all alike attended with life) feafons of deep inftruction, which I was made humblingly fenfible could not be the cafe, by any capacity of my own to render them fo, but by being admitted (however undefervedly) for a fhort time, by the Mafter of aſſemblies, into the heavenly treafury, where the faint's provifion, the armour of righteoufnefs, and the juft balance of the fanctuary, are all to be found; and where, as we deeply and quietly abide, we are furnifhed with an unerring perception of what, among the many offerings in the vifible church, proceeds from the divine repofitory, and what doth not; fo that individuals thus gathered, though in an obfcure exercife, may fay with the apoftle, and which I heard revived in one of thefe meetings, " in every thing I am inftructed." And as in the opening of fpiritual things, and being favoured in fome degree with a fenfe of truth, refpecting the fubjects of deliberation which come before thefe meetings, the natural difpofition fometimes prompts us to make publick remarks confonant with our feelings; I have, thus far, found it neceſſary to fet a double watch upon this fide, left I fhould ftep forward unbidden to put a hand to the ark, (the real ftate of which Uzza faw as well as I) and fo, like him, un-
availingly

availingly labour, and introduce death upon myfelf; proving unworthy of an admittance into the treafury, and of being entrufted with divine fecrets, which are not to be revealed but in the divine will, and under the fenfible direction of the High Prieft of our profeffion; that the bread which we minifter, being given us by Him, may alfo be bleffed, and that, however apparently courfe and infufficient, its efficacy and extenfive ufefulnefs may abound to thofe who are fed, and redound to His praife whofe will is our fanctification. As an attentive care on this hand is neceffary, I likewife perceived a danger on the other, when, in the fimplicity and nakednefs of truth, and confequently unadorned with any thing goodly in my own eyes, a right feafon has been difcovered to exprefs a few words, and through unprofitable diffidence, and undervaluing the fmallnefs of the appearance, I have put by thefe little openings to duty. This was more than once the cafe, during the fittings of the felect meetings this year, and which contributed to my own increafing weaknefs. So that, whilft we are defirous to keep our own hearts, and be preferved from prodigality in imparting our religious feelings, we ought alfo to ftand refigned to the fecret intimations of truth, in order to approve ourfelves good ftewards of the manifold grace of God; advancing from one degree of favour, acceptance, and communion with Him, to another, and thus become eftablifhed before Him as children without rebuke. The meetings for difcipline of women friends became exceedingly weighty to me, as the friend who was clerk laft year declined the office, and my name was mentioned by

divers

divers for that service. I sought to object, under an awful sense of the weightiness of that station, especially in so large and newly established a meeting, and with the feebleness of my qualifications for it; but I soon felt all resistance chained down in me, and a secret, fervent breathing begotten for that holy assistance, which I knew to be superior to every effort of my own without it: for though a degree of exertion is necessary, and the natural faculties of mind called upon to service, yet I saw they are no longer instrumental in helping forward the cause of truth and righteousness, than whilst they are actuated by divine love and life, and abide in the faith, without the government of which, they are no better than sounding brass, and a tinkling cymbal. Under this humbling persuasion, I took my seat, having E. T. and S. D. to assist; and the business of the meeting opened, which proved, in the several succeeding sittings, a profitable service, introducing women friends, more generally than heretofore, into an exercise on their own, their families, and the church's account; for want of which, great declension from the virtue of true religion, and the simplicity it leads into, has long lamentably spread among us as a people. And since, in the turnings and overturnings of the great Controller of events, a women's yearly meeting is established, and for these two last years hath been regularly opened in correspondence with the several quarterly meetings, in order more deeply to enter into the state of society, as it is seen in the truth, a necessity was evidently discovered from meeting to meeting, for friends to encrease their acquaintance with the light, which only makes manifest, and without which our

judgment

judgment is exceedingly imperfect; and when this is obtained, not only to work in it, but to work wifely in it, endeavouring to fupprefs a difpofition which is not purely intent upon reaching the witnefs in each other, even when under the neceffity of humblingly difplaying that chriftian virtue, of rendering good for evil, and of being willing to endure all things. Chriftian condefcenfion is one of the great wheels whereby the caufe of truth is advanced, among rightly exercifed members, in meetings for difcipline. When a burden refts on the mind of any, which in fimplicity is removed, it adds greatly to its value, and recommends it to thofe to whom it is offered, when fubmitted in the fpirit of true meeknefs, and no inclination difcovered to urge that out of the truth, which at firft was delivered with the favour of it; even though it may feem to undergo perfecution, by that wifdom in others which is from beneath, and is carnal; for a bleffing belongs to thofe who rightly endure perfecution, and being reviled, revile not again.

To difcriminate between our own fpirits, and a right zeal when contending for the faith, requires great finglenefs of heart, and opennefs to felf-conviction, which I have forrowfully obferved too few arrive at, or dwell in; and hence we are deprived of an increafe in the increafe of God, the fruit-bearing branches not being fo effectually purged, as to enable them to bring forth more good fruit. —O the beauty of the living branches, when they abide in the vine, draw their fap from the root, and retain only an holy emulation with each other! a preferving canopy would fuch form in

meetings for difcipline, as well as worfhip, and many who are light in their fpirits, refembling the fowls of the air, would be induced to lodge under it. No boafting, no felf-feeking, no fpirit that would rend or tear the tender feelings of any feeble traveller, could here have any place; becaufe being branches which bring not forth good fruit, they are cut off and caft into the fire. But as, in the prefent mixed ftate of things, and efpecially in thefe meetings, where friends are untrained to the publick exercife of their gifts, and unaccuftomed to fit under a diverfity of fentiments, occafions cannot fail of being furnifhed for the trial of chriftian virtues, I was renewedly convinced, of the neceffity which thofe who act in the ftation of clerks have to be clear in their views, by dwelling near enough to the fpirit of the gofpel, fo as to receive qualifications therefrom, in pure wifdom, to ftrengthen or make way for that lowly plant which is righteous, and boafts not itfelf in the garden of the Lord; but to which the promife and bleffing belong, " for all the trees of the field fhall know, that I, the Lord, have brought down the high tree, and exalted the low tree, have dried up the green tree, and caufed the dry tree to flourifh;" yea, the valleys are exalted and the mountains reduced, when the feed of immortal life reigns, and fways its pure fceptre in the affemblies of the people of God. The attention of my mind was, therefore, fecretly attracted to the Father of lights, by whofe powerful difcoveries I faw myfelf; and notwithftanding the bufinefs of the meeting almoft conftantly employed me, yet I was favoured to feel a frequent abftractednefs, and ample opportunities,

under

under a prevailing fenfe of my own weaknefs, fervently to petition the Lord to be with my fpirit, to keep me patient in my prefent employ, meek in my demeanour, and truly a fervant to His caufe and people. And I may with thankfulnefs acknowledge, to the praife of His grace, which is fufficient for all the wants of His children, that, however deficient in many refpects for the ftation, I comfortably felt divine ftrength and wifdom underneath; wherein the precious unity of the one fpirit, not only with the prefent, but divers abfent friends, confolated my often drooping mind. Notwithftanding the foregoing obfervations, the meetings, in general, were attended with living virtue, and the humble travailers refrefhed and inftructed therewith.

After the yearly meeting was over, my hufband and I ftaid a few days about London, as did my beloved companion R. J. to whom I ftill felt bound in the fervice which fhe was engaged in; and therefore fet out again with her for the weftern counties, the feventeenth of the fixth month. We took the meetings of Staines, Bafingftoke, Whitchurch, Andover, Salifbury, Rumfey, and Ringwood, in our way to Fordingbridge, where the quarterly meeting for Hampfhire was held.

It was a time of fome degree of favour and encouragement, to a few honeft-hearted friends in that county; fome of whom are under a renewed vifitation of divine mercy. From hence we went to the quarterly meeting of Dorfet, held at Pool; in which my dear companion was enabled to difcharge

charge her exercised mind of a load which she found there, in a powerful manner; the state of that county being very low, the living scarcely able to bear the dead. We then proceeded to the meetings of Shaftsbury, Marnhill, Sherborne, and Yeovil, where my dear husband left us intending for Bristol, and from thence to Ireland. On this occasion, I felt a secret breathing for the continuance of the Lord's protecting providence, both with respect to the safety of the body, and the preservation of our minds in His fear, and an increase in His favour.

From Yeovil we went to Puddemore, Longsutton, Ilminster, Chard, Bridport, and so to Exeter, where we found, as in some of the foregoing places, a few innocent, concerned friends; but the want of that baptism which initiates into the church of Christ, builds up the members into a spiritual house, a holy temple in the Lord, where He presides and ministers, was sensibly felt; and yet the language of encouragement to press forward to this state, appeared to us to be the language of truth. In general, the spirit of the world, though often disguised, so much prevails, that before the right foundation can be discovered, a specious pile of buildings wants pulling down; and therefore for ministers rightly to visit meetings and individuals in this state, requires soundness of judgment, strength in the pure faith, patient perseverance and righteous zeal; all of which, when I see myself, I feel the want of.* We staid their first day meeting

* The following passages are extracted from her letters :———9th of 7th month, 1786. As I trust our

meeting at Exeter, and then went to Kingſbridge, taking a little meeting at Newton Buſhel in our way,

alliance to each other in ſpirit, is ſtronger than the ties of nature, it is not (we may conclude) inconſiſtent therewith, to impart to each other without ſtraitneſs, in the circulation of mutual love and renewed ſympathy; for without this quickening experience, all our communications muſt be lifeleſs and inſipid. How excellent is the life of truth! the want of it in myſelf, and in others, is a daily burden to my mind; and the burden bearers, in places where we come, being very few, renders it ſtill more heavy.—To ſay that the ſtate of the ſociety is low in theſe weſtern parts, is ſo general, and ſo juſt a complaint, that there is a danger of its being taken up without feeling ſufficiently the ſpirit of mourning.

———" Thirteenth of 7th month 1786. We endeavour quietly to get forward; and by the continued ſuſtaining evidence, that the beſt ſtrength is gracioully near to aſſiſt in the needful time, and the bleſſing which makes truly rich ſometimes revealed in the midſt of our poverty, we are preſerved, thus far, in a degree of thankfulneſs to the great Supplier of all the neceſſities of His people; though often attended with the ſpirit of mourning over the ſcattered remnant of a once flouriſhing heritage. Though in ſome places there is but little to viſit, yet not being a people wholly given up to reproach, and the pure feed ſtill groaning for deliverance, a little room is left to labour; and here and there an exerciſed member dwells, with whom, whenever they were found, our minds could not but dip into near ſympathy; ſo that any little opening to ſervice, in ſuch deſolate places, ought not to be declined, but rather cheriſhed in confidence that the good Huſbandman will again plough and ſow His plantation, and bleſs the labour of thoſe He puts forth. I cannot ſay that this is an expectation which hath abundantly attended my mind, in our paſſing along; but, juſt as 1 write, a little hope is renewed, that the vineyard will again proſper by a right and neceſſary extirpation of the briers, the thorns, and the noxious weeds; and, by an holy cul-

way, and to Plymouth, where we attended their monthly meeting; which is in so weak a state, as to be far short of supporting the dignity of christian discipline in its own spirit; and this is lamentably the case in many other places. It is only as the gathered churches become sensible of their deplorable situation, look beyond their own natural abilities, to the well of life in themselves, and get low enough to draw water thereout, that a restoration of the power will be witnessed, which is Jesus in the midst of them. We also attended their meetings the first day following, which were deeply exercising; but our gracious Helper was near, strengthening to an honest labour; wherein the right way to the kingdom, was proved to be widely different from that wherein many are walking; and under this help, a degree of holy solemnity was felt."

———

In addition to the preceding journal, which appears to be left short of the visit, the following extracts have been made from her letters; which, though not containing a regular, continued account, may afford further information and instruction.

——"The

tivation, be prepared for the true plants, wherever scattered, being enclosed within divine protection, and rendered fruitful in holiness, so as to be fitted to receive the heavenly Visitant, and made able to endure the northern and the southern blasts. O that this hope may not perish, but prove true in a future day, when the earth is shaken of her rest!

―――" The prefent journey with my beloved friend, has been a frefh trial of the uprightnefs of my defire after dedication; for after returning from Ireland, I earneftly fought quietude and obfcurity, to fettle down among my valuable connections and enjoy their fociety, or the benefits of folitude; but the reward of peace was not the attendant of thefe profpects; nor did the cloud appear to reft upon my tabernacle: the words, " Time is fhort," were deeply infcribed upon my heart, fo that one thing or other bid me take a few more fteps in the tribulated path of gofpel obedience,"

―――" I have felt myfelf thefe few days back, as near the end of my prefent commiffion, my faith, patience, and every chriftian virtue, as to the point of land before us; and being fo far from home, aggravates the profpect, and gives me very much the feeling of a pelican in the wildernefs, out of the reach of almoft any other help, fave that holy Arm which leads about and inftructs, in what appears to us the moft deferted fituation, and moreover hath promifed to keep as the apple of the eye.

" Could I believe myfelf to be one thus provided for, and to whom the arm of power will continue to be extended, fome of my fecret cogitations would be lefs painful and gloomy, and with greater pleafantnefs, I could advance forward, though in a tribulated way. From Plymouth we came into Cornwall, taking Germains, Looe, Lifkard, Auftel, and Mevageffey meetings, in our way to Falmouth, where, and in its neighbourhood, we have met with

fome

some valuable friends. In these western counties through which we have come, viz. Hampshire, Dorsetshire, Somersetshire, and Devonshire, the society, as to the circulation of that life which we profess to be seeking the influence of, is indeed lamentably low. A worldly spirit and a state that is neither hot nor cold, greatly prevails; so that the few living members (for there is here and there one) are scarcely able to lift the standard of truth, or revive the remembrance of the law. But in this county, viz. Cornwall, things are better; a right zeal having sprung up in divers, to search into the real state of the church, and what is more, a care first to search themselves; an exercise greatly wanted among active members in many places. C. P.'s labours in these parts have been, we think, eminently blessed; and the good effects of such a faithful discharge of duty, and bearing a steady, uniform testimony to the truth, and against error, would, there is no doubt, oftener be found, if that was oftener tried. We get but slowly forward since we came into this county; for though I have mentioned some good in it, yet we find it close exercising work, to get clearly down to the good thing alluded to; and have staid longer in places hereabouts, than any where before. Yesterday was trying to my almost worn out mind; my companion got a little relieved in the morning, but I saw no way for myself all the day, though under a great weight; but so it is, we need patience and subjection in such times, lest we move before the waters have risen to their appointed height."

———" We

———" We have been favoured to get along without accidents, and have to acknowledge that, many ways, we are helped beyond our frequent expectation; finding, (as we suppose others do) discouragements on the right hand, and on the left; which, if suffered to prevail, would soon destroy that little grain of efficacious faith which removes mountains, and without which, however we may labour and waste our strength, such mountains of difficulty and unfruitfulness, as the christian traveller meets with, can never be removed. How necessary is it then to fight the good fight of faith: that so, when pure life is circulating, instead of knowing it not, we may be strengthened to lay hold of it, and to experience the inner man so renewed in us, as to actuate every service.—Here we see our own insufficiency, and how unavailing it is to depend upon our strength and judgment, in things belonging to ourselves or others."

———" I have been at meeting this morning at Collumpton, a small gathering of lukewarm professors, in the general; but a few solid young people afforded a comfortable prospect for the future. Silence was my lot here; but my spirit was deeply humbled, in feeling the baptizing virtue of truth near to purify my vessel, which I esteem more than the fairest qualifications for publick service; and am more and more led secretly to supplicate the increase of this solid experience and ability, to endure with christian firmness and patience those dispensations by which it is obtained. Nevertheless, I am often deeply tried in religious meetings, with such exceeding great strippedness of good, and intrusion of

thoughts

thoughts which I by no means approve there, that I mourn under it; and when any thing opens, which appears like a difcovery of truth, to give it to others when I am ready to perifh with hunger myfelf, is almoft irreconcileable; efpecially when after giving up to it, I find myfelf as poor when a meeting breaks up, as when it began. I can hardly defcribe what I fecretly fuffer from meeting to meeting, on this account; fo that when I am favoured with a fenfible evidence, of the fanctifying power of the Minifter of minifters yet dwelling in mine earthen veffel, abundantly doth my foul acknowledge, that the excellency of the power is not of us, but of Him, and that he hath a right to reveal it when and how he pleafeth."

She attended the circular meeting at Gloucefter, in the ninth month; from whence fhe returned pretty directly, into Yorkfhire, and was at the quarterly meeting for that county. In the forepart of the tenth month, fhe proceeded with G. D. and others to the County of Durham, and attended the quarterly meeting there. Of thefe fervices, no remarks can be added, as there does not appear any thing material of her own preferved on thefe occafions.

C H A P.

CHAP. V.

Family Visit at Sheffield.—Her Illness there.—Consideration of removing into Ireland.—Journey into Lincolnshire.—Removal to Ireland.—Journey into Holland, Germany and France.

IN the first month 1787, she was engaged with Reb. Jones and others, in a religious visit to the families of friends at Sheffield; concerning which she writes as follows:

———The visit here is got through, and I hope profitably so to many, and especially the youth, of whom here are great numbers; some of the apprentices are very raw, but others seem turning about with desire to find, and make, the right purchase. They are indeed, altogether, a great load of care upon the shepherds and shepherdesses in this place, whose concern I hope is increasing. It is pleasant to find increasing unity and openness among rightly concerned friends in this place, and that love which casteth out fear.

At the close of this family visit, she was taken very ill, with a heavy cold and an inflammation of the lungs. This disorder continued for several weeks, during which she was brought very low in body and mind. But the great Physician, on whom appeared to be her sole dependance, saw meet to raise her again, and to renew a considerable portion of health and strength. Of this illness, and the exercise of her mind under it, as well as of

her

her feelings in the review of it, some account will be conveyed, by the following extracts from her letters, written whilst she was on the recovery.

————I am now favoured with ability to answer your solicitude myself, and say, that the account you had of my illness was, I apprehend, not worse than the reality; having been reduced to the gates of death to all appearance, with an inflammation of my lungs, which had been approaching some weeks, and arrived at an awful crisis; at which time, by the merciful interposition of the good Physician, the disorder took a favourable turn, and opened again my prospects to this mixed state of things. My bodily affliction was great, but the conflicts and gloomy exercises of my mind, were not less, being involved in all the weakness and insufficiency of human nature, in endeavouring to attain to the spring of pure consolation, at the same time that, in unerring wisdom, it was sealed in my view: so that, upon the whole, it was a season of deep proving, and, I humbly trust, lasting instruction; by rendering more single the attention of my mind to divine discoveries, whereby our duty is seen, and strength to perform it acceptably received. To be found faithful in the great work of the present life, is an object of such magnitude, that all things else appear comparatively trifling, when we are looking into a state of eternal duration.

————The ways of wisdom are a great deep, and the designs of removing from, or restoring to, this uncertain and probationary state of being, are often for purposes which require a daily waiting for, and dependance upon the unfoldings of pure inftruction, in order profitably to difcover them. I confider this to be my own cafe, and often remember a remark of J. Woolman's to a friend, perhaps fimilarly circumftanced, " do we (fays he) get through with great difficulty, and yet recover; He requires that we fhould be purged from drofs, and our ear opened to difcipline."

—— I am favoured to continue recovering, though often reminded that in every fenfe I am a poor weak creature, and under abundant neceffity to hold faft the little ftrength I have, and patiently wait for the renewings of that life which quickens, and gives joy in the fpiritual creation. But I am ftill too carnally minded, too much difpofed to look outward, and too little to prefs through the oppofition of nature, to that true weightinefs of fpirit which I earneftly fought for in a late feafon of adverfity. Thefe things convince us that, in order to win the crown in view, we muft fight the good fight, and wreftle for that faith which only gives the victory.

The fubject of their removing into Ireland, and fettling there, had for a confiderable while, engaged her folid confideration; and the propriety of that undertaking was about this time attended with fuch clearnefs to her own mind, and that of her hufband, that they apprehended the time was near for their departure from this land. Divers of her letters written on this occafion, fhew her fenfe of the importance of this meafure, and how great and exemplary was her concern, that they

might

might be directed wisely and safely concerning it. The following have been selected from them.

———— Our minds have been under frequent, and sometimes, unprofitable concern how to dispose of ourselves. There seems an abundance of places to choose from, both in Ireland and here; but to know our right lot, is what we are both desiring singly to stand open to the discovery of, if conveyed to us ever so simply; the light which manifests it, be it ever so small, will, I believe, satisfy our fasting minds. We have need to be reduced low, that we may so obtain the knowledge of the divine will, as cheerfully to yield obedience thereto. Though we think we have waited long for instruction, yet as our opinions, of ourselves especially, are often very fallacious, it is not impossible but we are far from that state of self-nothingness and dependance, which I am sometimes ready to hope we are on the brink of. We are at present quite unbound to any place; perhaps to have no place of abode is the lot designed us; a lot that much opposes my inclination, but if right, however trying, it must be submitted to, and its consequences likewise, as the requirings of the day.

———— My mind has of late looked with more clearness than before, towards Ireland. It has been a subject of consideration, attended already with much anxiety; and now that I am apprehensive I have seen a right opening towards it, I wish to be preserved from looking back, or entering into unprofitable considerations bout it; but rather to leave the matter at present. on'y standing open to the discoveries

coveries of more light, either for or againſt it, and reſpecting the right time of moving, or of not moving at all, which I know to be the ſituation of my huſband's mind reſpecting it.———— I well know, that except we are in our right places, we can have no true enjoyment or expectation of ſupport under, or the bleſſing upon, our allotted portion of ſuffering; and we have proved both lands to have in them their ſhare of trials and probations; and know that things which look the moſt pleaſant in either, may ſoon, as ſome of them have already at times been, be embittered, and ſhaded with gloom. I wiſh however to number my bleſſings, for they are many, and far beyond my deſerts.

———— I often wiſh that I could learn to be ſtill when I have nothing to do, and inſtead of ſtraining my eyes in the dark, and watching the breaking of the day, to dwell quietly in the ward all night, believing in the light, and obediently working therein. The outward day breaks gradually upon us, and experience teaches us the certain indication of its approach, a dawning of light, which we are not apt to diſbelieve, nor doubt that the meridian of it will come in due time. And as in the outward, we cannot haſten that time, no more can we with reſpect to divine illuminations. Does it not therefore, remain to be our buſineſs, to wait for the light when a little of it appears, to believe in it, and that the fulneſs of the day will come, though we do not now ſee it; remembering that, " bleſſed are they that have not ſeen, and yet have believed." This is what I apprehend to be right to do, and

what

what I wifh to attain; but I would by no means infinuate, that I confidently believe myfelf to have arrived at it, in the profpect of removing to Ireland; meaning only, that after a ftate of anxiety, and tofling about with every wind of the fentiments of others, I feemed to get into refignation's harbour. I am however willing to ftand open to further conviction; and if the will fhould be gracioufly accepted for the deed, my poor bark excufed the expofure, and my dear R. G. fatisfied, (which I do not doubt if it is right) it will not be an unpleafant releafe from an engagement to which I now feel myfelf rather bound: for there are many in this nation, and in our own county, (fetting afide my near relatives after the flefh) to whom I am clofely attached, and from whom nature will flinch to part; but there are alfo divers of this clafs in Ireland, whofe friendfhip will, if my refidence there be right, greatly repair the lofs, and tend to fmooth the otherwife rugged path. This is looking at fecondary caufes, a view which I do not wifh often to take; becaufe to be in the place afligned, (whether I was known of mortals or not) where the great work of fanctification and acceptance in divine favour is going forward, would, I am fatisfied, afford a peace fuperior to all human confolations, and enable the truly abafed mind nobly to fay, " Although the fig-tree fhall not bloffom, neither fhall fruit be in the vines; the labour of the olive fhall fail, and the fields fhall yield no meat; the flock fhall be cut off from the fold, and there fhall be no herd in the ftalls; yet I will rejoice in the Lord, I will joy in the God of my falvation:" a glorious experience worthy our afpiring after! Whatever has a tendency to loofen our affections from mixed ftreams of refrefhment, and centre them in the great fource, the well in ourfelves fpringing up unto everlafting life, I apprehend more truly qualifies for fervice, than a fituation replete with opportunities, for the increafe of human wifdom and activity in the vifible church; which never fail to have in them their fnares, by gratifying felf, if given way to, in one fhape or other.

————What I have felt at times on the fubject of our removal, cannot be eafily defcribed; divine fupport and direction, if fingly fought to, under the weight of it, will be found fufficient to fuftain, and open the right way; but I apprehend that our fmall grain of faith, may meet with many trials and buffetings in our future fteppings; and oh that we may never make fhipwreck thereof!

May the ftaff of Ifrael be our fupport, feparately and together, and may we have no other dependance, is the fecret petition of my mind; for, in the undertaking before us, we may fay, that with our ftaff only we are paffing over this Jordan.

Having come to a conclufion refpecting their removal into Ireland, and obtained the concurrence of their monthly meeting, they proceeded to York and attended the quarterly meeting there; from whence, after taking a folemn and affecting leave of their near connections and friends, they fet forward for the county of Lincoln; the meetings of which, as well as fome others, fhe felt a defire to attend, in her

way

way to the yearly meeting. Soon after this trying separation, the following letter appears to have been written.* With divers companions in that service, she visited most or all of the meetings and families of friends in Lincolnshire, and attended several other meetings as she proceeded to London. Though but little of the progress of this journey is described in the following extracts; yet the feelings of her mind, and the instructive remarks set forth therein, will, it

---

* Last week but one was our quarterly meeting at York, which was favoured with the overshadowings of the heavenly wing. It was a parting time, and almost too affecting for my present weak state; but I endeavoured what I could to look beyond personal enjoyments, to that fellowship which is pure, standing with the Father and with the Son, and which admits of no change by outward separation, if we retain our integrity and places, in the adoption of children. On seventh day morning after, came the dregs of the cup of removal; a heart tendering farewell to my beloved connections at York, with the proprietors of the school, and some of their husbands. It was almost too much for my frame, faith being at a low ebb, and discouragements coming in like a flood; but in the opening of true vision, the spirit of the Lord was lifted up as a standard against them. As to the body, I have now parted with many who seemed interwoven with my existence: with divers of them it was gradual, and I esteem it a favour it was so: but though I am sensible, that in the church I leave both fathers and mothers behind; and as to brethren and sisters in the truth, they seem almost daily added to, and promise, according to their present growth, to be skilful servants in the family; yet the near unity my spirit has felt with some in Ireland, affords me a ray of hope, that should we be spared with life and strength, to enter into and rightly stand in our lots at Clonmel, we shall find every want supplied, and true yoke-fellows beyond our deserts.

it is apprehended, render it proper to infert them here.

———— We are favoured to get along as well as we might expect, we hope in fome degree of fympathy with the ftate of the beft things in this defolate county; but upon the whole, my mind is and hath been favoured with a calm, efpecially for thefe few days back, which tends to promote the reftoration of health, and ftrengthens with a good degree of refignednefs, to look forward to the profpects before me; and fo far from confidering the purfuit of them a hardfhip, I efteem the end propofed thereby, a favour of which I am unworthy; for what is there worth living for, but to be found in the difcharge of our duty?

————We are now in the Ifle of Axolm, vifiting a few defolate profeffors, who are like fheep having no fhepherd; and yet in a place as much neglected as perhaps any in the fociety, we are comforted in finding a feed alive, refembling Jofeph in Egypt, and may fay, for my own part, that I have felt the moft folid reward for a little labour here, of any fince leaving York. It is not after the fight of the eye, or the hearing of the ear, that we can judge aright.

————They that fuffer with the feed, fhall reign with it; but it muft not be in our way, nor in our time. Patience is due on our part, and the exercife of that grain of faith which we have received; for, " by faith the elders obtained a good report," I prefume of the Lord, rather than of men. Then let us

not

not be afraid of the trial, for its efficacy is proved thereby. O that I was ftronger in this fpot! for even fince we left York, and particularly on leaving it, I have feemed to be reduced to the loweft ebb, and nature hath foreboded difcouragements beyond what I thought I was able to bear. But this is not always the cafe; for fometimes, when every thing elfe is fhaded with gloom, the foundation is moft clearly revealed, and its ftanding fure incontrovertibly known and believed in; fo that all things have appeared poffible to him that believeth, and the ways of the Moft High difcovered to be higher than our ways, and his thoughts than our thoughts. Here I love to repofe myfelf, and ftand refigned to every difpenfation which has the remoteft tendency, not only to let me fee the work of my day, but to refine and qualify for it.

—— I have recovered fo much, that I have now fcarce any thing to complain of refpecting the body. To be fure it is not very ftrong, but it has thus far proved able to bear all that was laid upon it; which is encouragement to myfelf, and alfo to others, to perfevere in yielding ourfelves up, under the power of the crofs, to every opening of duty, feeing that all things are poffible to them that believe. And yet I fainted in my mind many a time, and feemed to be one of thofe who have no faith: fo that, on reflecting upon this little embaffy, the profpect and the progrefs of it, it feems as if it was all done for me by that good Hand, which requires the paffivenefs rather than the activenefs of the creature, in profecuting His defigns. Though I now give a pretty good account of the body, I may alfo add,

add, that, sometimes, my mind gets encompassed with glooms and discouragements, which nothing can dissipate, save a state of resignation and quiet dependance upon the everlasting Arm of Omnipotence; and this is often so hard to attain, that I am afraid of falling in the struggle, when a hope is again revived, of being under divine protection, and that the day's work is really going forward. This, at times, introduces a quiet serenity, and strengthens to leave the things that are behind, and press forward to those that are before. The sympathy of my friends under my late trials, has been considered a favour of which I am unworthy; and there is undoubtedly no better way of securing it upon the foundation of gospel fellowship, than by learning to live without it, and looking singly to the Rock from whence all good things are hewn, and the hole of the pit, the humbling dispensations of infinite wisdom, from whence they are dug.

Soon after the yearly meeting at London, they proceeded for Clonmel in Ireland, where she was favoured to arrive in safety, in the 6th month 1787, with her health much improved, and under a good degree of peace and satisfaction of mind; which continued for some time after her arrival, as a source of consolation and encouragement she writes as follows :

——— Our removal has altogether been blessed with a good degree of that peace which passeth understanding, and attended with such circumstances, thus far, as we have great cause to be thankful for. An unmixed cup of comfort in human life, is what

my

my short passage through the world, has taught me not to look for, and a small degree of religious experience, not to pray for; and yet to pray for those things which are really good for us, will ever require the renewings of that Spirit which only breathes the will of the Father. Nature shrinks at suffering; sometimes I am ready to anticipate a draught of it, proportionable to the late and present degree of favour; and sometimes I am flattered with a language that tells me, " it is already drunk, and that the bitterness of death is past." An humble, resigned mind is however always our duty and interest to press after. It has a fortification in itself against the varied assaults of Satan, and a sufficient portion of Gilead's Balm for every afflictive dispensation of infinite wisdom; both of which, if my natural life is spared, will, I do believe, be my companions, and prove frequent trials of an abiding and advancement in that gospel Spirit, which loveth, hopeth, and endureth through all.

Her mind had frequently, for a considerable time before this period, been impressed and closely exercised with an apprehension, that it would be required of her to pay a religious visit to some parts of Germany and France: and, a few months after her settlement in Ireland, this concern increased with such weight and evidence, that she was constrained, in resignation, to spread it before the friends of their monthly meeting; who, after solid deliberation and sympathy, concurred therewith, and gave her their certificate of unity and approbation. She received also the near concurrence of their quarterly meeting, and that of the morning meeting

of

of ministers and elders in London, and set forward on this journey in the 3d month, 1788, in company with her husband, George Dillwyn and his wife, and Mary Dudley; who were also bound to this service, and engaged therein with the unity of friends.

The following parts of her letters on this occasion, describe the previous exercise of her mind, and contain a pretty regular, though short account of the journey, from the commencement of it, to its conclusion.

12th month 1787. My mind after a season of deep trial and exercise, was led to visit, in what appeared to myself an extraordinary degree of gospel love, many in that country, and some parts of Germany contiguous thereto; fully believing, according to my feelings, that there were spiritual worshippers in those parts.

12th month 1787. If the prospect before us be in divine wisdom, we have great cause to acknowledge that it is unfathomable, and past our finding out, because of my incapacity, in every respect to perform such a journey to the honour of the great Cause. I wish, however, now to leave caring too much about the future, and endeavour after quiet resignation; well knowing, that by taking ever so much unprofitable thought, I cannot add one cubit to my stature, nor make one hair of my head white or black; and also hoping, that when it comes to the trial, the will may be accepted for the deed; which I have no doubt will be the case, if the province

vince meeting, or my sympathizing friends, advise me against it; or if no friend of superior weight in the ministry, proves under the like concern, and admits us in their company. Discouragements of various kinds crowd in at times upon me, but when gospel love flows from the living fountain, it overpowers all selfish considerations, and shews me my own unworthiness to be, in the least degree, employed in the divine hand.

1st month 1788. Our situation at present, requires at least a grain of that faith which has power to remove mountains; for, truly vain is the help of man, in cases where the pure seed is to be exalted. A sense of our insufficiency to do any good thing without divine assistance, will, I trust, whatever our trials or temptations may be, so humble us, as wholly to prevent a vain dependance upon any thing of our own; but surely there is as much need for watchfulness and prayer at this day, as when the disciples were immediately recommended to it.

1st month 1788. My mind is often under a load of exercise on my own account, and in care lest the precious cause should suffer by me. The present is a time of deep trial and searching of heart, lest we should be meddling with, or doing, any thing which is not in the clear discovery of gospel light. When I consider how little I am experienced in the station wherein I may be likely to move, the newness and peculiarity of the service in prospect, and even the weakness of the outward tabernacle, (which to be sure I think least of) my feelings suggest the applicableness of the saying, " I am a worm." This however

however cheers me, that without fome degree of clearnefs, we need not, neither fhall attempt to move.

2d month 1788. I have been of late confiderably indifpofed, but upon the whole am much better, though every day fenfible of having (by fome means or other) a very broken conftitution. If it do but laft until the portion of work allotted me is finifhed, that is enough, even though it be performed under the preffure of bodily infirmities; all which may be no more than neceffary to keep the mind to its proper centre, and direct its attention, fingly to an inheritance undefiled, and which fadeth not away.

3d month 1788. According to prefent appearances, we, (I mean our little company) ftand in abundant need of the whole armour of light. We are about to embark for a country, the language of which none of us know, and in expectation of a path wherein we can fee no footfteps, and which muft be attended with new and various trials. May our truft be in the Lord alone, who is able, in feafons of the greateft difficulty, to encreafe our faith, and make way for us where we fee no way.

————Having the concurrence of friends, we left London and proceeded for Harwich, where we were detained feveral days for want of a fair wind; during which time we had two meetings, and afterwards, (23d of 3d month) the wind turning in favour of our leaving that port, we embarked; but it was fourth day night, the twenty-feventh, before we

we landed at Helvoetfluys, which was neverthelefs a favour, and I hope efteemed fo by us all. We got to an agreeable Englifh inn there, and after a pretty good night's reft, fet forward towards Rotterdam, by way of the Briel and Delf, and came in fafe rather late at night, it being there a great day's work of about twenty-five miles. We travelled in an open waggon the firft feven miles, the road being fo bad that no other carriage could get along with fafety, and the reft of the way went in their boats called Treckfchuyts, which are drawn by a horfe, at the rate of about three miles an hour. This is a very pleafant and eafy way of travelling, and it was through a country made as agreeable by improvements as it is capable of, being very flat and marfhy. Many of the inhabitants followed us through fome towns, and gazed exceedingly at us; and fome of them, as well as they were able, manifefted a love which met that in us that drew us hither; but the ftrangenefs of our language to each other, was a continual difcouragement; yet as it was not of our own bringing on, we endeavoured to keep quiet under it, and fecretly defired that our minds might be fo influenced, as to convey to them, in filence, that which is better than words. We have now got into fo new a line, that it is no wonder if we fhould be more than ufually blind; and it will be well, if fome of us fhould be alfo more than ufually dependant and patient refpecting our fteppings; for being feparated and remote from our friends, and fome of difpofitions rather hafty than otherwife, there is, no doubt, a danger of fometimes preffing forward with too much earneftnefs, and thereby of preventing the
completion

completion of thofe little fervices, in one way or other, which are intended for the purchafe of our own peace at leaft. Though Holland was not much in the profpect of us who came from Ireland, yet we have been favoured with fomething more than a hope, that we are thus far in our places, and feel a comfortable and ftrengthening unity one with another therein. The defire of my mind is at prefent ftrong, that, though in ever fo much weaknefs, we may be enabled to pafs through the country in that finglenefs and dedication of heart, which may preferve us from condemnation.

We ftaid three days in Rotterdam, and had two publick meetings at the meeting houfe belonging to friends; there are a great many Englifh people in that city, and the attenders of our meetings being principally of that clafs, we had no need of an interpreter. There are fome ferious people with whom we got acquainted, and to whom our vifit feemed acceptable, but no profeffors with us, except one perfon, who cannot be expected, in his prefent ftate, to throw much light upon the teftimony of truth; but he was very willing to render us fuch fervices as were in his power, which we took kind.

From Rotterdam, we came forward to Amfterdam, by way of Leyden, Haarlem, &c. and were kindly received by our friend John Vanderwerf. Here our minds, generally, got very low on divers accounts. Several of us were poorly with complaints in the ftomach, &c. which ftrangers are fubject to, before their conftitutions come to bear the difference of their meat, drink, air, &c. The few

few under the name of friends in this great city, yielded us little of that strength which is the fruit of sympathy of spirit, and inward acquaintance with divine requirings; and which if right, would have been truly salutary and cordial to us at that time, as we looked upon ourselves to be then embarking upon the most arduous and discouraging part of our journey; having a great distance to travel, entirely unacquainted with the country, strangers to all their different languages, except a little French, and no interpreter to accompany us. Under these complicated trials, our faith got into the furnace afresh. This was much the case with me, and my dear companions felt no less. However, as we endeavoured after resignation, and were sometimes replenished with strength patiently to wait for renewed manifestations of duty, way opened, by degrees, to get clear of that place. We attended their little monthly meeting, the business whereof was transacted in the Dutch language; so that we had not an opportunity of judging much about them; except that their appearance, and the feelings of our minds, convinced us that true religion is at a low ebb among them; and yet there is something tender which loves truth, and with which, a family visit among them, made us better acquainted.* We had also three publick meetings there, which

---

* We were comforted in the belief that their solitary situations are divinely regarded, and hope that divers of their deficiencies in some points wherein we have been otherwise taught, are counterbalanced in the sight of holy compassion and justice, by the sincerity of their intentions, and the discouragements in many respects peculiar to them, which we, by experience, know little

which were attended by many of the inhabitants of different defcriptions; but there are a few with whofe company, both in and out of meetings, we were comforted. They are a ferious religious people, not connected with any fociety, and believing in the fpirituality of all true worfhip. We paid a vifit to one of their families, which confifts of a widow, her fon, and two daughters, none of them young. They are people of confiderable property, which they devote very much to the fervice of the poor. They were affectionately kind, and demonftrated their unity with, and attachment to our principles, as far as they had heard them in the meetings which they attended, and were fully convinced of the neceffity of an inward work, and that all true worfhip muft be performed in fpirit and in truth. In a religious opportunity which we had with them before we parted, the cementing influence of gofpel love flowed among us like a ftream. From this family, we were furnifhed with letters of recommendation to fuch as themfelves in Germany, fome of whom we have feen to our fatisfaction. During our ftay in Amfterdam, we were interpreted for, by John Vanderwerf, or one of his fons, both in publick and private. It feemed ftrange, and rather hard to us women, efpecially at firft; but we foon got over it, and had reafon to hope that our
religious

about. The keeping up of a meeting for worfhip every firft day, in their weak ftate, is an act of faithfulnefs, which we might be often ready to faint under, were we in their fituation, feparated from the ftrengthening communications which religious fociety affords, (not having received a vifit of this kind for four years) and being defpifed among the worldly minded.

religious communications were not materially affected; our friend feemed to have an awe upon his mind when he ftood up, took off his hat, and delivered, fentence by fentence, what was expreffed. Thus after fpending eight days at Amfterdam, and being deeply tried in that place, our minds were ftrengthened to leave it, (the 9th of the 4th month,) with a renewed truft, that the great Shepherd of Ifrael, who knows his own fheep in every trial and fituation, however remote from the knowledge and confolation of their friends, would fuperintend us, and gracioufly reveal himfelf for our help, in the needful time. We effayed to proceed by way of Utrecht, (where a few books were diftributed, and much love felt for the inhabitants) Nimeguen, and through part of the king of Pruffia's dominions, into the Elector of Bavaria's to a place called Duffeldorff, where we again made a little ftop, finding a few who could fpeak Englifh, and moft of them French. Here we commenced acquaintance with a folid, religious man, named Michael Wetterboar, to whom we were recommended by the people whom I have mentioned at Amfterdam. Being gathered to the principle of truth, and engaged to conform to it, as revealed in the line of his own experience, he walks much alone in a dark and diffipated place. He was a kind friend to Claude Gay, when paying a fimilar vifit to our's in this country, many years ago, and was rejoiced to fee us. He lamented the lonefomenefs of his fituation, and faid that his mind was ftrengthened by the vifit. From hence we went eighteen miles and back, out of our road, to Elberfeld, where, as at many other places, for

want

want of an interpreter, we fuffered what often appears to us an unavailing baptifm for the teftimony's fake. But perhaps it is not fo much fo as we are apt to think : the ways of the Moft High are not our ways, nor his thoughts our thoughts; we know not but this deeply humbling path, and the fecret exercifes we have daily to pafs through without any vifible relief, may have a ufe beyond our finite conceptions; fo that it is fafeft to leave thefe things, and outward confiderations about them, in the hand which can blefs, and render fruitful, the things which are not, by caufing them to bring to nought the things which are. However, we found an opening to fome folid converfation with a few in this place, and underftood that there are many religious people there; but we were difcouraged by the difficulties we found in getting an acquaintance with them; fo we returned, after ftaying one night, to Duffeldorff. We left that place, and paffing through a dark country, arrived in two days at Newvied, the 18th of the 4th month. We have had very little rain fince we came upon the continent, confequently the roads are dry, but being for the moft part a deep fand, we have not been able to travel over it fo quickly as is defirable. Thirty miles a day, is I think nearly the average of our expedition, though we moftly travel poft. The vehicles are heavy, being generally covered waggons or clumfy coaches. We moftly prefer the former, as ourfelves and luggage meet the beft accommodation in them. The inns are pretty good, and the people refpeƈtfully kind to us, and in that line but little difficulty occurs in making ourfelves underftood. Our road has

lain

lain upon the banks of the Rhine, and furnished us with prospects of a country extremely beautiful, and, in some places, for miles together, covered with vineyards. But the pleasure which we might innocently have derived from those scenes, has met with continual damps, by the gross prostitution of sacred things which, in the crosses and images thickly scattered upon the road, give pain to every feeling whereby spiritual worship is promoted. The Roman Catholics are very numerous in many parts which we have passed through; but, in most places, the Protestants enjoy the privileges they desire without interruption; and among them there is undoubtedly an awakened, sincere hearted people. On our arrival at Newvied, we found a great change in the face of things, it being a new and pleasant town, inhabited by serious Protestants, and principally by the Moravians; though there are about twenty families of the Menonists, and as many of a people who call themselves Inspirants, but by others are often called Quakers. We were directed to a Moravian inn, which proved very agreeable, feeling ourselves in that family very much as if we were at home. Here we were soon visited by several of the Moravian brethren and sisters, some of whose minds appeared unprejudiced, and intent upon spiritual improvement; which drew them often to our apartments, and opened a door for the communication of such gospel truths, as, from time to time, occurred; and we had a comfortable hope, that they dropped into some of their minds as seed into good ground. We had the advantage in that place of an interpreter, a young man of the Moravian œconomy, who cheerfully befriended us on many occasions; and though,

though, at the firſt, he appeared under difficulty in communicating religious matter which was new to him, yet before we went away, his underſtanding ſeemed more opened, and his feelings much more cordially diſpoſed to the principle of truth as we profeſs it, and to the ſeveral branches thereof. We had a publick meeting in that place the evening before we left it, after a week's deep exerciſe and ſecret ſuffering; but this opportunity furniſhed us with renewed cauſe, to put our truſt in the gentle puttings forth of the Shepherd of Iſrael, and in the revelation of His power, which we humblingly find is ſometimes withheld, until the feaſons of our greateſt extremity. The young man, our interpreter, readily accepted his office in the meeting, without any previous requeſt, and performed it with great ſolidity. Our viſit to that place was cloſed by a ſeaſon of divine favour, in a family which cheerfully received the teſtimony we had unitedly to bear, to the efficacy of ſpiritual worſhip, and the neceſſity of preparation for it; and in much love and tenderneſs of ſpirit we left Newvied. " O the depth and extent of the riches, both of the knowledge and wiſdom of God! how unſearchable are his judgments, and his ways paſt finding out !" We had abundant cauſe in our travels through Germany, to ſay, that we were led in paths which we knew not, and frequently reduced to a ſtate of extremity. We were ſenſible, according to our meaſures, of the miſt of ſuperſtition and idolatry which overſpreads a great part of the country; and alſo had, at times, revealed that moſt ſure word of prophecy, which penetrates the obſcureſt receſſes of Sion's travellers draws them into hidden fellowſhip one with another, and unites

them

them in the fufferings of the precious feed, though differently fituated in the world, and their profeffion in it various. Thus were we led in paths which we knew not, and ways we had not feen, and were often incapable of finding out thofe whom we thus felt, and when we did difcover fuch, we were unable for want of a knowledge of their language, fully to communicate to them : but trufting in the all-fufficiency of almighty help, for the fupply of all their needs, we were favoured, when dedication of heart had been attained, and the green paftures of life opened, to lie down befide the ftill waters, and leave the event of our travel to Him who bleffeth, or blafteth, at his pleafure. From Newvied we came to Wifbaden, a place in great requeft for warm bathing, there being feveral boiling hot fprings in the town, from which the water is conveyed to private cifterns, where it cools for ufe. There feemed fomething rather attractive in this place to our minds, and yet, as was often the cafe, difcouragements prevailed over our beft feelings, and we proceeded to Frankfort, a day's journey. There we ftaid two nights; but though we had letters of recommendation to religious characters, yet for want of being able to make ourfelves underftood, we had no converfation with any but a Pietift who fpoke Englifh but poorly, and who, after fome difcourfe on religious fubjects, left us with profeffions of love. From Frankfort we proceeded to Bafle, a large proteftant town, where we arrived the 3d of the 5th month. Here our minds feemed arrefted, and all efforts towards purfuing our journey were painful, until we had fettled a few days under our exercife, and embraced, though in the crofs, fuch opportunities as

opened

opened for relief. Having some letters of recommendation to serious people, they were presented to them; in consequence of which, several visits were paid us, and we observed in some rather a critical investigation of our principles. They were cautious of embracing us until they perceived the doctrines we held; after which there was great openness in some of their minds, candidly to receive such communications on religious subjects as from time to time opened. One of them understanding the English language well, was, in several instances, a very friendly interpreter to us; and his mind being acquainted with divine illuminations, he often discovered symptoms of conviction and sensibility, when, as a channel, the openings of truth were passing through him. In a large company to which we were invited, this person, observing our disposition to silence, kindly and feelingly proposed and requested a compliance of the company. We were favoured, to our thankful admiration, with the humbling influence of divine love, and strength renewedly to bear testimony to the necessity of an inward preparation for the solemn act of true worship, which requires neither forms nor ceremonies, to render it acceptable to the Father of Spirits. The opportunity was concluded in solemn supplication, which our friendly interpreter rendered, sentence by sentence, into the Dutch language, with a reverential awe, whereby the liveliness of it was preserved. We had also a comfortable season of retirement in the family of another of our friends there, whose wife and daughters profess not to see the necessity of a religious circumspect life, as he, and his eldest son do; but they were affectionate

ate and attentive to us, and we had reason to hope, received no unprofitable impressions by this little act of dedication. This person conducted with true brotherly kindness towards us, discovering great simplicity of heart, and an openness to receive the truth, where-ever or however he might find it; being experienced in that great work of repentance unto life, and ceasing from many entanglements in the world, which he believed had a tendency to enslave his mind, and to keep him in a state of separation from divine favour: so that to meet with fellow pilgrims who could tell him a little of their knowledge of the right way, seemed like marrow to his bones. We have several times fallen in with persons who kindly entertained Claude Gay, in his lonesome travel through these parts; and in Basle we have found two agreeable religious old men, with whom he was hospitably sustained for three weeks. They are of a people called Inspirants, and often by others Quakers; but upon an acquaintance with them, especially at Newvied, we found them no less active than other professors in singing, praying, preaching, &c. in their congregations. They appear to be descendants of the French prophets; and among them there is an honest hearted number to whom the love and language of the gospel flowed with more openness, and appeared to be received with more simplicity, than among some others. To these two elderly men we paid several visits, which were not unattended with instructive conversation; but this did not afford that relief which our exercised mind seemed to want, nor could we comfortably see our way from the town, until we had, in their family and among such as they

H might

might invite, borne teftimony, by our example alfo, to the neceffity of filent waiting.* It was a feafon obtained with difficulty, and paffed through in tribulation of fpirit. The candle was not eafily put into the candleftick, and when there, evidently fufpected by thefe people, not to be in its right place. But before the meeting clofed, publick teftimony was borne to it, and to the refurrection of that life which is the light of men, being the only qualification of fpirit, to come forth from that ftate of darknefs and death in which we are by nature, and to perform any religious duties, or acceptable fervice to the Lord. At the clofe of this opportunity, we parted with thefe two men in love, though not a perfect unity of fentiment, which appeared more fully by an affectionate letter which one of them fent after us. There was alfo in this place, and in moft others where we ftopped, a prejudice againft women's preaching, which encreafed the difficulty our minds often felt in obtaining relief among a people of a ftrange language; but though our efforts were few and feeble, yet as far as dedication clothed us, and we were careful not to caft away our confidence, we had ever caufe gratefully to acknowledge, that great recompenfe of reward was vouchfafed, and the foul ftrengthened to return to its reft, under a renewed fenfe that the Lord had dealt bountifully with it. The kindnefs we have

---

* To put the light into the candleftick, fo as to bear, even in private, a teftimony to the truth, and fpiritual anointing in filence, is here a greater trial of our love and faithfulnefs to the caufe, than any can readily believe, who have not been led among thofe who are ignorant of a ceffation from their own works.

have met with in many places, exceeds what we might have expected, having several times experienced so much of the promise fulfilled, that we have met with brethren and sisters, who, though not altogether of the same profession, are fellow travellers in the christian path. Sometimes a wisdom appears in our being stripped of that outward help, so desirable, of an interpreter; as in our present circumstance, if any good is done, there is no part of it wherein the creature can glory. There is one thing which exposes us, that does not often suit the disposition of our minds, which is, that at the best inns (where we generally go) we must always dine and sup at the ordinaries, where there is often a great resort of company. If there is any use in this mortification, it will amply make up; the only testimonies which are publickly borne this way, are by our men friends keeping on their hats, and refusing to pay for the musick which sometimes accompanies our meals. We took a coach from Basle * to Bern, where we staid over a first day pretty

* The following letter was written at Basle the 9th of 5th month 1788.

As it is probable we may leave Basle without taking leave of thee, and acknowledging thy kindness with a gratitude due to it, and feeling in my heart a christian salutation, I take the liberty, this way, of expressing my desire for thy increasing knowledge of the mysteries of the kingdom of God; which our blessed Lord thanked his Father for concealing from the wise and prudent, and revealing unto babes. The sacred influences of divine light upon our understandings, are cheering to the mind, and animate its efforts to obtain the liberty of the children of God: and as we wait in this light, and believe in its manifestations, we are favoured to see more light, the means appointed to procure it are revealed to us, and strength given to follow.

pretty much in private, save that an agreeable solid man, an Inspirant, paid us some visits, I believe to mutual satisfaction. We heard of a religious exercised
But as it was prophetically spoken of the Saviour of the world, that there was no form or comeliness in him, that when we should see him, we should desire him, so the simplicity of his gospel is found to be. Nothing more strongly opposes the will, wisdom, and activity of the creature, than in all abasement, singly, to depend upon the promised Comforter, the Spirit of Truth, the anointing which an Apostle said the true believers received and had abiding in them, the unspeakable gift purchased by the precious blood of the Lamb, and dispensed in infinite mercy for our salvation, which, through its converting, purifying power is effected; for he gave himself for us, that he might redeem us from all iniquity, &c. Nevertheless the glorious end for which this sacrifice was made, ought to be advanced to, and our dependance increase upon the smallest discoveries of the spirit of Christ, though to the natural mind there may be no form nor comeliness in them: but it may sorrowfully be said, with respect to His inward appearance the second time without sin unto salvation, that he came to his own, but his own received him not; yet let us remember for our encouragement, that to as many as did receive him, he gave power to become the sons of God. So that if we surrender ourselves as clay into the hands of the potter, and our wills to the refiner's fire, we shall, this way, be made living partakers of the sufferings of Christ, being fools for his sake, and, according to our measures, conformable to his death. This is an experience which closes the lips in awful silence, and restrains the imagination from feeding upon the Tree of knowledge; without which restraint, there is a danger of our not sufficiently embracing the excellent example of Him, who was led as a lamb to the slaughter, and as a sheep dumb before her shearers. The spirit of this world, in any of its false refinements, cannot preside here, neither can any righteousness of our own; because we humblingly see with the apostle, that it is not for any of these work

exercised coachman for whom was left a book or two, he not being at home. And thus, after secretly suffering, as in many other places, we took our departure for Geneva, travelling through a very beautiful country the last twenty miles, by the lake of Geneva, and in prospect of the Alps; which were covered with snow in the latter end of the fifth month, although the weather was very hot with us. These, with the steep and craggy rocks of Switzerland, and pines of various kinds growing spontaneously upon them, and forming shades and wildernesses, compose a scene in nature truly magnificent; indeed for six hundred miles back, the prospect of mountains spread over with vineyards, with the grandeur of the Rhine, flowing below them, and its banks adorned with variety and abundance of fruit trees in full blossom, would have afforded a scene of pleasure to spirits at liberty for such enjoyment. But our hearts were on the whole too sad to be captivated thereby; a seed attracted us in sympathy, which was not so visible, nor had carried with it these sensible delights; and for it, in part, we travailed in spirit. We spent one day and two nights in Geneva, where being informed that John Eliot and Ady Bellamy were
waiting

which we have done, but of the mercy of Christ, that he saveth us, and by those means which he died to obtain, even the washing of regeneration, and the renewings of the Holy Ghost. Fervently desiring that thy sincere mind may, through the humbling processes of true spiritual baptism, be led, in the faith and patience, to the rest which is prepared for the children of God. I remain in gospel love,

Thy Friend,

S. G.

waiting for us at Lyons, we hafted to them, and found their patience tried by a week's detention in that town. We joined them, and became comfortable; and fpending one day to reft and be refrefhed there, took a boat, and rapidly poured down the Rhine, one hundred and thirty two miles in feventeen hours, to a place called Pont St. Efprit, from which we came to Nifmes and Congenies, the 22d and 23d of the 5th month, having travelled nine hundred and fifty miles from Amfterdam. It now looks pleafant to think of being foon among our friends, and a people to whom we may fpeak without an interpreter; for in that refpect our fituation is a fort of exile, but greatly made up, by a fecret fenfe, more often renewed to us than we might have expected, that we are here in the appointment of Him who gracioufly regards the fparrows, fo that not one of them falls to the ground without His permiffion: and truly thefe innocent open hearted people are of more value than many fparrows. We entered Nifmes, with fuch a peaceful ferenity upon our fpirits, as portended the acquaintance we have fince commenced with minds panting after the waters of Shiloh, and the ftrengthening effects of true gofpel labours. We went next day to Congenies, about four leagues. Our arrival drew out of their habitations the people in general; fome looked at us with aftonifhment, and others with countenances which put me in mind of Mary's falutation to Elizabeth. Thefe foon acknowledged us, and drew us into the houfe of a fteady, valuable widow, where we were folemnly faluted and received, and our minds melted together; and fuch a ftream of gofpel love flowed, as fome of us

thought

thought exceeded what we had before experienced, though no words were used to exprefs it. We obtained lodgings at the houfe of a perfon not profeffing with them, with a view not unneceffarily to interrupt them in their ufeful employments, and to be at liberty ourfelves to go among them as there appeared a fervice; but we only lodged there one night, and that with difficulty, their defire to have us among them, and to render us their fervices in their own way, was fo ftrong, that, after contending the point, we gave way, and returned to the widow's where we were entertained with every thing of the beft they could fupply. Our friends are moft of them poor, induftrious people; but we were favoured with all that was needful, though thofe things we call fo are fcarce, the country being generally overfpread with vineyards, oliveyards, and mulberry-trees. It can hardly be thought how comfortable we were: peace of mind fweetens every inconvenience. We found thefe people different from our fociety in their outward appearance, and in their want of fettlement, and fufficient quietude in their religious affemblies; but the humility and fimplicity of their meetings, attended with a lively confcioufnefs of their own weaknefs, make them ready to embrace every offer of help, that is fuited to their capacity and progrefs in the truth. There are a few of them, among the younger fort particularly, who furnifh a hope that there will be a fociety in this dark part of the world, eftablifhed upon the right foundation. We foon found, that to be ufeful to them, the vifitors muft be weak with the vifited, and in chriftian condefcenfion bear with them, until truth opened a door of utterance to shew them a more excellent way. Their monthly meeting was held on first day, wherein, of their own accord, they laid open their discipline, by reading their minutes or agreements acceded to on their first setting up these meetings; which, for consistency with their profession, are, in general, superior to our expectations. But it extends no farther than to a care over their poor, and one another's moral conduct; they have no other tenets, nor any testimonies, recorded, by which they may be distinguished; and our little band were not without a guard, with respect to proposing, or urging any thing to them, which they have not, at present, a capacity rightly to adopt and support. At Congenies, and in its neighbourhood, we spent two weeks; visited all their families; attended their monthly meeting; had a meeting for conference with the elder rank; a youths meeting, and a very satisfactory publick meeting with the inhabitants; and divers solemn opportunities unforeseen; all which brought us into near sympathy with them, and often deeply humbled and baptized our spirits on their account, as well as our own. Our parting was a very affecting one, but under a comfortable sense that the Shepherd of Israel has them under His gracious care. From Congenies we went to Giles's about twenty one miles, where there are between twenty and thirty who profess with us, as they do at Congenies; but they do not appear so much awakened in their minds, nor so earnest to be visited. They received us, however, with great kindness, and were pleased with the visit, which perhaps may be profitable to some beyond what we can now see. As without faith it is impossible

sible to please our all-wise Director, so it is impossible to persevere and hold to the end in His service, and in the humiliations which the creature meets with in it, without this precious ingredient, which is his own peculiar gift, and silences all fleshly reasonings. After having three meetings at Giles's, we came to Nismes, and there took coach for Lyons, one hundred and fifty miles. From that we travelled post, by way of Roane, Fontainbleau, Paris, and Versailles, to Alençon, where we arrived the 2d of the 7th month, several of us being weak and weary, after having travelled near six hundred miles from Nismes. In our way to Lyons, we passed through Dauphine, where some of our minds were not insensible of an attractive influence: but having no certain information of some we had heard of there, and several of our company strongly bending homewards, it did not seem the time easily to find them out.

Truly there is a hidden, precious seed scattered up and down, not only in these parts, but in Holland and Germany, measurably gathered, both from the superstitious, and the vain world; and seeking a foundation whereon they may rest the sole of their feet. This appeared beyond all doubt, both from a little knowledge which we obtained in those countries of some, and from that most sure word of prophecy, which penetrates the obscure recesses of Sion's travellers, and unites them all together in the ocean of gospel love. At Alençon, we were affectionately received by John De Marsillac, and courteously by his wife, who, through the whole of our visit there, which was three days, appeared

appeared to enjoy the company of their vifitors. Here we endeavoured to take frefh counfel about the way of proceeding to England, which ended in the conclufion, of George and Sarah Dillwyn and John De Marfillac going to the Ifland of Guernfey, to vifit the few friends there; and T. E. A. B. M. Dudley, my hufband, and myfelf, to London directly, by way of Dieppe, which we purfued accordingly, and arrived in London the 13th of 7th month 1788.

We have had a folitary and exercifing travel; but through infinite kindnefs, are again reftored to our friends, and fome of us to our native country. We attended the quarterly meeting of London: the fight of fo many friends was new and reviving to us; and the renewed evidence, that the Lord had been mercifully with us, that he had led us about, and inftructed us, and tenderly preferved us when, in child-like fimplicity, we depended upon his counfel, afforded, and ftill affords, abundant caufe to praife him for his mercies paft, and humbly hope for more.

Thus, after a journey of more than two thoufand five hundred miles, attended with many difficulties, and clofe exercifes of body and mind, fhe was enabled to return to her home at Clonmel, in the 8th month 1788, under the comfortable fenfe of divine favour and protection. Some parts of her letters written after her return, on a retrofpect of this vifit, appear to be worthy of infertion.

———We

———We have had, since leaving York, many new scenes of trial, and new demonstration of providential care; especially in the course of the long and deeply proving journey which we undertook, in hope that the Hand of Omnipotence led forth to the Continent. The state of mind in which I was involved previous to it, the inexpressible humiliations and besetments which attended the accomplishment of it, and since that, the commemoration of unmerited support, with the renewed discovery of human frailty, seem to change, in many respects, the face of this world to me. Not that I am redeemed from the love of it; but that I have learned to expect less from it; seeing more and more, that this is indeed a probationary state of being, and that our sufferings and joys in it are no otherwise important, than as they affect our attachment to the one great object of eternal good, and our communion with it in the silence of all that is fleshly.

——— It is a joyous consideration, that the glorious light of the gospel is emitted from the Sun of Righteousness; and that, though instruments may be used to bear testimony to it, yet that he, before whom all nations are but as the drop of a bucket, the small dust of the balance, and who takes up the isles as a very little thing, can, when they fail, do his work without them, and " glorify the house of his glory." I humblingly reflect upon our late journey on the Continent, and am bound to acknowledge (however as an individual I have failed in truly saying, " thy will be done") that the word of the Lord is faithfulness and truth. My mind is
settled

creating and converting word of Omnipotence, the pure feed of divine life was vifited with greater efficacy, than the difcouragements which we were under, allowed us to know at that time. But ah, poor Amfterdam! yea, poor Rotterdam! and many, many places on that fide the Continent, touching whofe inhabitants my foul, at times, fings mournfully to its well-beloved!

C H A P.

CHAP. VI.

Her Concern respecting a Boarding School for female Youth.—Visit to Friends Families in Cork.—Journey to London.—Visit to Dunkirk, Holland, Pyrmont, &c.—Her Return—and Decease.—Testimonies concerning her.

IT may now be proper to take some notice of a concern which had weightily engaged her attention, respecting the propriety of opening a boarding-school at Clonmel, for the religious care and education of female youth. This subject had, for some time, been deeply pondered, both by herself and her husband; and had, at length, so matured in their minds, as to afford an evidence that it would be right to set forward the work.

Their motives for this undertaking appear to be purely disinterested, and with the single view of promoting a guarded and religious education of children; being themselves in easy circumstances, and under no necessity to pursue this employment, for family support.

When we consider the susceptibility of youth to early impressions, with the general permanency thereof on their minds; and reflect that they are soon to participate in the concerns of life, and will, in a few years, be the principals on this stage of being; we cannot but perceive the extensive importance, both to individuals and the community, of an early moral and religious education; nor be surprised

mankind, should feel it her duty to cultivate this sure ground of general reformation, and to encourage others, upon pure principles, to engage in an employment so truly honourable and productive of good.

Though under doubts and discouragements of mind, arising chiefly from the humble sense of her own weakness, and want of qualifications for so arduous and important a service, she was enabled to open the proposed institution, the month after her return from the Continent.

She was much concerned that the children committed to their care, might be preserved in innocence, and trained in the paths of piety and virtue; and when not called from home on religious service, laboured faithfully in advancing such measures as tended to promote the solid advantages of this institution.

On the subject of this school, there does not appear to be much remaining written by herself: a few of her letters have, however, been collected, expressive of her tenderness lest she might interfere with other institutions; and of her cautious steppings in this concern; with divers other instructive sentiments; most of which have been extracted, and are as follows:

——— The prospect of removing to Ireland in any line, continues to my mind very awful; and undertaking a matter of so much consequence as
the

the propofed fchool, is not lefs fo: but if our friends whofe judgments we efteem, feel uneafy with it, and freely exprefs themfelves, it will rather be a relief than a difappointment; efpecially as we have no intention of getting, or faving money by it to ourfelves. If we are but favoured to fee the work of our day, and found faithful in the performance of it, though ever fo humbling to flefh and blood, I fometimes think, it is all that I defire.

———— I do not like the thoughts of crowding new inftitutions upon friends, impofing objects, or doing any thing which has the remoteft appearance of oppofing our own, or others' profpects, by dividing or fcattering the little ftrength, which, if put together, might prove no more than fufficient for one undertaking at firft; though afterwards, it might increafe for whatever further openings might be perceived in the truth.

———— I have, at times, been much depreffed with a fear of interfering with the fchool at Mountmellick, and difcouraging the valuable friends engaged therein. I felt moft eafy to write them a few lines, with a view, as I tell them, " to open a door for a free communication of fentiments refpecting what we both have in view;" expreffing my love and efteem for them, and belief, that as both they and we are difinterefted in our views, defirous of promoting the fame caufe, and rightly directed, we fhall move, either feparately or together, with a comfortable degree of unity and fympathy; and requefting their opennefs with me, in faying whether any thing has occured to them, on hearing of

our

ragement to them, and which is in our power to afford; whether they wifh us to be united in our undertakings, or think that two fchools will anfwer; and laftly, whether they do not think it will be better for them fteadily to purfue their own profpects, until our houfe is opened, (if ever it fhould be) and then to ftand refigned, either to unite or keep feparate, as at that time appears beft. So much feemed a little relief to myfelf to fay, feeling great affection and tendernefs towards them; at the fame time that my own faith is nearly tried. I, however, feel a hope as I am writing, that if our offering is not accepted, but proves like David's propofing to build the houfe, that, neverthelefs, we fhall feel that fecret fupporting language, " thou didft well, in that it was in thine heart, &c."

———Doft thou not wonder at the undertaking we have in view? My dear R. G. has kindly condefcended to make ample preparations for a boarding fchool for girls, and has built a confiderable addition to our prefent dwelling; which ftands upon an ifland, in a navigable river called the Suir. It is about a hundred yards acrofs, and near a quarter of a mile long; has on one fide of it, the quay and town, and on the other, cultivated mountains, which feem almoft to hang over it. The profpect from the front of the houfe, is through the garden and a pafture, to the river and valley, and is terminated by a very high and rugged mountain, feveral miles diftant. The place is altogether very commodious, and pleafant for the intended purpofe; but how we fhall meet with

fuitable,

suitable, disinterested persons for undertaking the immediate care of the children, &c. is not clear; a hope however cheers us, that if our views are right, and deserving a blessing, all things needful will be afforded us in the needful time. I should like to have such, for almost every station in the family, as possess a sincere concern for the prosperity of the work, and find a dedication in their own hearts to it; being afraid of drawing any, merely to gratify ourselves, that have not some such foundation to support them in seasons of trial, which, generally, more or less, attend the most upright and disinterested designs.

———I have had a very low dull time of late about this undertaking, from a fear that we shall not be found equal to it. I do not mean, in the sight of men, for probably we could not please all, let us do ever so well; but I mean in the sight of Him whose blessing is more craved and panted after, than the most specious appearances it can wear.

———Having formerly mentioned the discouragements of my mind in the setting out of the school we are engaged in, it is but just also to say, that things respecting it now wear a pleasanter aspect; with a hope that that which was sown in weakness, seems, through divine help, (for to that only it can be attributed) rising into greater strength. The minds of some of our precious charge are evidently encreasing in verdure, by the dew of heaven; and, in the general, innocence is to be felt from the influence of their spirits.

Our

THE LIFE OF

Our helpers alfo grow (we hope) in the root of true religion. Indeed, did the world, or our religious and civil concerns with its inhabitants, fpeak no more trouble to us than what we find upon our little ifland, it would be too great a ftate of profperity for human nature profitably to be indulged with; for even that calls for a watchfulnefs and induftry, which the flefh is at enmity with, and which I fear being found wanting in. To feel an evidence that we are under the care and blefling of the Shepherd and Bifhop of fouls, after conflicting doubtings refpecting it, is fuch a cordial as reanimates the foul to fight the good fight of faith, and to lay hold on eternal life. In feafons of favour this has been the cafe; but it is hard to lay down all thefe precious gifts, ftill to walk as the mafter walked, to teftify, by our dedication, that we believe he came to fave finners, and, as to the means whereby his glorious work is promoted, to fay, " not my will, but thine be done."

In the 12th month 1788, fhe engaged, with other friends, in a vifit to the meetings and families of friends, in the city of Cork: and during her employment in that fervice, the following letters appear to have been written. Though they do not exprefs much account of the vifit, yet they may be acceptable, from the inftructive remarks they contain, and the weighty and concerned fpirit which they manifeft under this engagement.

———We have been fteadily engaged with fitting in four families a day; and though we often

feem

seem ready to give up, and feel like imprisoned spirits, yet, upon the whole, we have no just cause to be discouraged; best help being near to strengthen us with might in our inner man, or such a proportion of it as is necessary for the performance of, and perseverance in, the work of the present day. As doing the will of our heavenly Father, is the only thing really worth living for, I wish to consider it as an unmerited favour, to know what that will is, and to be furnished with any degree of capacity to do it.

———The season of the year, the closeness of the city, and the complicated occasions of heaviness and depression, in the view of the state of things here, all contribute to suffering, both of body and mind; so that were we clear of unprofitably adding thereto, we do not lack a pretty full cup thereof. Indeed we have no business to seek for a portion or baptism, differing in nature from that which the great Pattern himself submitted to, and which the true seed here and elsewhere, have still, for wise purposes, to experience.

———Whether any good may come of our labour and travel here, must be left: it is the blessing only which can render this, and every other endeavour of the poor servants, effectual to the building up of any drooping member in the most holy faith. My soul has in the course of our visit to the families of friends in this city, passed by the gates of death. But the deceitfulness of my own heart is such, that it cannot be removed by pleasant things; nor does fitness for the little services we are engaged in, spring

spring out of the most sensible and gratifying operations of the spirit; but out of these unsearchable baptisms, which, neverthelefs, demonstrate they are of the Holy Ghost and fire, because they leave an empty temple, a temple ready to be filled with the presence wherein there is life. According to my small knowledge of good, I may assert that, after all, the joy of the Lord is our strength; and were it not that, in the beginning of this visit, my spirit had been sweetly consolated therewith, I very much doubt whether, from many of my feelings and deep provings since, I should have held out until now: peradventure it possessed some of that sacred efficacy, which Elijah's forty days sustenance is distinguished for, and thereby, to the praise of that grace, by which I am what I am, my confidence has not wholly failed me in the deeps.—All that is within me prays, that as we have been mercifully strengthened to drink, in this place, a bitter cup, we may not, in our own wills, refuse any dregs which in infinite wisdom are intended, in part, to constitute the cup of salvation. But the flesh is weak! A few have refused us, and whether their hearts will relent, is yet to try. We cannot however but sympathize with a tried, afflicted remnant in this meeting, whose hands I do believe, will grow stronger and stronger, be more and more instructed to war, and their fingers to fight; for however the boasters over the pure lowly seed may exalt themselves, yet they cannot stand in the day of judgment, nor prevent the fulfilling of the promise, that the law shall be magnified and made honourable. I concluded to stay third day meeting; and though, as is often my lot, speaking to men

did

did not relieve my inward oppreffion, yet in proftration before the almighty Helper, who in abundant mercy is touched with a feeling of our infirmities, there was a fecret fuftaining evidence, of living again in His prefence, whereby thofe bones that were broken did rejoice. Thus are the poor of the flock helped in their extremities, and encouraged to maintain their confidence in the omnipotent gathering arm of Ifrael's Shepherd.

—— May we not be afraid of fuffering; for in this land however, they that dwell with the feed, muft dwell in a low fpot, and give up their names to reproach. " If ye were of the world, the world would love you, but becaufe ye are not of the world, the world hates you: it hated me before it hated you." To be of this happy, though afflicted number, is more to be defired than to join ourfelves in affinity with a fpirit which, inftead of fuffering with the feed, wars againft it, in the wrath and cruelty of the king of the locufts which came out of the pit; a fpirit that cannot ftand in the day of judgment, but which, being airy and unfettled, leads from the quiet habitation, and leaves the mind without a ftay. How excellent, yea how much to be defired is that ftate wherein, through holy chaftifement and fuffering for the feed's fake, that precious feal of adoption, the language of Abba Father, is feelingly obtained and breathed! This is indeed a Something in ourfelves wherein we can rejoice, an unmerited gift which excludes all boafting, a prefervative from moving in the line of others' experience, further than it is made our own, or

from

from having our rejoicing in them. Were the active members of our society, more generally and individually gathered to this deep inward feeling of the life of truth, and the evidence of its operations in themselves, how much more effectual would their labours be, in building up one another in the most holy faith? I am afraid for myself; I long to be more truly weighty in my own spirit; not to assume a consequence among men, or to plume myself with borrowed feathers; but really to be preserved in company with the seed, and through its operations, to live, move, and have my being, in the church especially. A series of deep exercises has fallen to my lot, on account of the law and testimony of truth in this province, and near sympathy with some who dare not let it fall to the ground, without discovering themselves, and on whose side they are. These find it to be a day of trial, of perplexity, and of treading down; and there are so few, even among the well minded, who are skilful either in lamentation, or in war, that the work lies heavy on a few; and sometimes I am afraid, that the ointment made after the art of the apothecary, gets unpleasantly tinctured by the dead flies (the unquickened efforts for the cause) being cast into it.

—— Though I often find it my duty to wash and anoint, rather than appear to men to fast, yet the secret travail of my soul is sorrowful, and beset with many discouragements unknown but to itself, and its almighty Helper; and I find, that the more deep and hidden my exercises are, and the more I seek for strength to unite myself, in a covenant

nant never to be broken, with the Beloved of my soul; the more I am capable to diftinguifh the confolations of the Spirit, the pure unerring Spirit, from every inferior or corrupt fource of gratification to the natural fenfes. I know my experience of this is but very fmall, and yet, as far as I have attained, I have abundant caufe to admire the wifdom there is in the paths of true abafednefs and felf-denial; yea, the fortrefs they lead to, and the fafety there is in them.

Never are we favoured with a clearer perception of our religious duty, in little as well as greater things, than when our fpiritual eye has been purged, by the miniftration of fome baptifm that has afflictingly removed every film of felf-love; which difcovers itfelf by an over-attention to our own reputation, to the eafe of the flefh, and a defire for pleafant things in fpirituals as well as temporals. Ah! may we think nothing too near or too dear to part with, for the fecret acceptance of the Beloved! The very putting forth of his hand, as through the hole of the door, little as the intimation may feem, is a powerful call to admit him in the way of his coming, however it may oppofe our own way.

She attended the half year's national meeting at Dublin in the 5th month 1789; and from thence went to York, where fhe made her relations and friends a fhort vifit, and proceeded pretty directly for the yearly meeting at London; which fhe attended, and returned home with an evidence, that, in this journey, fhe had been occupied in her proper place. This is agreeably teftified by the following

ing letter, which is the only one that has appeared on this occasion.

———— Our little flock looks pleasant and healthy. Our joy was mutual at meeting yesterday, and home is felt by us to be a peaceful retreat. In a little sitting which we had at home in the evening, there seemed some ability to lie down as beside the still waters; a consoling experience: and on looking back upon our late journey, though there was no great professed draft to it, a hope arises, that, consistent with our religious duty, we were going on with the work of the day.

In the latter part of the year 1789, she felt her mind drawn to have some publick meetings in divers places, where none of our society dwell, particularly at the town and garrison of Kinsale; where, as well as at other places, these services tended to open, and spread the knowledge of the truth. Concerning her visit to the abovementioned place, she writes thus:

—In much fear, and I trust humiliation of spirit, I have been to the town of Kinsale, and suffered to have appointed, through an apprehension of duty, a publick meeting there. It was large, nearly as much so as the house belonging to the society would admit. There appeared to be about two hundred people, who generally behaved with decency and solidity, and the meeting was owned with the gathering influence of Israel's Shepherd; which, in time of silence, was I thought comfortably experienced. We also paid a visit to the fort, and particularly

ticularly to a large company of deserters, who are collected there for transportation, many of them good looking young men; and I also ventured to remind some of the officers, of their religious and civil duties. It was altogether a service much in the cross, and deserving of no reward, for want of timely resignation to it: but, in unmerited mercy, I was favoured with a peaceful calm, which my beloved companions also enjoyed, and earned with honest labour.

She was, indeed, much concerned, and laboured in her measure, for the propagation of that holy principle, which is the light, and life of men; and she counted nothing too dear to give up, or part with, for the promotion of this pure word in their hearts. A renewed evidence of this appears, in a fresh instance of dedication to a very trying and arduous service. During her late travels on the Continent, her mind had often sympathized in secret, and been united in gospel love, with a precious seed scattered up and down in those parts; but which, it seemed not then the appointed season to visit in person. This time now approached, and, as she apprehended, in the openings of divine wisdom; so that she believed it her indispensable duty, to give herself up, in pure resignation, to this service; which appeared in her view, to comprehend a visit to Dunkirk, Holland, Pyrmont, and some other parts of Germany. Under the weight of this important concern, she experienced the near sympathy of friends of the monthly and quarterly meetings to which she belonged, with those of the national meeting in Dublin, and yearly select meeting in London; who concurred in teftimonials of their unity and approbation. Thus ftrengthened by the feelings and concurrence of the church, and by a fimilar concern of her friend George Dillwyn, fhe fet forward to engage in the work before them, in the 6th month 1790; accompanied alfo by her hufband and Sarah Dillwyn, who felt their minds engaged to enter with them on this journey.

Her letters written under the profpect of this vifit, during the progrefs of it, and upon its conclufion, appear to form, in general, fo regular and connected an account of it, that nothing further appears neceffary, than to lay the extracts from them before the reader.

2d month 1790. I feem very like one who hath no refting place on earth, or any confolations here in which I dare to truft; but if I am found worthy, in the fmalleft degree, to refemble the great and holy High Prieft of our profeffion, it is enough. As to the performance of great works, I look not for it; my mind is taught to believe that I have no right thereto, or reafon to expect that an inftrument fo feeble, and fo little a time in ufe, is likely to be owned, in any extraordinary degree, in the difcharge of my fmall part of the great work. But my fpirit hath often been dipt into fympathy inexpreffible, with a feed in thofe parts, of which I have not yet attained the outward difcovery, and peradventure, this fecond vifit may prove like fifhing, and catching nothing. This I defire to leave, and to attain to a daily and fimple reliance upon

unerring

unerring direction, which the creature knows muft be attended with a dying daily.

2d month 1790. We ftand in need of care, both of our own, and that of our friends; our endeavours for peace being, in many refpects, in a line rather new and important, and in which we defire to be preferved from moving further, than the good Shepherd leads and goes before.—It has not been without a portion of deep exercife, and frequent baptifms, known only to the Searcher of hearts, that I have obtained fo much ftrength as to caft my burden for a time upon the church; and fince they have taken it, and I believe fome of them felt it, my relief has, beyond my expectation, been effected.—But this is temporary. I know, in a fpiritual fenfe at leaft, that bonds and afflictions await me; yet with thankfulnefs may acknowledge, that, feeling the everlafting arms to be underneath, none of thefe things at prefent move me.—My capacity to promote the work of righteoufnefs on the earth, is very fmall; but according to that capacity, I long to be found faithful, not counting my life dear unto myfelf.—I have not heard of any companion in the little fervices before me, nor do I feel any anxiety on that head; believing that, if the concern is right, fuitable fellow labourers will be provided, without any toiling interference of mine.

3d month 1790. May my mind be preferved in ftability to the end: for that I both watch and pray, well knowing that when I lofe that, it muft be diftinguifhed mercy indeed, that preferves my poor little veffel from total wreck. As a very hard gale

gale of even fair wind may occasion great danger, so I perceive that the urgency I feel, at times, in my spirit, to do the Master's apprehended will, may render frustrate the gracious design, if ballast be not on board. I never felt my mind so sensibly sustained in the prospect of any journey before. I esteem it an unmerited mark of the great Shepherd's condescending care, who hath, blessed be his Name, richly replenished my soul with faith, and so abundantly ministered its sister virtue, patience, that my frail tabernacle being at times overcome, the language of my heart is similar to that of the Spouse; " Stay me with flaggons, comfort me with apples, for I am sick of love."

This is a dispensation which I do not expect to continue; for when a testimony of this love is called for, when difficulties are to be encountered, both within and without, when we are to be offered up a sacrifice in the service of the christian faith, oh how inconstant is the human heart! how many substitutes for obedience, how many subterfuges does it find! Remembering these things, the wormwood and the gall, yea the anguishing exercises attendant on our late journey, my heart is humbled within me, and preserved from expecting the journey in prospect to be unmixed with similar trials; or even to see in it, gratifying demonstrations of that glorious work, which, in gospel vision, is beheld to be begun in the German Empire, and many other parts of the globe less known to us. On any presumption of this sort, I have not dared to take one step; but have much desired that my spirit may be deep enough, according to my measure,

sure, to suffer and rejoice only with the pure seed, whether obviously the fig-tree blossom, and fruit be on the vine, or not.

———On second day morning, at the yearly meeting of ministers and elders held in London the 17th of the 5th month, our certificates were read; which, far beyond what I durst have looked for, created expressions of gospel unity and church encouragement, that were not entirely unseasonable to my mind; feeling myself as poor as seemed possible for spiritual existence. But what also greatly contributed to lift up my head above the overflowing billows, and say to the winds and the waves, " Be still," was the indisputable evidence, that the Master had separated for a similar work, my beloved friend, George Dillwyn; under which his oppressed mind was constrained publickly to acknowledge, to his own and others relief, that he believed it to be his duty to go with us. How precious is that help, which is dispensed in better wisdom than our own! and being the fruit of mercy, it is often reserved for the moment of extremity. It was a very solemn uniting season; the spirit and the bride (the church) appeared cordially to unite in the same language of encouragement. I greatly desire a heart capable of humbly and reverently returning acceptable obedience for these favours, in the few feeble steppings through my future pilgrimage. Trials I have learned to expect, having a disposition that will not suffer me to be exempt, until it becomes lost in the ocean of gospel love. In ourselves, as in the world, there is trouble; oh that our acquaintance may become more and more intimate

intimate with Him, in whom is the fulnefs of undefiled peace! Then may we rejoice in every tribulation, which has urged us to lay hold on eternal fubftance. No female companion appearing, our former valuable fellow traveller, Sarah Dillwyn, was naturally looked to, and no obftructions occurring, Ratcliffe monthly meeting (of which fhe is a member) cordially teftified its approbation therewith, and granted her a certificate. Thus we four being banded, left London (Jofhua Beale accompanying us) on the feventh day after the yearly meeting. There we met with many friends like bone of our bone, and flefh of our flefh; yea, fo cemented have fome of us at times felt, as fully to convince us that it was the work of both grace and nature; the latter of which, in our many feparations, is learning I truft to be more and more fubject, and to furrender its will to the divine will, which indeed fweetens many bitter cups, and ftrengthens us to fay amen to every requiring of truth. Without this experience, how are we like bullocks unaccuftomed to the yoke! The yearly meeting was large, and fatisfactory in a good degree; but fuch affemblies, compofed of minds fo various, have generally a confiderable portion of exercife and weight for the feeling part of its members; and it is an unfpeakable favour that there are fuch preferved in the church, whofe fpiritual faculties are fo alive, that, like watchers on the walls of Zion, they can give an alarm at the new and various attacks, which our common and unwearied enemy is making upon truth's ramparts: and it is alfo a diftinguifhable mercy in our poor fociety, that there are, among the younger part

of

of it, fuch as, by the livelinefs and faithfulnefs of their fpirits, promife a fucceffion of ftandard-bearers.

We were at Rochefter on firft day, at the monthly meeting at Canterbury on third, and got to Dover that evening; from whence we failed next day for Dunkirk, and had a fine, but flow paffage, being on the water fixteen hours. Here we found John De Marfillac waiting for us; and Jofhua Beale, alfo uniting himfelf to us, we became fix in number. The day we arrived, was their week day meeting; and it may with thankfulnefs be acknowledged, that it was mercifully owned with divine refrefhment, and the communication of counfel from the living fpring thereof. And what tended to heighten our joy, on fitting down with the friends here, was the fcene which we had beheld juft before. What they call the hoft was carried about, with fuch a proceffion of the army, corporation, clergy, and little children, as I never faw before, or could have fuppofed; there being many thoufands both of people, and images of filver, pewter, and wood; hundreds of candles near fix feet long; abundance of rich filk and other veftments; barefooted and fhaven headed friars; mufick, drums, &c. cannon firing, and bells ringing. So that, after all this ftir, to fit down with our friends, under our own vines and fig-trees, and meafurably to partake of fubftantial food, was truly joyous; and more efpecially fo, under the belief that the one fhall decreafe, and the other increafe. We fpent a full week at Dunkirk, to a good degree of fatisfaction, perceiving the bleffing that thofe new fettlers may be in that land, and at this important juncture, if they wifely keep to, and are gracioufly kept by, the preferving unchangeable principle of truth. They are at prefent worth vifiting, and their number is likely foon to be increafed from Nantucket.

After having four publick meetings in Dunkirk; (at all which divers not of our fociety attended) and feveral private ones, we proceeded to Oftend, (B. R. going with us) here we fpent a day to fatiffaction, finding a man and his wife from London belonging to the fociety, who had not feen any reputable friends for feven or eight years. Though they had the marks of being, in fome degree, robbed and fpoiled, yet there was alfo fomething in them to vifit, and which accepted the teftimony of truth, as far as related to themfelves. Divers books were alfo fcattered, and not without a hope that the bleffing accompanied fome of them; for even in this little fervice, there is a great difference in our feelings. It is often like cafting bread upon the waters, and, fometimes, without hope of return in any day or age. From Oftend we continued our courfe along the coaft, by way of Bruges, Flufhing, and Middleburgh; at the two latter of which, we folemnly paufed, and alfo expofed ourfelves to the obfervation and acquaintance of the people; intimating to fome our errand, and making inquiry for fuch as were feeking the truth. With fome fmall exception, they appeared to be in their ftrong holds, and fenced cities, intent upon this world's gain, which is, with too much propriety, called their god. However, a few books were left among them;

them; and finding the fon of a friend at Middleburgh, we had an opportunity of religious retirement with him, and of dropping fuch counfel as opened therein. He appeared, by his acknowledgement and attention to us, to accept the vifit kindly; but his fituation is exceedingly unfafe. From Middleburgh we went to a little port, called Campveer, and there hired a veffel to take us to Rotterdam. We had a very pleafant paffage, our minds being favoured with much tranquillity; and after a thirty hours fail, arrived at our port, the 18th of the 6th month; where, as we expected, we entered into a frefh trial of fidelity to the precious caufe. Here we ftaid three days, vifited fome former acquaintances, who were very kind; and commenced new ones with fuch as feemed to underftand how to receive difciples in the name of difciples. To one or two of this clafs, our minds were particularly united. Being there on a firft day, we had two publick meetings, both confiderably attended, but efpecially the latter, which was alfo a truly folemn and profitable opportunity. Between Dunkirk and Rotterdam, we had divers opportunities of difseminating the knowledge of the principle of truth, by the diftribution of books, and fome conferences in a private way; but had no publick meeting, though our minds were in feveral places, brought under a confiderable weight of exercife; which feemed to anfwer no more end, than the people's walking round the walls of Jericho; and were it not that we are convinced, even from outward obfervation, that the Lord is at work in the kingdoms of men, and making a way for his own feed, we might conclude, that the fortifications which this world's fpirit hath erected,

erected, particularly in Holland, will hardly ever be taken down. We went pretty directly from Rotterdam to Amsterdam, where we had our share of secret dippings and discouragements; but not expecting great things in our setting out, or desiring to be borne up above a feeling of what we are, and the oppression and obscurity of the true seed, we are the less exposed to a spirit of dismay; and engaged at times, in simplicity, to sit down together, professedly to wait for the guidance of truth, or a discovery that the cloud rests upon the tabernacle. In these seasons, we have been strengthened, and cemented in best unity, and also encouraged to hold on in a path to be trodden more by faith, than sight.

In the publick meetings, of which we have attended three, we experienced painful exercise; and yet I thought on first day, that both the sittings were, upon the whole, solid and lively. We received accounts of our brother, Joseph Grubb, being in a very declining state of health, which had made its appearance before we left home; and being in partnership with my Robert Grubb, and the care of business forbidden to my brother, my husband thought it his duty to offer him all the relief he could; a tranquil mind respecting outward things, being of unspeakable consequence to the latter part of a man's life: this, without any anxiety about our own property, and a presentiment before we left home, that he would hardly go through the journey, induced us, though much in the cross, to separate. We were detained at Amsterdam longer than we expected; one occasion
of

of which was the printing of some extracts from Hugh Turford's writings, with an addition from Mary Brook on silent waiting, which some of our company translated into French. It contains very suitable matter for the present age, and is an acceptable publication to J. M. and B. R. to distribute in France, and also convenient to us in this journey, as many understand French. We have a large stock of other books, very eligible for our purpose, which the meeting for sufferings has given us for distribution. The 6th of the 7th month we came to Utrecht, where J. M. being tender took cold, and was confined next day to the house; and as he did not ail a great deal, it suited our plan of spending one day quietly together, before we parted, he and B. R. having concluded to go from hence to Dunkirk, and J. M. from that place to his home. This has been a trial to us, but knowing J. M's attention to best direction, and also his desire, if right, of keeping with us, we dared not to persuade him to suit our inclinations and convenience; and therefore, after enjoying each others company, in sweet fellowship and tenderness of spirit, we parted; our little band then consisting of George and Sarah Dillwyn, J. B. and myself, with the most arduous part of the journey in prospect. Perhaps this stripping of outward help is wisely dispensed to us: in that light we view it, and dare not dispute divine sufficiency. Soon after our friends were gone, we concluded to pay a visit to a family of Amsterdam, (with which we were acquainted when there before) who now reside at their country house about half way from that city to Utrecht; and accordingly

accordingly fet off, and arrived about five, and were received more like near relations united on the beft ground, than as people of another nation and profeffion. We alfo met here two women of confiderable account on a vifit; to one of them particularly, our minds were nearly drawn, and the little inftruction which was in our power to communicate, from the exercife of our minds, broken French, and the ufe of the fcriptures, to particular paffages of which we directed them as they occurred, was received with a religious fenfibility, which greatly united us together, and which words cannot fully fet forth.* Though we often lament our

---

* Some time afterwards, fhe wrote the following letter to one of the women of that family. Remembering thy requelt to hear from our little company when we returned from Germany, and being now fo near you, I felt an inclination to tell thee, and thy valuable brother and fifter, that, through the merciful direction and care of providence, we have got along to a good degree of fatisfaction, and been favoured, upon the whole, with a moderate fhare of health. We purfued our journey from Utrecht, by way of Arnheim and Munfter, to Pyrmont; there we ftaid two weeks, and then went to Rinteln, Minden, Ofnabruck, and Bilefeld, and fo, by way of Munfter, to Crevelt, Duffeldorf, Mulheim on the Rhine, Elberfelt, and from thence to Cleves. We found a few in many of thefe places, who, being weary of the ceremonial part of religion, are defiring its living fubftance, and to be true worfhippers in fpirit. Thefe have many difficulties from within and without; but if they depend, fingly, upon divine help, and ceafe to recommend themfelves by their own dead works, we have a hope, that they will gradually retire from the confufion of the carnal mind, to the true fheepfold. Were the profeffors of chriftianity more generally acquainted with the undefiled reft, which the redeemed

our ignorance of the language of this people, and its attendant inconveniencies, yet I was never more convinced of the influence of truth qualifying to speak to one another in our own tongues, though utterly incapable in any other language, than that of the spirit; for in the present case, we were not sensible of either us, or the cause, suffering under our apparent disadvantages. We cannot always judge why we are so led, and why so destitute of some outward accommodations to the service, which human prudence would naturally point out; but I may acknowledge that, on this account, I never was more contented and supported in an humble trust, that the good and Almighty Hand is with us in " these mortifying labours." We left Utrecht on seventh day morning, and came to Wageninge, which is an agreeable little town. The inhabitants were greatly surprised at seeing us, but became uncommonly civil and courteous; in part owing to a man who drove us from Utrecht, who by some means, unknown to us, conceived so favourable an opinion of us, and seemed furnished with

mind is strengthened to gather to, they would detect the fallacy of unsanctified forms and ministry, and rejoicingly receive the eternal Witness for God in themselves, for their Lawgiver, Friend, and Comforter.

We reflect with satisfaction upon our visit to Middlewaart; not only in remembrance of your affectionate hospitality, but also of the uniting virtue of truth upon our minds, which left a pleasant favour after we separated; and now reviving, with renewed desire for all our preservation, and increasing intimacy with the good Shepherd of his sheep, I salute thee, my dear friend, in sisterly affection.

S. G.

with such materials for description, that where-ever we stopt, he was sure to influence the people in our favour, and they united in testimonies of affection and kindness. We spent all first day in Wageninge; had a little, but solemn and refreshing meeting of our own company, and had also the company of a young Priest of good character. He and George Dillwyn conversed (I believe intelligibly) upon some important subjects in French, though perhaps neither of them were fully acquainted with the language; but the best sense being present, that defect was made up thereby.

We left a few suitable books with them, which were very kindly accepted; and our parting was with apparent sentiments of affectionate esteem. We also gave books to divers others, and had a satisfaction in spending this little time among a kind, simple hearted people. The people of the inn are particularly of this description, their conduct manifesting a pleasure which they had in entertaining us. These comfortable spots and feelings, somewhat resemble Elijah's food, on the strength of which he had to travel many days. As neither the great work, nor the capacity to do it, is ours, so we may be emboldened to hope, that our acceptance will stand in proportion to our obedience to that we have, rather than to that we have not. From Wageninge we came to Arnheim, where we spent one day agreeably, were at the house of very civil people; and though we did not commence much acquaintance, yet were satisfied with our little detention there, and to one or other left several books. Here we met with a kind man who speaks English well, says he was seasonably, and effectually served by a friend in England,

when

when he was a ftranger there; and this is (no doubt) an additional inducement to lay himfelf out to oblige us, which he does with the appearance of much fincerity. Thefe journies, I fometimes hope, will in future open my heart with more cordiality to ftrangers; for " knowing the heart of a ftranger," a deficiency herein would be doubly culpable. The next place we went to was Doefburgh, where our feelings were rather unufually pleafant; but we did not find any ftop thereby in our progrefs. The landlady at the inn where we ftopped, appeared and approved herfelf to be far from the common fort, for dignity of manners and folidity, if not religious weightinefs of mind. Her conduct to us was truly friendly, manifefting an affection and liberality becoming other parts of her character. We gave her a Barclay's Apology in Dutch, and feveral books in French, which fhe appeared fully qualified to read, and in a good degree to underftand : fhe wanted much to pay for them, but on any terms was glad to receive them; and after looking over the fummary, promifed to lend them among fome of her neighbours. Germany is a country very unlike the Netherlands, both in the face of it, and in the manners of its inhabitants; the people being kept in a ftate of greater fervility under princes of fmall territories. Our difficulties in the way of travelling commenced when we left Holland; for after gliding along in Treckfchutes, upon their quiet waters, we got into waggons, the beft publick conveyances the country afforded, and the roads being extremely bad, we were jolted to a degree not eafy to fuppofe; and for want of knowing the language, were impofed upon, and induced to

take

take our paffage in the poft waggon, underftanding that we fhould have it to ourfelves, arrive feafonably at our lodgings the two nights in profpect, and have time enough for reft. But inftead of thefe fine things, after they got our money, a Capuchin Friar, and a very ill looking man, were put in with us, and we kept in this fituation, with two meals wanting, through a dark rainy night (the wet coming in upon us) until three o'clock the next morning; when, after two hours reft, we were fummoned again, and without ftopping to take any meals, fave our dinners, travelled on until we arrived, about one o'clock next morning, at the gates of Munfter, a fortified city; where we had to wait for an entrance more than half an hour; and then had to find our lodgings among a people of a ftrange language, whofe principal object was to get from us all they could. This is a hint of the manner in which we got along, and I mention it to fhew the inconvenience ftrangers are fubject to, and how different the fare of thefe countries is from that of England; at the fame time an acknowledgement of providential care is abundantly due from us. Our minds, during this extraordinary trial of body and fpirits, were remarkably fuftained with cheerful tranquillity, and an abounding defire to comfort one another in this painful imprifonment. We were alfo preferved at the time from fuffering in our health, and found that part of two days reft in Munfter, recruited us finely.

Our ftay in that city was very fatisfactory, finding it to be a place of confiderable opennefs. One man in particular, a profeffor of languages in the univerfity univerſity, who was ſick, received our men with brotherly affection and joy, had very ſatisfactory converſation with them, and was glad to receive divers of our books, ſome of which he intended to put into their publick library. He told them of a relation of his, in a part of Germany where we have not been, who is fully convinced of our principles, but who has not dared openly to avow them; and ſaid, that in ſome other parts, there are many ſuch, which we have ſince found to be the caſe. A ſerious young nobleman, a pupil of his, intending to take a tour to England, was deſirous of being recommended to ſome friend in London, in which George Dillwyn gratified him. Many other opportunities occurred of caſting books into the hands of ſerious people, and in an imperfect way intimating to them ſuch truths, as at that time we were furniſhed with. From Munſter we came by way of Warrendorf, Padderborn, &c. through Weſtphalia, to Pyrmont, which we reached the 23d of the 7th month. Here our minds were ſoon comforted in the belief, that there is a ſeed in theſe parts, which, however hidden from the world, and the many churches profeſſing the chriſtian name, are preſſing after an eſtabliſhment on the right foundation. Our minds were greatly favoured with peaceful ſerenity, and a ſteady reliance on providential care; ſo that inſtead of difficulties depreſſing, they rather animated our ſpirits to preſs forward, towards the fulfilling of our allotted portion of travail and exerciſe, and to bear up one another, according to our ability, through all. Nevertheleſs, there have been ſeaſons when Satan did not fail to ſuggeſt to the weakneſs of my mind, that

we

we were running in vain. But to all our humbling encouragement, after we arrived at Pyrmont, and particularly in the second meeting there, among a simple hearted, seeking people, we were convinced that it was not so, and that infinite kindness would also preserve us from labouring in vain. It was an opportunity wherein (to the praise of the grace which we depend upon) we may say, that, for a time, " the seed reigned over all." Visitors and visited experienced it to be a season of uncommon contrition, and during the extension of the holy Wing, our spirits seemed gathered into perfect unity; so efficacious is divine life and love! It appears that two years ago, there were about twenty in Pyrmont, who being uneasy with the dead formality of many professors, met together in their own houses, sometimes reading, singing, or praying, as they apprehended most right. They underwent considerable persecution on this account from the avaricious priests, who persuaded people not to do business with them; and being generally low in the world, they suffered in this respect; but it appears that they were not hindered thereby from meeting together: yet their rest, not being a pure one, was broken up; some of them finding their reformation from what they saw to be wrong, was very small, concluded there was something more substantial than what they had yet experienced; and this being suggested to the rest, occasioned a division among them. A few returned to the profession they had left, and the others ceased to meet together; yet it is wonderful to see the brotherly kindness which distinguishes them from others. They call themselves friends, and with

much

much propriety, to each other. We spent about two weeks in Pyrmont, with satisfaction of mind. For three rooms, three beds, fire, candles, and the use of the kitchen, we paid 15s. per week, found our own provisions, cooked them ourselves, with the assistance of a girl, and an elderly man, one of the friends who spoke English pretty well. He marketed for us, interpreted on more important occasions, and served us with great solidity and cheerfulness. In many respects, we felt as if we were at home, though among a people, few of whom knew what we said; but they told us by signs, that they felt that which was better than words, and which required none to set it forth: O! that we may be preserved in, and feel more and more bound to, our own line and measure of duty; that as the work is the Lord's, the management of it may also be in his wisdom, and tend to his glory; and then no matter how low and abased the creature becomes. During our stay at Pyrmont, we had many meetings, some of which were uncommonly contriting opportunities, wherein their doubts seemed to subside, and the virtue of truth to sweeten and refresh their weary spirits.* In many respects they are weak, and yet so sincerely desirous to obtain " the one thing needful," that we entertain a hope, that some of them will increase in steadfastness to what they know to be right. Our minds are often involved in discouragement and conflict: the weakness of our frames, and perhaps the

---

* At one meeting we had the company of four men, who walked the day before near twenty miles, to sit with us; and that of another man, who came about forty, also on foot.

the prospect of the unfinished part of the work, may be the occasion of these. But let us remember, that until they are overcome by the power of victorious faith, it is our seed time rather than harvest, and therefore we are called upon, by merciful and heart-solacing intimations, to sow in hope. Whether any apparent fruits ever appear from this journey, we seem comfortably satisfied at times, that it will not be lost in the unlimited family of the one universal Parent; and if we are but favoured to keep the word of his patience, so as to hold out to the end, and return without condemnation, it will not be lost to us. We set off from Pyrmont for Rinteln upon a different plan from that on which we had travelled before; for having a man to do little services for us when there, who is one of their friends, and speaks English well, we saw an extraordinary convenience would attend our taking him with us; and therefore have taken a light waggon, and a pair of horses, which saves us imposition and trouble in procuring carriages, &c.

Our man conducts himself with great propriety and simplicity, as our friend, guide, interpreter, and servant; being charioteer, and doing a great deal for us besides. We spent a week at Rinteln, and had several meetings among them, besides private religious opportunities, in several of their families, and left some of our books for a university in that town. In our way here, we came through a skirt of Hanover, where we beheld, in the improvements of the country, and the appearance of the people, a cheering resemblance of England. About Rinteln, there are near twenty of
those

those who call themselves friends, and some of them we believe to be lively spirited people, and considerably experienced in the inward work of religion; of whom we have a comfortable hope, whether they are ever known to our gathered, visible church, or not. We are now in this country under a frequent sense of inward poverty, and with many confirmations that, of ourselves, we can do nothing; yet trusting that best wisdom has turned us into this little field of labour, we dare not, with our present feelings, desert it; but we go on from spot to spot, as we apprehend is most in the line of our duty. From Rinteln we proceeden to Minden, where we found a little company of sincere hearted, and exercised christian travellers, who appeared glad of our visit, and expressed a belief that it was in divine appointment for their good. They seemed more desirous for a right opening to sit down together in silent waiting, than to enter into conversation about what they had already experienced. We had several solid, and I hope edifying, meetings among them, to which several came from the country many miles on foot, which demonstrated their earnestness to be helped on in the right way; among these was a blind woman who gets her living by spinning, and who walked seventeen miles to meet us. She is an example of christian fortitude, and true nobility; for on our asking her, if she was not under difficulties in procuring herself a living, she gratefully answered, that her friends sometimes helped her, that she knew she was poor, but when she reflected upon her supplies, and the query revived in her mind, " if she lacked any thing," the acknowledgement always

ways succeeded, " nothing, Lord." She told us, with great humility and tenderness, that her knowledge of the truth was not obtained by books or outward means, but by the operation of the divine principle in her own heart. I hope we have been preserved, thus far, from drawing the inward attention of those whom we have visited, to ourselves, or attaching them in the affectionate part to any representation of good. The secret, sympathetic exercise which we have felt on their account, and in company with them, hath, I do believe, brought us all at times, to the renewed discovery of the everlasting foundation; and we have a hope that some of these will acceptably build thereon. We here met with great civility, and tenderness of spirit, from a counsellor and director of this place; but the cross is a mighty stumbling block; he often makes me think of Nicodemus: when we left the town, he kindly went before us to an inn on the road, where he had provided coffee, and convened several of the friends to take their last leave; a parting which I hope was attended with true solemnity, as well as brokenness of spirit. With tears he expressed his desire, that He who said he would be with his disciples to the end of the world, would go with us, and bless his own work. Next day we travelled towards Buer, and dined sweetly in a field, on provision which we took with us, whilst our horses were eating corn. We then turned a little out of the road, to visit a man and his wife, whom the Priest is persecuting for absenting themselves from his place of worship. He has got the Magistrate to fine them near twenty shillings, (which is a great deal for them) and they refusing

to

to pay it, from an apprehenfion of duty, have
fuffered diftrefs of their goods, with chriftian fimplicity
and firmnefs. After fpending near two hours
with them (I hope to our and their edification)
we came on to Buer. In the neighbourhood of
this town live a little company of Zion's travellers,
with whom we had a meeting; and our gracious
Helper being near, by his good fpirit, rendered it
an humbling and refrefhing opportunity. We have
many encampments, and when we fhall get through
this wildernefs, is very uncertain; for my part, I
fee no way yet! This blindnefs is, probably, to try
my patience, of which I feem, at times, to have a
reducing ftock; but am fecretly fupported, in
knowing Him in whom I have, through holy help,
believed. We have great caufe to be humbly thankful,
for that portion of fure direction and ability,
which, for our inftruction as well as comfort, have
been revealed in the midft of our weaknefs, and
become as a table in the wildernefs, furnifhed with
food wifely adapted to the neceffities of weary and
hungry travellers. It feems very fingular, when I
recollect myfelf, that we are keeping houfe in Pruffia,
and confiderably united to fome of its inhabitants,
who were lately entire ftrangers; and, in
degree, feel as if we were at home, though fo
far from that which is called home. It is a little
like being in a new world, yet fo near
the old one, as to be diftinguifhed for fimilar
evils, and that *fafhion* which paffeth away, when
truth, which is ftrongeft of all, takes its poffeffions.
It is very pleafant in thefe journeys to feel this
fentiment lively upon our fpirits, " the earth is the
Lord's," &c. We went from Buer to Ofnabruck

the

the 26th of the 8th month, where we spent several days under considerable exercise of mind, and not finding that our visit was likely to be attended with any use, and being also fatigued various ways, we were so discouraged, that we were about concluding to leave the town next day, though we thought the way to it had opened as clearly as to most places we had been at; but on feeling further about it, we thought it safest to try a little longer, and not move in the dark. Our situation was unfavourable, being at a Roman Catholick Inn where the Protestants are afraid to come, and our Friend and interpreter having no acquaintance in the place. Thus we continued until seventh day evening, without any thing satisfactory occurring, except giving a few summaries * to some shopkeepers on whom we had called, and having the company of a young woman who had inquired concerning us, and discovered a serious desire to be with us, and to have some of our books: she appeared to us to be possessed of much sweetness, and valuable sensibility. On seventh day evening, our men called upon the merchant, on whom they had a letter of credit, who speaks English well, behaved with great kindness, and soon apprehending their errand, (having some knowledge of the society in England) went with them to an overseer of part of his business, who was a religious man, and discontented with the ceremonious part of the world's worship. They found this person a little shy at first, but he soon opened to them with simplicity, and discovered himself to be a man who was

awakened

* These were books containing a summary account of our principles.

awakened to a profitable fenfe of his own ftate, and to a fincere defire to be led in divine counfel, to greater acceptance than the fhadows of things could yield him. He came with them to the inn, and we fpent the evening agreeably together. He told us of a few more in the town of his fentiments, who met together every firft day evening, to read, &c. and on being afked, if they would be willing to fit with us after our manner, he expreffed his own inclination fo to do; and after inquiring of others, told us next morning, that it was agreeable to them all. In the morning, we were furprifed and comforted with the fight of a very folid feeling young woman from Buer, in the capacity of a fervant, who had walked fifteen miles to meet us, in confequence of a fecret draft in her own mind, without having any reafon to expect, from what had paffed, that we fhould be at Ofnabruck fo long. After getting her fome refrefhment, we fix fat down together, and had a ftrengthening opportunity, wherein dear George Dillwyn miniftered to us. At four in the afternoon, we had a meeting with about eight more, among whom was an officer, who behaved folidly. It was a time of favour, and I believe deep inftruction to fome there, who had not before feen the neceffity of ceafing from their own works, and depending only upon the renewal of divine life in the foul, for qualifications rightly to worfhip. After meeting we paid a vifit to one of their friends who was fick, with whom we were led into fympathy and filence, and to whom we imparted fuch counfel as truth unfolded at that time. Thefe were relieving circumftances to us, and fet us at liberty, comfortably to depart on fecond day morning for Hertford or Herwerden. We therefore fet off with the profpect of a pretty eafy day's journey, but found the road very rough, and in many places dangerous, and more of it than we expected; fo that we were grievoufly jolted, and out until near ten at night, very contrary to our inclination; for we tried much to get lodgings in a town a few miles off, but the people would not take us in. We appear very ftrange to many here, but fo different to a few who are acquainted with the truth, that the diftinction of countries feems almoft loft, and proves the cementing virtue of religion. At Hertford we were vifited by two religious men, who come under the defcription of thofe called friends in thefe parts; and they were encouraged to faithfulnefs. Our men alfo vifited a lawyer, who being difcontented with the ufual ceremonies of religion, &c. keeps much to himfelf. Next morning as we were at breakfaft, propofing to depart, there came two men from different parts, who had walked many miles through the rain to meet us. One of thefe men, fome time ago, refufed to be married by the Prieft, in which, and in other things, he bore a fteady teftimony, under perfecution, againft an hireling miniftry. The opennefs, kindnefs and folidity of his manners and countenance, were pleafant to us; and being evidently acquainted with filent waiting, we had a folemn inftructive opportunity together. From Hertford, we proceeded to Bilefeld, a town where, and in its neighbourhood, there are many religious people, and particularly agreeable as to the outward; but it was a vifit attended with as

deep

deep baptifm, and continual travail of fpirit, as we have experienced in any place that we have been in; which, with the providential openings, and ftrength to vifit the precious feed in the needful time, tended to convince us that we were in the way of our duty; a moft cheering evidence, in this dreary wildernefs, and a full reward for all our little toils. At this place there are fome who live feparate from all publick profeffion, who under an apprehenfion of being turned out of the way, were afraid, for a while, to give us any of their company: but being alfo afraid to let the opportunity flip, we were invited to one of their houfes, to confer with feveral of them on fuch fubjects as might occur, in order to know a little of each other. Both fides were fomewhat furprifed to find fo much fimilarity of fentiment, refpecting the ground and teftimonies of truth. They told us, that if there were a people there, who ceafed from all forms or activity of their own, and fat down in fimple dependance upon the operation of the heavenly gift, they would embrace them with brotherly affection, and rejoice to unite with them herein; but they were loath to believe, that they two or three might be required to bear fuch a publick teftimony; nor were they willing to unite with us in fo doing, for fear of the people whofe eyes are much upon them. They are people of confiderable account, and are very fearful of drawing the lower clafs of their neighbours to themfelves; and being of Nicodemus's clafs, like better to obtain and enjoy, their religious knowledge in private. We had, neverthelefs, feveral opportunities of folid conference together; which were attended with great unanimity and cordiality; the laft of which was particularly owned with the circulation of divine virtue, and with ſtrength fully to relieve our minds towards them. We were very kindly invited to the houſe of a merchant, who appears to be a very ſincere man. We paid him and his daughter a morning viſit; but they were not content with that, and therefore preſſed us to ſpend firſt day evening with them. In the morning of that day, we ſat together in the inn, where we had the company of an honeſt man, who came on foot ſixteen miles to be at meeting with us, and alſo of four others, of the town. In the afternoon, as J. B. was taking a ſolitary walk, he was met by a ſerious man, who deſired his company to a houſe a little way out of the town; he complied with his invitation, and when they got there, they found fourteen people met together, for the ſake of religious improvement, who ſoon made their requeſt that we would all go and ſit with them. I was laid down, in a tried ſituation of mind, when J. B. brought the invitation which had in it ſo much of the right favour, that we embraced it, and immediately ſet off, having above an Engliſh mile to walk. By the time we got there, they were about twenty in number. We ſoon ſettled down into a ſilence truly ſolemn, which laſted a conſiderable time without interruption of any kind; and when the channel of inſtrumental miniſtry opened, the precious life mercifully continued, and our parting was under its tendering impreſſions. This circumſtance, of dropping in with a people of whom we had had no intelligence, and with whom we contracted no further acquaintance, with the ſenſible feeling of divine care over thoſe who are as ſheep having no ſhepherd,

herd, affords altogether a sweet and pleasant reflection; accompanied by this encouraging truth, that " the Lord can make a way, where there seems to be no way:" O that He may gracioufly continue thus to favour us! After this opportunity, we went to the aforementioned merchant's, and were treated with genuine hospitality. After supper, there came in eight or ten persons with the expectation of a meeting, in which they were not disappointed; and I hope it was edifying to them, George Dillwyn having suitable and lively matter to communicate. We had also a religious sitting with a family from Elberfelt, a lively spirited couple, and another person with them. After spending five days here, and bearing the cross as faithfully, perhaps, as in some places where a more open door was ministered, we departed in much peace, and under the belief, that the power of truth is making its own way in that neighbourhood. In our way from Bilefeld, we stopped at a large village called Guterflots, where there are many well disposed people. We staid one day there, and sat with a few people who met us at one of their houses; after which, and distributing a few books to others in the town, we went forward to Munster. We are often very weary, and the accommodations we meet with but indifferent, compared with those of England: the roads are also bad where we have already been, which, with the construction of the carriages, occasion us sometimes to be grievously jolted; and yet we have no cause to complain, having our consolations as well as toils; as it seldom happens that Zion's travellers are qualified to salute each other, even in a thorny difficult way, but the immortal birth, in some degree, leaps for joy. This experience, with the belief that the Lord is at work in the kingdoms of men, and even graciously rewarding such feeble endeavours as ours, with a morsel of the bread that the world knows not of, render any little services of ours as objects unworthy the notice of ourselves, or our friends. From Munster we went to Crevelt. We found our discouragements on entering it, being refused admission at one inn we went to, and at the next, we had such a crowd gathered about us, with such shoutings and rudeness, as greatly frighted our horses, after we were out of the carriage, and our driver had alighted, so that they ran away, and he following, and taking hold of a chain behind, was thrown down, and his head, to appearance, much hurt against the wheel. Some of our feelings were low enough on this occasion. But through the continued kindness of providence, our man soon recovered, being able to move about next day; and the people of the house conceived such an affectionate respect for us, and treated us with such true civility, as made our situation so far comfortable. We also gradually made so much acquaintance, as afforded a degree of hope that our going to Crevelt was right, and that our secret and known exercises there, will not be in vain. About the time of our concluding to come away, our company began to be more sought; which opened the way for the disposal of some of our books, and I feel a secret hope that they will be blessed to some there. We came to Duffeldorf where we staid one day, and had the enjoyment of M. Wetterboar's company. He seems aged, but is alive in the truth. We proceeded to Mulheim, where we arrived the 23d of the 9th month. It is a town about two miles from Cologne, like a Goshen on the confines of Egypt, where many awakened, and some truly religious people reside. We commenced an acquaintance with a few, who have got a clear insight, from the work of truth in themselves, into the gospel dispensation, and the spirituality of the christian religion; concerning these we have encouraging prospects; yet not without a mixture, knowing something of Satan's devices. They received us in the name of disciples. We had divers religious opportunities with them, and parted under the precious sense of divine love and life. We paid a visit to a merchant's wife, a woman of amiable character, who through religious concern, has got into a despairing condition. It was attended with great satisfaction to ourselves, from the sweetness which attended our own minds in her company, and in that of her husband's, who seems bending under the affliction, and likely to profit by it. She often expressed an earnest wish, that she had seen us at a time when such a visit might have been blessed to her; but said, that now it was too late for any thing that was good to be offered to her. This was, however, very far from our sense. Now, through the renewal of unutterable mercy, and never failing help, my soul acknowledges a relief and answer of peace (as far as relates to this service) which I am sure my little endeavours, and compelled dedication are unworthy of. We have had many discouragements since we came to the continent, and many baptisms into death: we have also partaken largely of providential care, and been favoured, from time to time, when refignation was attained to, with that direction whofe effects have often proved its rectitude, and ftrengthened our faith; and my foul, at times, has been put into the capacity of lying down as befide the ftill waters. Some of the laft openings, or fenfe of duty, have been the moft trying and in the crofs; but being yielded to, and the work performed, a comfortable retreat hath been clearly and fweetly founded from this large field of arduous labour; and at a time, when an opennefs among the people was manifeftly increafing. This I efteem an inexpreffible favour, and fuch a one as they only can be fenfible of, who have gone under the weight of fimilar mountains, and been involved in the fear of being mifled.

At Mulheim, fhe drew up and figned a letter to Leopold the Second, King of Hungary, &c. fince Emperor of Germany, in which her companions united. For fome time before her arrival at this place, her mind had been very weightily exercifed with the important fubjects expreffed in this letter; infomuch that, at one period, fhe was under an apprehenfion that it would be required of her to go in perfon, and relieve her mind to the king. But from this very trying fervice, fhe felt herfelf comfortably releafed, and the mode of addreffing him by letter, was fatisfactorily fubftituted. The addrefs was intrufted to the care of a reputable merchant of Cologne, who engaged to forward it without delay. The following is a copy of it.

To

To LEOPOLD the Second, King of Hungary, Bohemia, &c. &c.

Among the numerous congratulations awaiting thy acceffion to the imperial crown, accept, O King! our chriftian good wifhes and folicitude for thy prefent and eternal well-being. We are confcious that we have no claim to the liberty of addreffing thee, but from a belief that the Lord Almighty, who ruleth in the kingdoms of men, and giveth them to whomfoever he will, hath inclined us to leave our habitations to vifit fome parts of this country, and now engages us, in gofpel love, to exprefs our fecret and united prayer, that thou mayft be an inftrument in his holy hand, for the advancement of that glorious day, fpoken of by the prophet, " when fwords fhall be beaten into ploughfhares, and fpears into pruning hooks, when nation fhall not lift up fword againft nation; neither fhall they learn war any more." The great defign of our univerfal Parent, in fending his beloved Son a light into the world, is for his own glory in the falvation of mankind; and for this gracious end, he hath given to all men a meafure of his own eternal fpirit. To co-operate with Him herein, dignifies human nature, and is particularly deferving the moft fcrupulous attention of princes. The fmalleft revelation of this heavenly gift in the believing foul, having a degree of omnipotence in it, brings into fubjection the natural will and wifdom of man, and difcovers to us the noble purpofes of our creation; it diffufes that true benevolence which characterizes genuine chriftianity, and renders dear to a prince, the happinefs of all, even the meaneft of his fubjects; imprinting upon his mind the fuperior value of an immortal foul, to all worldly acquifitions. Through the neglect of a principle fo pure and important, how hath the rational part of God's creation been facrificed to the irregular paffions of fovereigns; and many unprepared fouls precipitated into an awful futurity! That the gofpel difpenfation is intended to remedy thefe evils, and promote the government of the Prince of Peace; that the Gentiles are to come to its light, and kings to the brightnefs of its arifing, are truths to which the facred records abundantly teftify. May this be thy happy experience, O king! that fo the power thou art providentially intrufted with, being fubfervient to divine wifdom, thy example may influence the minds of other princes, who alfo beholding its excellency, may unite in encouraging their fubjects to decline, in mutual charity and forbearance, whatever is contrary to the purity and fimplicity of the religion of Jefus. And may'ft thou be enriched with all fpiritual bleffings; that thefe added to thy temporal ones, may not only perfect thy happinefs, but perpetuate it beyond the narrow limits of time, and qualify thee, acceptably, to caft down thy crown at the feet of Him who is King of kings, and Lord of lords, who lives and reigns for ever and ever.

George and Sarah Dillwyn, of Burlington, New Jerfey, North America.
Sarah Grubb, Clonmel, } Ireland.
Jofhua Beale, Cork,

Members of the religious fociety of friends in thofe countries and Great Britain, commonly called Quakers.

Mulheim on the Rhine,
29th of 9th month called Sept. 1790.

A

A short time before her return home, on a review of some parts of this journey, she wrote as follows.

In many places, we found a people who were discontented and weary with the mere profession of christianity, and the deadness of those forms and ceremonies with which it is incumbered; and who were convinced of the sufficiency of the heavenly principle. These, having been mercifully visited with a lively sense of the spirituality of true religion, received us in the name of disciples, and rejoiced in being directed to the christian's rest. This true sabbath, was, however, imperfectly understood by many of them, for want of ceasing, when they met together in little companies, from all activity of their own, and depending singly on the quickening. virtue of truth, to qualify them for, and lead them into, such services as are most acceptable, and most consistent with the duty of true, spiritual believers. Some of this people appeared to be so near this great point, as soon to discover and acknowledge it; but their increasing testimony thereto, will, if rightly borne, prove the closest trial which they have yet met with. We are indeed convinced, beyond all shadow of doubt, that there is a choice heritage in Germany, and in other parts of the Continent, who are gradually retiring to the true sheepfold; but, at present, they are, like the disciples, secreted in an inner chamber for fear of the Jews. Our visit to this people, though attended with a degree of suffering, hath been productive of solid peace.

Her mind being thus comfortably releafed from this field of labour, fhe proceeded from Mulheim to Cleves, and from thence, through Flanders, to Dunkirk, and arrived at London the 27th of 10th month 1790; and feeling a defire to vifit her relations at York, &c. before her return home, fhe went pretty directly for that city; where fhe ftaid a few days, very much to the comfort and fatisfaction of her relatives and friends there. At this time fhe laboured under evident indifpofition of body; but the fweetnefs of her fpirit, and the cheering effects of meeting again her beloved connections, with the profpect of foon returning to thofe at Clonmel, fupported her in a great meafure above it, and encouraged her to fet forward and proceed towards home; which fhe did by way of Ackworth, Sheffield, Manchefter, &c. At thefe places, fhe was again refrefhed by the company of divers near and dear friends: it appeared, indeed, by thus encompaffing, in this fhort vifit, fo many of her beloved connections, that, as the time of her fojourning here was foon to clofe, fhe was enabled and permitted to wind up the labours of her day, with the mutual confolation of feeing again many of thofe with whom fhe was clofely united, and bidding them a final farewell in mutability. At Ackworth, fhe fpent the night with a near and beloved relative, to whom, in much brokennefs of fpirit, fhe thus expreffed herfelf: Oh! my dear, I think fometimes that I fhall foon be gone; it feems, as if my day's work was nearly done, and on looking towards home, as if I might not be long there."

She

She reached Dublin in time for the half year's meeting, and in the select meeting there, gave an account of her late journey, with great meekness and humility of spirit; ascribing nothing to the creature, but rendering to the Lord the praise of His own works. From hence, she proceeded directly for Clonmel, (having account of the small-pox being in the family) where she was favoured to arrive the 12th of the 11th month, much relieved from a severe cough which had lately attended her, though greatly exhausted in her strength and spirits. On her way from Dublin, she writes thus to a friend:

To be strengthened rightly to fill up our appointed measure of sufferings for the body's sake, whether at home or abroad, is a mark of divine favour, and will be succeeded by undefiled rest.—I am now returning home, under a grateful sense of Providential care, and in peaceful poverty of spirit.

The following is extracted from a letter which she wrote at Clonmel, a few days after her return.

I can now once more salute you from home, in renewed and endeared affection, and gratefully acknowledge the multiplied preservations of our never-failing Helper, in thus far bringing through a variety of exercises, from which the natural mind cannot relieve itself. I reflect with solid satisfaction upon my visit at York, &c. and am glad I paid it, though I feel myself a poor worn-out creature. The 24th of the 11th month she set off from Clonmel to attend their quarterly meeting at Cork;
previous

previous to which she wrote the following letter to a friend:

My present affliction hath gained great afcendency over my mind, fo that I feem faft lofing my hold, and fenfe of Him that is invifible; and remembering fome paft exercife, when I was in danger of lofing the beft life, I am ready to fay, with mournful Jeremiah, " caufe me not to return to Jonathan's houfe, left I die there." I know that nothing hath yet occurred, which needs to fcatter a well regulated mind from the fource of good; but I am left to fuch a fenfe of my own wretchednefs, that even the grafshopper or things comparable to it, are become a burden. To attend a quarterly meeting under fuch impreffions, is a profpect which I need not defcribe; but I fear to make a prey of thy fympathetic mind. May I be preferved from a murmuring difpofition, by which the holy Spirit is grieved!

At the quarterly meeting, fhe delivered in, an humble account of her late miffion, appeared in divers acceptable teftimonies, and at the clofe of the meeting was taken ill. This laft conflict of nature, which was at times very fevere, continued about ten days, when it pleafed infinite wifdom to remove her from the toils and troubles of mortality, to a manfion of everlafting reft, on the 8th of the 12th month 1790, and on the 12th her remains were attended to the burying-ground by many friends. It was a folemn, memorable time; and living teftimonies were there borne to the fufficiency of that power, (which had fo eminently qualified her for his

his fervice,) to raife up and abilitate others to follow her footfteps. During her illnefs, which was at the houfe of her beloved friends Samuel and Sarah Neale, fhe dropped a few expreffions, worthy of prefervation, which have been collected and are as follow: In a meffage to a young woman who prefided in the fchool at Clonmel, fhe faid; Salute her very affectionately. I defire the fympathy of her fpirit, and that fhe may be endued with additional qualifications to bear her own, and our joint trials, under thefe complicated circumftances. Tell her, I have been much favoured with quietnefs of mind from the firft, though a ftranger to how the prefent afflictions or trials may terminate; but the grain of faith and hope which is mercifully vouchfafed, I efteem preferable to all knowledge. She further faid; give my dear love to all our young women; I hope that each will be preferved in their refpective lines of duty. I know their tendernefs for me, but would be forry they fhould let down their fpirits too low; for I believe that truth would rather increafe, than leffen our ftrength, at fuch times as thefe. The children are all affectionately remembered by me: I hope they will each endeavour to lighten the general burden, by their fobriety, and doing that which they know to be right. I am trying to get my mind to a fettlement, that all things work together for good; but it is hard to get at it. She feveral times faid: " I muft go. You muft let me go." And nearly the laft words fhe fpoke were repeating that paffage of fcripture, " my peace I give unto you."

Four

Four days before her deceafe, fhe dictated the following weighty, inftructive letter, to a particular friend. Thy falutation met me, though apparently out of courfe, in the right time; being under impreffions, which make time and circumftances of little account, compared with the unlimited confolations of the Spirit, or a preparation to receive them at the Divine Hand. My foul, though encompaffed with the manifold infirmities of a very afflicted tabernacle, can feelingly worfhip and rejoice in nothing more than this, that the Lamb immaculate is ftill redeeming, by his precious blood, out of every nation, kindred, tongue, and people; and making a glorious addition to the church triumphant, whofe names will ftand eternally recorded in the book of life. I exprefs not thefe things from a redundancy of heavenly virtue, but from the foul-fuftaining evidence, that, amidft all our weaknefs and conflicts of flefh or fpirit, an intereft is mercifully granted in Him, who giveth victory over death, hell, and the grave.

Thus hath the fetting fun of this humble follower of the Lamb, gone down in brightnefs; and though fhe hath been called away as in younger life, (being only in the 35th year of her age) yet her day's work appears to have been compleat, and, with refpect to herfelf, every meafure worth living for, filled up. Honourable age is not that which ftandeth in length of time, or that which is meafured by number of years; but wifdom is the gray hair to man, and an unfpotted life is old age. May we who remain behind, whilft we deplore the church's lofs in the removal of fo ufeful

ful and dignified a fervant, be encouraged to imitate her example, and to furrender ourfelves in faithfulnefs and dedication to all the Lord's requirings: that fo, when the refidue of our days is accomplifhed, we alfo may be favoured to receive that blefled declaration; " well done, good and faithful fervant, enter thou into the joy of thy Lord, and into thy mafter's reft."

A Teſtimony

THE LIFE OF

A Teſtimony from our monthly Meeting for the County of Tipperary, concerning Sarah Grubb, deceaſed.

Our minds being deeply affected by the recent great loſs which the church hath ſuſtained, in the removal of our beloved friend, Sarah Grubb, daughter of our friends William Tuke and his late wife Elizabeth of York, we feel it incumbent on us to give forth a teſtimony concerning her; for as the memory of the juſt is bleſſed, ſo the remembrance of this dignified and eminently uſeful member in the church militant, is precious to many; to whom ſhe was a nurſing mother, raiſed up, by a thorough ſubmiſſion to the operation of the divine hand, to the ſtature of an elder in the truth, though, as to years, ſhe had ſcarcely attained the meridian of life. She was a woman of extraordinary natural abilities, ſtrength of judgment, and clearneſs of diſcernment; and being favoured with the viſitation of heavenly love in the morning of her day, and ſubmitting to be brought into that paſſive nothingneſs, wherein the veſſels in the Lord's houſe are formed and fitted for uſefulneſs, ſhe witneſſed an early preparation for ſervice, coming forth in publick miniſtry about the 23d year of her age. After exerciſing ſome years the precious gift committed to her, to the conſolation of many, ſhe joined in marriage with our friend Robert Grubb, and very ſoon after manifeſted the fruit of entire dedication, by viſiting the meetings of friends in Scotland, where her ſervice was truly acceptable, and continued in ſuch a line of devotedneſs, that in the courſe of about five years ſhe viſited moſt, or all the meetings in Great Britain

tain and Ireland. About three years since, she removed with her husband to reside within the compass of this monthly meeting; wherein she was deeply exercised in spirit, for the arising and spreading of life, and frequently and earnestly engaged in exciting her brethren and sisters to diligent labour after it. In ministry, she was found and edifying, not only like the scribe instructed to the kingdom, bringing forth out of her treasure things new and old, but qualified by pure wisdom, to bring them forth in the demonstration of the spirit and with power, in the authority and becoming gravity of the gospel, being in her delivery an example to all concerned in bearing a publick testimony for the Lord's cause. The view of coming to settle in this nation, was accompanied with a sense of divine requiring, to establish a school, for the education of the daughters of friends in useful learning, simplicity, and that unaffected piety into which truth leads its followers; which she was enabled to accomplish, we trust, to the lasting advantage of some of the rising generation. Soon after her coming to reside among us, she, in consequence of a concern which had for a considerable time rested on her mind, engaged in a religious visit to Holland, some parts of Germany and the south of France; in which she was joined by several friends, and wherein she was eminently gifted for the service to which she was called; her ministry, private admonitions, and exemplary deportment, reaching the witness in many minds; so that her fervent labour, and the sweet favour of her exercised spirit, we believe is still felt, and will be long profitably

fitably remembered in thofe parts. After her return, fhe paid an acceptable vifit to feveral parts of this province, and had meetings where none of our fociety dwelt, much tending to fpread the knowledge of the truth. And laftly, under the prevalence of gofpel love, and earneft folicitude that the fheep not yet of this fold might be gathered to the teachings of the great Shepherd, fhe again left her own habitation, and engaged, with fome of her former companions, in a very arduous and exercifing vifit to Dunkirk, Holland, and fome of the northern parts of Germany; wherein, we have reafon to believe, fhe had eminent fervice, to the confirming of many vifited minds in the faith, and promoting the bleffed caufe of truth and righteoufnefs; in which glorious work, her intrepid fpirit fhrunk not from fuffering: the extending of the government of her dear Lord and Mafter in the hearts of the children of men, and the promotion and increafe of His fpiritual kingdom over fea and land, being nearer to her than her natural life, or any other confideration, fhe was brought to a willingnefs to be fpent therein. In her return, fhe attended our national meeting, and in the meeting of minifters and elders, giving an account of her late journey, under the influence of that humility which was fo confpicuoufly the covering of her fpirit, fhe afcribed all to Him, whom fhe knew to be the Author of every good work, in thefe expreffions: " we have done but little, but the Lord is doing much;" concluding with, " return unto thy reft, O my foul! for the Lord hath dealt bountifully with thee?" as though prophetick of that

everlafting

everlafting reft, into which fhe was fo near being gathered: for her bodily ftrength being confiderably impaired, by almoft conftant exercife and fatigue, it proved unequal to the force of a diftemper, which foon after feized her frame, and, by a rapid progrefs, terminated thofe afflictions of which fhe had fo largely filled up her meafure, for the body's fake, which is the church.

She attended our quarterly meeting at Cork, returned a lively account of her journey, and was acceptably exercifed in the meetings there; after which, fhe was confined by ficknefs at the houfe of our dear friend Samuel Neale, near that city, where, among other weighty expreffions, fhe uttered the following, "I have been much favoured with quietnefs of mind from the firft, though a ftranger to how the prefent afflictions or trials may terminate; but the grain of faith and hope which is mercifully vouchfafed, I efteem preferable to all knowledge." In a letter which fhe dictated to a near friend four days before her deceafe, fhe faid, " My foul, though encompaffed with the manifold infirmities of a very afflicted tabernacle, can feelingly worfhip and rejoice in nothing more than this, that the Lamb immaculate is ftill redeeming, by his precious blood, out of every nation, kindred, tongue and people, and making a glorious addition to the church triumphant, whofe names will ftand eternally recorded in the book of life. I exprefs not thefe things from a redundancy of heavenly virtue, but from the foul-fuftaining evidence, that, amidft all our weaknefs and conflicts of flefh and fpirit, an intereft is mercifully ly granted in Him, who giveth victory over death, hell and the grave." Which, with other corroborating circumstances, clearly evinced, where her hope and dependance were, and that her refined spirit was prepared for its glorious manfion, into which we have no doubt it was admitted. She departed this life the 8th of the 12th month 1790; and after a folemn meeting being previoufly held at the meeting houfe, wherein, and at the graveyard, feveral living teftimonies were borne, her body was interred in friends burying ground, in Cork, the 12th of the fame; aged about 34 years.

Her converfation was innocently cheerful, which endeared her to the youth of both fexes, and gave her much place and influence with them. To her beloved hufband, fhe was a truly affectionate wife; to her friends a near fympathizer in affliction; and being clothed with that charity which feeketh not her own, and breatheth peace and good will to all, was ready to reach forth the hand of help, fo that the whole of her conduct was an uniform confiftency with her holy profeffion, and the purity of thofe doctrines which fhe furely believed and was engaged fo extenfively to publifh. May fhe, being dead, yet fpeak with a prevailing language to us all who are left behind; "follow me as I followed Chrift;" that fo we may die the death of the righteous, and our latter end be like theirs.

Given forth at a monthly meeting for the county of Tipperary, held at Clonmel by adjournment, the 13th day of the 2d month 1791.

Signed

Signed in and on behalf thereof, by many friends.

The annexed teftimony concerning our beloved friend, Sarah Grubb, has been read in our quarterly men's and women's meeting for Munfter Province, held in Cork the 21ft of the 2d month 1791, with which we have near unity.

Signed on behalf of our men's meeting by
RICHARD ABELL, Clerk.

And on behalf of our women's meeting by
MARGARET GRUBB, Clerk.

Read, and approved, in our half year's meeting for Ireland, held in Dublin, from the 1ft of the 5th month 1791, to the 5th of the fame inclufive, and on behalf thereof figned by
JOHN DAVIS, Clerk to the meeting this time.

A Teftimony of York quarterly Meeting concerning Sarah Grubb, late Wife of our Friend Robert Grubb of Clonmel, in Ireland.

This our valuable friend, having been a member of this meeting until within the four laft years of her life, and the remembrance of her being precious to many of us, we feel our minds engaged to unite in a fhort teftimony concerning her, with defires that many, from her pious and excellent example,

ample, may be ſtirred up, according to their different meaſures, to follow her as ſhe followed Chriſt.

She was born in the city of York, in the year 1756, and was favoured with a guarded and religious education, which, with the divine bleſſing upon it, preſerved her from many dangers and follies to which youth are often expoſed, and prepared her heart for that open reception of the truth, and entire ſurrender to its dictates, which remarkably diſtinguiſhed her through the more advanced periods of life. But though ſhe was early under the viſitations of divine love, yet being of a quick and lively diſpoſition, joined to great natural abilities, ſhe found it hard work to ſubmit to the lowlineſs and ſimplicity of the croſs of Chriſt ; and endured many ſore conflicts before ſhe ſurrendered her will to the government of the Prince of Peace. Whilſt under the Lord's preparing hand for the work of the miniſtry, ſhe experienced many deep baptiſms of ſpirit; but He who knew her ſincerity, and earneſt deſires for His holy help and direction, gracrouſly ſuſtained her in this proving ſeaſon, and in due time brought forth living offerings, to His own praiſe, and the comfort of many minds. In the exerciſe of her miniſtry, ſhe was careful not to move in her own time and will, nor to exceed her gift ; but to be attentive to the ariſings and continuance of life, with patient reſignation and dedication of heart.

Her love and gratitude to the Father of mercies, and her fervent concern for the proſperity of his cauſe on earth, made her unwearied in her labours to promote it, and to be willing to fpend and be fpent for his great Name's fake. She was an example of true humility and abafednefs of felf, feeling that all her fprings were in the Lord, and that though the creature may at feafons be honoured, yet every good and perfect gift came from above, and called for unfeigned acknowledgment. To the neceffity and powerful efficacy of the pure principle of light and grace in the foul, fhe bore many living teftimonies, and recommended, above all things, the clofeft attention and obedience to its holy manifeftations, as that alone which can preferve from the fpots of the world, redeem the mind from its fpirit and enjoyments, and confer that peace which the world can neither give nor take away. She beheld and mourned over the breaches and wafte places of Zion, and we believe laboured honeftly, according to the ftrength received, for the repairing thereof, and the reftoration of ancient beauty and fimplicity. Her fuperior abilities, fanctified by the humbling operations of the holy fpirit, qualified her for extenfive fervice in the adminiftration of the difcipline of the church; wherein fhe was concerned to act, under a degree of that covering, which ought to influence every religious movement. Of a folid and weighty fpirit, fhe was engaged to dig deeply for the hidden treafure, and laboured to dwell near the fpring of divine life: yet infinite wifdom faw meet to fuffer her at feafons to experience great inward poverty: but under thefe proving difpenfations, fhe murmured not, being refigned to the will of her Lord and Mafter, and made willing " to fuffer with him, that fhe might alfo reign with him." And having partaken of

L the

the fufferings and confolations of the gofpel, fhe knew how to fympathize with the exercifed and mourning fpirit, dealing her bread, when qualified, to the hungry foul, and pouring in the wine and oil to the help and refrefhment of many. And as this devoted faithful fervant of the Lord was thus inftrumental in glorifying His name among mankind, and promoting the divine government in their hearts, fo fhe became more and more refined, and redeemed from all vifible enjoyments; until, in unfearchable wifdom, He who put her forth and went before her, was pleafed to " cut fhort the work in righteoufnefs," and to remove her, we doubt not, from His church militant on earth, to his church triumphant in heaven.

Read, approved, and figned, in, by order, and on behalf of our quarterly meeting held in York, by adjournments, on the 30th and 31ft of the 3d month 1791 by

MORDECAI CASSON, Clerk to the meeting this time.

ELIZABETH TUKE, Clerk this time.

APPENDIX:

APPENDIX:

CONTAINING

AN

ACCOUNT

OF

ACKWORTH SCHOOL,

OBSERVATIONS

ON

CHRISTIAN DISCIPLINE,

AND VALUABLE

EXTRACTS

FROM MANY OF HER

LETTERS.

SOME

ACCOUNT

OF

ACKWORTH SCHOOL,

ADDRESSED TO A

FRIEND IN AMERICA.

Dear Friend,

THE following imperfect account of Ackworth school is presented to thee, in confidence that thou wilt not expose it, and yet with a hope that it may privately aid thy endeavours to establish a school, for the religious education of youth, in another part of the world; an engagement worthy of thyself, but requiring something better to render it truly succefsful.

As religious concerns cannot, any more than those of a civil nature, be rightly carried forward without order and method, it becomes a very important inquiry, what rules and adjustments of things pertaining thereto, are consistent with the spirituality

spirituality of their origin, and when these are found, they call for great care in officers and their superintendents, to keep them in their proper places, left that which is begun in the spirit, should be sought to be made perfect in the flesh.

There is a moral rectitude, fabricated in human wisdom, which is beautiful to the natural eye, seizes on the passions, and draws from a superficial judgment, an inconsiderate approbation of what, perhaps, when it is scrutinized into, has sprung from a love of popular applause, and tends to settle those who are active in it, in a rest and enjoyment of the work of their own hands.

To know the first spring of action, is a noble attainment; and if it prove pure, then carefully to keep it so, is a work (thou well knoweft) of far greater magnitude; and which will tend more to the regulation of a school, than a fine-spun system of positive rules, untinctured with faith in the sufficiency of divine aid, immediately communicated.

To obtain a right form is surely of absolute necessity, because regularity is one of the wheels whereby the intended work is to be effected; and perhaps some useful order may be gathered from the following pages, which I hope will not be implicitly adopted. Indeed, I have been thoughtful, in the course of my penning them, whether such as are rightly influenced to promote an education consistent with our holy profession, would not be better furnished with qualifications to settle even

civil

ACKWORTH SCHOOL.

civil concerns, without a model of the experience of others; feeing that the fountain of divine wifdom is inexhauftible; that for the conducting of temporal things, there can be no order like that which immediately flows from it; and that a very fmall digreffion of our attention from this fource, is often fucceeded by many erroneous fteps.

To thy prudence, therefore, I commit this little work, believing thou wilt not ufe it improperly. If it afford thee any ufeful reflections, in times of relaxation from the weight of gofpel fervice, be the means of opening for me a door of accefs into thy clofet, make me a partaker of thy treafure, and fometimes revive me in thy remembrance for good, I fhall be fully fatisfied. One obfervation further occurs to my mind, for which, as this is all a piece of freedom, I fhall not apologize. As nothing can be faid to be truly religious, (whatever the firft defign may be) but what is religioufly conducted, a very fpecial care ought to be maintained to the pointings of truth, in choofing inftructors and fervants for a fchool; who fhould be more directed to the fchool of Chrift themfelves, than loaded with injunctions about trivial matters, and their conformity to them confidered as their qualifications. No law or rule ought to be fo framed, as to interfere with their religious duties; and when any make a wrong ufe of the liberty truth allows, great care fhould be exercifed, left alterations take place, which have a tendency to circumfcribe the righteous with the tranfgreffor; for where this is the cafe, people of an outward, fteady conduct, a cringing temper, and
who

who know but little about revealed religion, seem to be most adapted to such an institution. These may, to the utmost of their natural abilities, preserve order, and prefer the works which most recommend them to those in superior power, being as earnest in their endeavours, as any, to promote the establishment of civil authority, and of a great many specious forms: but the vitals of the institution being oppressed, and the spirit and life of every act of duty to the children, and of christian discipline among them, disregarded, the whole body must gradually grow diseased and corrupted.

Education is a subject so copious, when unfolded to the inward attention of those to whom the care of children is rightly committed, as to require a better assisted pen than mine, to do it justice; but this I believe, that simplicity, godly sincerity, and a righteous zeal and tenderness, with an improving and imparting knowledge of useful things, can hardly fail of rendering a person who is under a secret sense of duty, qualified to undertake it.

To be sensible of the divine influence, to propagate the knowledge of it, and so to prefer it to all other considerations, as to walk worthy of its blessing being shed upon our endeavours, is the Alpha, and the Omega, of our profession. That " the blessing of heaven above, and of the deep that lieth under," may rest upon thee, dear friend! crown all thy labours, sweeten all thy bitter cups, and render invincible the habitation of thy spirit, when storms may assail it, and discouragements wait

wait at the threshold of its door, is the present fervent breathing of thy truly affectionate friend,.
SARAH GRUBB.
Foston, 1st month 5th 1786.

SECT. I.

Ackworth school is an institution intended for the religious education of children, members of our society, between the age of nine * and fourteen, and particularly of those whose parents are not in affluent circumstances. It admits of three hundred, viz. one hundred and eighty boys, and one hundred and twenty girls. They are paid for, at their entrance, by a bill of admittance of eight guineas value; for which they are provided with board, learning, clothing, and other necessaries, for one year; four shillings and four-pence are also then deposited, as an allowance of one penny per week for pocket money. This school is under the immediate care of two committees, in each of which there are twenty-eight members; one is constituted of friends of London, and held there; the other of friends in the neighbourhood of Ackworth; divers of whom are twenty, thirty, and some forty miles distant from the place.

Each committee meets once a month; when the general state of the institution is considered, particular regulations proposed, complaints received, the intended resignation of services reported, and friends

* The present limitation of age is between eight and fourteen.

friends appointed to inquire for a fupply of affiftants, &c. &c.

As it often happens that divers friends are at Ackworth the night before the fitting of the committee, or early in the morning, three of them infpect all bills of parcels, and the treafurer's accounts ; and report to the committee the ftate thereof, the number of the children admitted and returned fince laft month, and thofe that are upon the lift for admittance: others examine the improvement of fuch as are likely to depart the enfuing month ; and, generally, religious opportunities are taken with them, and an account given thereof to the committee. Copies of the minutes of each committee are tranfmitted to one another, and neither of them conclude upon any thing new, of importance, without mutual approbation. Several friends, once a year, give up to an appointment to fpend fome time in the houfe, in order to value the ftock, to fettle all accounts, and to take a more general and minute furvey of the ftate of the family, than could be done at any other time with fo much propriety : and generally, on vifits to the family, at other times, the company of women friends has been defired, a number having their names down on the committee's books for fuch fervices. Agents are appointed in each county, who undertake to negociate the bufinefs between thofe who fend the children, and the inftitution, by providing bills of admittance and certificates, and giving notice of their readinefs, &c.

A

ACKWORTH SCHOOL.

A general meeting is held at Ackworth once a year, conſtituted of friends appointed to attend it from the ſeveral quarterly meetings. Here the ſtate of the inſtitution is intended to be laid open; all ſubjects of doubt, and eſpecially ſuch as the two committees could not agree upon, to be referred for candid difcuſſion and determination, and new regulations or rules eſtabliſhed.

A large number of friends from diſtant parts, is appointed to infpect the children's advances in learning, &c. and to obtain a knowledge of their teachers abilities, a free and honeſt repreſentation whereof is thought abſolutely neceſſary. This general meeting adjourns to a ſuitable time in the yearly meeting week, when their minutes are read, and a report made from thence to the yearly meeting at large.

N. B. The infpection of the female fide of the houſe is committed to the women friends, aſſembled at the general meeting at Ackworth; who appoint different committees to examine the different departments, have free conferences with the officers, infpect the girls improvements, take religious opportunities with them, and report the ſubſtance of their obſervations, and the propriety of ſuch amendments as occur to them thereupon; after which, minutes are formed, and a copy of them ſent into the mens meeting.

There are stationed in the family, a treasurer and his wife, to whom is committed the superintendence of the whole.*

The boys have generally four or five masters, whose salaries are from 25 to 100l. ‡ per annum, intended as proportionate to their services, and abilities; and there are also some apprentices. The number of the schools is four, and the masters keep much to the distinct branches of learning for which they are best qualified; as one, reading, another writing, a third arithmetick, &c. and the children pass in classes from school to school, except the little ones, who are principally kept under the care of one master.

The apartments for teaching are so commodious as to render all crowding unnecessary, especially at writing; the desks, though in one continued length, have nevertheless such divisions, by openings for each boy's books, &c. that there need not be any interference, if they keep their places.

Ten or twelve of the eldest and most solid boys, are chosen monitors, who lend some assistance in the schools, particularly in settling the children to their places, and taking care that each has his own.

About

* These serve the institution without a salary, which greatly adds to their authority.
‡ 100l. was the salary of the principal master; but this office being discontinued, no salary is now so high.

ACKWORTH SCHOOL. 247

About ten minutes before every meal, a bell is rung, at which the children are quickly collected in ranks, either on the open ground, or under a colonade which shelters from wet and heat. The masters stand in the front in their own divisions, whilst the monitors survey them behind and before, taking care that their buckles are in order, their hair combed, and if any be dirty, to send them to wash.

Here the masters have a frequent opportunity of making useful observations, giving general directions, administering counsel, and selecting out offenders for the table of disgrace; which is no otherwise distinguished, than by being detached from the rest, and having no cloth upon it.

When the second bell rings for meals, they advance in couples with great regularity to the dining-room, (the least going first) and divide at the foot of the table, one going up on one side, and the other on the other; by which means they are seated with dexterity and expedition.

A general silence immediately ensues, which, by an intimation from one of the masters, is soon broke, and all begin their meal; but no conversation louder than a whisper is allowed, during the time of eating, and no more in that manner than is necessary for transferring their victuals from one to another, when some have too much, and others too little, the latter of which are freely supplied by the masters, if they ask.

When

When all appetites appear satisfied, and a meal is ended, silence again takes place, after which, with an intimation of quietude, and sedateness, they are beckoned to depart. They unite again in couples at the foot of the table where they parted, and walk steadily out of the room into the places appointed for play, where they disperse. It is thought necessary, that one of the masters should bestow a general oversight on them in these times of relaxation, with no more interference than is absolutely necessary.

SECT. III.

The same order is observed among the girls, as with the boys, at school and meals; they have seldom less than four mistresses whose salaries are from 12 to 25l. per annum; these teach sewing, knitting, spinning flax, reading, and the English grammar. Writing and arithmetick are also taught by one of the masters, who is particularly set at liberty, part of every day, for that purpose, and has a certain division of girls each time; but the committees are desirous, that some of the female teachers should be qualified to instruct in these branches of learning.*

A wise attention is paid in the girls schools to quietude and regularity; each is to know her own business, and the time for applying for instruction about her work, &c. There are two or three apprentices for whom there is a considerable sphere of

---

* These branches are now taught by female instructors.

of action, in assisting the mistresses, as there are many more articles of care among the girls than the boys; such as large stocks of goods to be made up into wearing apparel, cutting up work, teaching various branches of the executive part, and dealing out haberdasheries to the children. A discreet allotment of care and employ to these, preserves the mistresses from too oppressive a load of anxiety about smaller matters, and gives them an opportunity, in their respective schools, to cherish a necessary recollection of mind, enabling them more sensibly to partake of a measure of divine strength, by which alone they can govern with right authority and tenderness. They have also monitors, who have similar offices to the boys. The reading mistress has seldom more than one class in her school at a time, which consists of six or eight, and they read paragraph by paragraph, all standing so remote from her, as to render a proper exertion of their voices necessary, by which they are inured to read audibly. The mistress or assistant teacher, to whom is committed the care of spinning, attends to that employ only a few hours each day; the rest of her time being taken up with mending the children's linen, especially that of the little ones, and instructing five or six girls at a time in that art, having them, and that kind of work, in a room wholly set at liberty for the purpose. The eldest girls take it in turns, one or two at a time, to assist the mantua-maker, who is supplied with plenty of work. They also take it in turns to work with the laundress every week, in washing, and getting up small linen, and in waiting at meal-times at the house-keepers table; and one in turn

is

is under the peculiar direction of the treasurer's wife, who keeps her pretty much to her own parlour, and employed in her work. Two of the girls are weekly appointed to sweep the lodging rooms every day, and all the girls make their own beds, (as they sleep in couples,) which are curled hair mattresses laid upon rails; they have a bolster, an under blanket, a pair of sheets, two upper blankets, and a counterpane of single furniture check, but no curtains. A chest with partitions stands at the head of every bed, and furnishes two girls with conveniencies for the keeping of their clothes, having two drawers at the bottom for their small linen.

Their apparel in general, and especially such as passes through the washings, is marked with the initials of their names, and the number of their bill of admittance.

The girls are provided with work by the institution, and for their improvement, finer needlework is taken in for hire than the family can furnish them with; and when that falls short, child-bed linen is sometimes made to sell, in which superfluous work is guarded against.

The girls and boys go to bed in the same order; and all their clothing is so folded up, and laid upon their chests, that though there are twenty or thirty beds in a room, yet after they are settled in bed, there is scarcely one article of clothing out of its proper place, and consequently no interference in putting them on. The lodging rooms have several

ral ventilators in the ceiling. One or more of the miſtreſſes, or ſteady apprentices, ſleep in each, and a healthy cheerfulneſs and decorum are preſerved through the whole.

SECT. IV.

At meeting the boys and girls enter in the ſame method, the boys firſt, a maſter leading the way; the leaſt children immediately follow, and are ſeated on the uppermoſt croſs forms, the reſt regularly ſucceeding according to their height; and coming in by couples, they fill two benches at a time, and very ſoon get all ſettled. The monitors are placed on a ſide bench, which gives them an opportunity of inſpecting the behaviour of the other children, and of inſtructing them by their example, the maſters and miſtreſſes are placed at little diſtances, on a ſeat one ſtep higher, by which they can over-ſee the whole. They depart with no leſs regulari-ty than they come in, the children joining again in couples; and in ſuitable weather, they take a circular walk round the area in the front of the houſe; after which, they are adviſed to retire to reading, a conſiderable library of friends books being provided, part whereof is produced on a firſt day.—The children every evening ſettle to read, the boys and girls ſeparate; and they all, with the family, are collected once a week for that purpoſe, previous to which, they quietly ſettle down in ſilence for a little while, then one of the maſters reads a chapter, and about ſix boys, and as many girls, read ſix or eight verſes each; after which, they pauſe again, until it is judged a ſuitable time for the children to withdraw, which they do, not in couples as on other occaſions, but ſingly, going immediately to bed, and at ſuch a diſtance from each other, as to admit of no converſation by the way, the teachers paſſing with them in certain diviſions, preſerves the quietude without interruption. They generally riſe at ſix in ſummer, and ſeven in winter, and go to bed at nine in ſummer, and eight in winter. It is a rule that every child, on admittance, ſhall have a certificate ſigned by a medical perſon, expreſſive of his or her being in health, and having no infectious diſorders, or apparent ſores; and if a child has not had the ſmall-pox, the parent or guardian ſignifies, whether, if the contagion ſhould break out in the family, they chooſe inoculation. Whenever an illneſs of any kind appears, the ſubject is conſigned to a ſteady matron in the ſtation of a nurſe, who has convenient apartments for the reception of ſuch; and an apothecary in the neighbourhood has a ſalary for attending at ſtated periods, whether he is wanted or not, and as much oftener as occaſion requires; the drugs are kept in the houſe at the expenſe of the inſtitution, and the nurſe has the care of them.

N. B. The children's dreſs, if not ſo when they come, is modelled to a certain ſimplicity, which meets with the general approbation of the moſt conſiſtent part of the ſociety; and ſuch apparel as is provided by the inſtitution, is of a ſubſtantial, and rather courſe texture, but neat in its colour and make, and a care is exerciſed over it, which preſerves it ſo to the laſt. An exact uniform in colour, &c. has not been adopted.

S E C T.

SECT. V.

The houfe-keeper has the general care and command of the kitchen, the keeping, giving out, and providing the houfe linen, fhe gives an account what victuals and stores are wanted, fees to the proper ufe of them, and delivers an account to the treafurer of her difburfements, once a month.

There are two chamber-maids, whofe bufinefs it is to make the boys and family's beds, to fweep their lodging rooms and the ftairs, every day except meeting days, to affift in getting up linen, mending fheets, the boys fhirts and ftockings, and alfo to help in wafhing and combing the boys. The nurfe likewife affifts in mending linen, but nothing is to interfere with her fervice to difeafed children.

Two cooks are found fufficient; they contrive their bufinefs fo as to have little hurry at meal times, and on the evening preceding meeting days, the victuals are fo prepared for next day, that little more is neceffary, having in fummer, cold meat, or fruit-pies, and in winter, boiled plumb puddings, which only require one perfon to ftay at home, to keep the coppers boiling.

They have one fervant whofe bufinefs is principally wafhing difhes, &c. A fteady, and rather elderly man, is generally kept for renewing the fires, and jobbing about. There is one dairy-maid, who has the care of the milk of upwards of twenty cows, affifts in milking them, and makes the butter,

ter, &c. The laundrefs's work is only to infpect and affift in the wafhings. A mill, fomething like the bleachers, is ufed for large clothes; it is in a building detached from the houfe, and is wrought by a horfe; the linen is wafhed in bags, being firft forted and foaped; two wafher-women are provided for one day, who, with a man that is kept in the capacity of a carpenter, can, with induftry and the laundrefs's affiftance, accomplifh all that is fuitable for that engine. Thefe wafhings come every week. One man has the care of baking and brewing, in which is included the children's dinners, when they have baked meat or pies, and making the bread, &c. There are 80 acres of land, and two men in the capacity of farmers, who, with a labourer occafionally, find fufficient employ in raifing a little grain, taking care of the cattle, affifting in milking, going to market about three miles diftance, and fetching coals from the pits a few miles. The treafurer, his wife, the houfe-keeper, with all the mafters, (except thofe who have families) miftreffes, nurfe, and mantua-maker, eat together at the houfe-keeper's table; and the other fervants fit down regularly together in the kitchen, where order and folidity are made incumbent for every fervant to obferve. A taylor and fhoe-maker, who have families, are ftationed in cottages adjoining the houfe, and have falaries fufficient for their fupport. Single men lodge and board in the houfe, being found neceffary to fleep in the boy's rooms. The family is fupplied with vegetables from a large garden on the premifes, and the care of it committed to a man in the ftation of gardener, and his affiftants.

N. B.

N. B. Admitting into the family such as are not in profession with friends, is guarded against.

SECT. VI.

Inconveniencies have been found by recommending persons with too partial an eye to their private interest, and obtaining for them a comfortable asylum; so that some who were not objectionable in their own spheres, and within the compass of their own abilities, have obstructed the right order of the institution, and have necessarily become objects of disapprobation; being defective in those faculties which were peculiarly requisite for the stations to which they were introduced: whereas some others, from a secret apprehension of duty, and an upright desire for the good of the institution, have, under discouragements and much diffidence, before their qualifications were ripened to publick view, been put into offices; and yet these have in due time, been wonderfully opened in religious and civil usefulness, and have become as pillars in the support of right government in the family. It has been found expedient, from which great advantages have arisen to the family, that friends who travel in truth's service, and those that come disinterestedly on the business of the institution, should be freely accommodated in the house; any expense occasioned thereby, being more than compensated by their religious concern and endeavours for the prosperity of the whole houshold. Nevertheless, inconveniencies and unnecessary expense have evidently arisen by the children's connections, and those thofe who only come from curiofity, having free accefs to the accommodations provided by the inftitution; and therefore an inn has been opened in the neighbourhood, * where people may be agreeably entertained, and enjoy, as if they were in the houfe, every privilege of feeing the children, obferving the order of the family, and attending religious opportunities. As a library of fuitable books is provided by the inftitution for the children's ufe, and as others of a very different tendency have unwifely been fent by their connexions, it has been found expedient to forbid the introduction of any publications but what firft undergo the teacher's infpection.

Divers advantages have arifen by the fchool's not being limited to the children of friends in ftraitened circumftances; as thofe who had their outward affairs in good order, might be expected fo to have extended their care to their offspring, as that their example among the more ignorant and lefs guarded youth, might promote folidity and good order in the family: and in cafes where that care had not been fufficiently extended, the good of fuch children, not lefs than others, appears to be the object of the fociety's concern: and as their parents were not prevented from contributing to the fupport of the inftitution, fo as amply to allow for the additional expenfe above the ftated fum, and even to exceed it if they thought proper, no reafonable objection could arife on that account.

By

* As the premifes belong to the inftitution, the committee has fome control on the tenant.

By this means the houfe was more eafily fupported, and that diftinction in the fpirit of the world, which is the bane of religious fociety, was in fome degree removed. Thus children intended to fill different ftations in life, being fet upon an equality, with which nothing interfered but their merit or demerit, has proved a great encouragement to friends in low circumftances to fend their offspring, when they found there was no defign publickly to mark them as objects of charity; which, no doubt, from diffidence in fome, and an unwillingnefs to be denominated *poor* in others, would have been generally fo difagreeable, as that the number of three hundred children could fcarcely have been found, whofe parents would have fubmitted to receive a national benefit, if thereto the badge of poverty had been affixed. As the poor in civil, much more in religious fociety, are entitled to neceffary and comfortable accommodations, and thofe who are in eafy circumftances, upon the principle of loving our neighbours as ourfelves, have not a right to more, fuch an education as is fuited to the one, may not be inconfiftent with the other, if inftead of training them for children of this world, the cultivation of their minds, as followers of Chrift, be the principal object in view. A friend may, for procuring the neceffaries of life, be in eafy circumftances, fupport an honourable appearance among men, and a generous hofpitality towards his friends, being of thofe who rather defire to give than receive; and yet, if out of a large family, he wifhes to fend three or four to fchool, and thinks it his duty to provide the moft guarded ed education, it may be quite inconſiſtent with his abilities, and the education he wiſhes them to have, to place them in a more expenſive ſituation than what, upon an average, they coſt the inſtitution at Ackworth: to prevent ſuch a friend from the benefit of ſo generous a deſign, is incompatible with the avowed concern of the ſociety for the welfare of its youth. Our judgment of one another's circumſtances in life is often erroneous, and it hath ſorrowfully appeared, that many have been ſtrangers to their own; and ſome who might be unkindly judged for ſending their children to Ackworth ſchool, becauſe of the appearance of affluence, which they unwiſely ſupported for a time, have proved unable even to bear the expenſe of keeping them there without the aſſiſtance of their friends. There have been objections in the minds of ſome friends to an open door for *all* children whoſe parents approved the plan of education, from a ſuppoſition that the houſe would be crowded with ſuch as might be otherwiſe as well provided for, and that the poor would be excluded the benefit and preference they ought to receive from ſuch an inſtitution; and alſo, that the annual ſubſcriptions expected from all the monthly meetings in the nation, would be too much appropriated to the uſe of thoſe who might afford to pay for their children elſewhere; from whence, diſcouragements being thrown out to friends in eaſy circumſtances ſending their children, the ſchool has much fewer candidates, and the deſign of it not ſo fully anſwered. Theſe objections would be removed, if friends were more liberal and unconfined in their views, as to numbers

bers or stations in life, and were so far from excluding, either the rich or the poor, as to be concerned for, and feel after the propriety of extending their accommodations, and diffusing their endeavours for the admission of all who offered, and by opening a door for those of ability to pay sufficiently for their children, they might also provide a means for the relief of such as require the help of others in bearing their burdens, remembering that, " the liberal deviseth liberal things, and by liberal things shall they stand."

Upon the whole, it is evident that all children ought to be considered as proper objects of such an institution; for, in general, even the situation of the rich, as to their prosperity in the truth, is as much to be compassionated as the poor; being often educated with ideas and impressions more repugnant to gospel simplicity, and less inured to the self-denial of a christian, than the offspring of some who labour under difficulties in temporal things. When parents are wise enough to feel disposed to place their children in a situation, so favourable for the growth of virtue, and so opposing the ambitious views, and presumptuous endeavours after self-exaltation, it would be greatly to be lamented, if such were excluded from a seminary, which under the peculiar care of the society, is better inspected, regulated, and furnished with religious officers, than private schools can often experience. And as, by this institution, a religious education and improvement in useful knowledge, is offered to the acceptance of friends for their children, upon moderate terms, and a place large enough for the prefent prepared, there is no doubt but that by an indifcriminate mixture of children belonging to our fociety, divers advantages to their future fteppings in life may arife.

There is in one quarterly meeting, a fund for the affiftance of thofe, whofe parents and monthly meetings may be unequal to bear the expenfes of their children's education, &c. This fund has been extenfively beneficial; the intereft is appropriated to pay one half the eight Guineas for each object; and the reft left to be raifed either by the children's connections, or their monthly meetings.

For the further information of thofe who may be, in fome meafure, ftrangers to this inftitution, a ftate of the accounts refpecting the fame for the year 1791 is fubjoined.

A Report of the State of Ackworth School, the 31ſt of the 12th Month, 1791.

An Inventory of the Eſtate and Effects belonging to, and of Debts owing by, this Inſtitution, the 1ſt of the 1ſt Month, 1792.

A Report of the State of ACKWORTH SCHOOL, the 31ſt of the 12th Month, 1791. The Income and Expenditure this Year have been as under, viz.

INCOME.   £.   s. d.
Donations and Legacies, as per Liſt   -   392   7   0
Annuitants deceaſed   -   -   -   -   -   250   0   0
Annual Subſcriptions, as per Liſt   -   -   871   6 10
Bills of Admiſſion; 287 with Children ⎱
  educated, at 8l. 8s. per Annum   -   ⎰   2410 16   0
Ditto, Over-time, 66 Weeks, at 5s. per ⎱
  Week   -   -   -   -   -   -   -   ⎰   16 10   0
Intereſt of 3 and 4 per Cent. Annuities   -   226   0   0
John Fothergill's Annuity, 1 year's dividend   50   0   0
Rent of New Inn, and Land, 1 Year 24l. ⎫
Ditto, of a Cottage and 5 Acres of   ⎬   35   0   0
  Land, 1 Year   -   -   -   -   11l. ⎭
Balance of Farm Account   -   -   -   -   356 16 11½
Total Income this Year   -   -   -   - 4608 16   9¼
Total expended this Year   -   -   -   - 3971   4   2¼
Increaſe in Favour of the Inſtitution   -   637 12   7
Balance of Stock the 1ſt of the 1ſt ⎱
  Month, 1791,   -   -   -   -   -   ⎰   8712   5   6¼
Improvements on the Eſtates ſince they
  were purchaſed, eſtimated at 1000 0   0
The following articles reckoned
  in laſt year's Inventory are
  diſcontinued, viz.
Improvements at N. Inn 34 0 4½
Trees in the Garden   40 0 0
Cart-houſe, &c.   -   -   90 0 0
Waſhing Mill   -   -   100 0 0
                          ─────────
                              264   0 4½
                          ─────────
                                   £.735 19 7½
Errors in Bills of
  Admiſſion   -   42   5   0
D° in ſtating the coſt
  Prices of 3 & 4 per
  Cent. Stocks   487 15   0
                  ─────────
                        530   0   0
                  ─────────
                                        205 19   7½
                                        ─────────
Balance of preſent Stock, the 31ſt of ⎱
  12th Month, 1791, as per the fol-   ⎬ 9555 17   9
  lowing Inventory   -   -   -   - ⎭

EXPENDITURE.   £. s. d.

House Expenses; in Provisions, Coals, &c. 1880 0 9¼

Clothing for Children - - - - - - 831 16 7¼

Salaries and Servants Wages - - - - 545 4 10

Interest paid to Annuitants, at 5 per Cent. 212 1 0

Repairs, including the new-making and enlarging of the principal drain from the building - - - - - -   124 14 6½

Conveyance of Children at 2d. per Mile, exceeding 50 Miles - - - -   130 10 8

Stationary - - - - - - - - 60 19 4½

Furniture, Bedding, Linen, &c. for Wear and Tear - - - - -   100 12 11½

Apothecary Account; Salary, Drugs, &c. 42 4 4

Contingencies - - - - - - - 17 17 5¾

Garden - - - - - - - - 25 1 8

Total expended this Year - - - - 3971 4 2½

An INVENTORY of the ESTATE and EFFECTS belonging to, and of DEBTS owing by, this INSTITUTION, the 1ſt of the 1ſt Month, 1792.

BELONGING TO THE INSTITUTION. £. s. d.

	£	s	d
The Eſtates at Ackworth, coſt	8952	11	0
* Improvements on ſaid Eſtates	1000	0	0
New Office for the Secretary, built this Year, coſt	83	18	10
Conſolid. 4 per Cent. Annuities 5500l. coſt	4328	15	0
Three Months Intereſt due thereon	55	0	0
Conſolid. 3 per Cent. Annuities 200l. coſt	143	5	0
Six Months Intereſt due thereon	3	0	0
John Fothergill's Ann. ¼ year's Intereſt due	25	0	0
New Inn and Land, half Year's Rent due	12	0	0
Cottage and 5 Acres of Land, 3 Quarters due	8	5	0
Furniture; Linen, Bedding, &c. on hand	1673	4	8
Farm; Cattle, Hay, Oats, &c. ditto	678	19	0
Houſe Expenſes; Proviſions, Coals, &c. ditto	473	9	9½
Clothing for Children, ditto	312	13	7
Stationary; Books, Paper, Quills, &c. ditto	151	15	4
Contingencies; Money lent on leaving School, to be returned	5	16	0
Ditto due for 45 Children who have had the Small Pox	47	5	0
Garden; Dial, Utenſils, &c. therein	16	12	9
Bills of Admiſſion; due for 4¼, and Forty-Seven Weeks	51	13	0
Drugs, Medicines, &c. on Hand	45	17	11
Materials for Repairs, ditto	24	15	8
Balance in the Treaſurer's Hands	107	14	8½
	18201	12	3¼

* The Money expended under the Head repairs, (which includes Improvements ſince the Eſtate was purchaſed) in the courſe of more than twelve Years, amounts to near Four Thouſand Pounds.

OWING BY THE INSTITUTION.	£.	s.	d.
Annuities at 5 per Cent. on the Life of a Subscriber and Nominee	4150	0	0
American Committee, due to them	2679	16	10¼
Childrens Account, due to 299 now in the House, being for Time unexpired	1357	6	0
Barclays and Tritton, due to them when outstanding Drafts are paid	429	3	8
Bills of Admission, for 3¼ for 1792	29	8	0
Balance of Stock in favour of the Institution, the 1st of the 1st Month, 1792	9555	17	9
	18201	12	3¼

AN

ACCOUNT

OF

YORK SCHOOL.

The following account of an inſtitution at York, written by Sarah Grubb, was alſo found among her papers; and as ſhe was one of its ſupporters, and it appears to be connected with the preceding ſubject, it is judged proper to introduce it in this place.

AS the ſchool at Ackworth did not receive children but within certain limitations as to age, &c. ſomething further, by way of appendix, was found neceſſary; viz. a ſchool ſomewhat ſimilar to Ackworth, which could receive girls of any age or deſcription, whoſe parents or guardians inclined to ſubmit them to the rules of the houſe; where a ſteady religious care might be exerciſed, uninfluenced by any pecuniary conſiderations, and inſtructions afforded in uſeful learning and houſewifery.

One

One friend having felt her mind under a folid concern for the eftablifhment of fomething of this kind, imparted it to divers others, as truth opened the way; and they finding a concurrent engagement, were willing to unite a little property and attention, for the opening and carrying of it forward; in expectation that others would be concerned to fucceed them, for its future continuance and fupport.

As an overfight fuperior to what might be expected from fuch as fhould be placed in the ftation of miftrefles, appeared to be proper, one friend, (her hufband uniting therein) offered herfelf to the fervice; and feveral religious young women of improving abilities, were engaged to ftep in, for a time, as teachers, &c. without expectation of any pay or reward, fave that peace which is the eonfequence of difinterefted faithful labour.

A fum was accordingly raifed, a fuitable houfe provided to accommodate about thirty girls, and furnifhed in a plain, ufeful manner, at the expenfe of the proprietors; except the parlour and a lodging room, which the fuperintendents were intended more particularly to occupy, and which are furnifhed at their own expenfe.

They alfo pay to the inftitution an ample fufficiency for their own living in the family.

Simplicity of manners, and a religious improvement of the minds of youth, were the principal objects in view of the friends who eftablifhed this fchool; and therefore, whatever has a tendency to obftruct this work, is cautioned againft, and fuch
apparel

apparel as the children bring with them, if deemed inconfiftent with the plainnefs which truth leads into, is not allowed during their refidence here; nor fuch literary publications as unprofitably elate the mind, and give a difrelifh for the purity of gofpel truths; but a knowledge of ufeful hiftory and geography, as additional branches of learning to thofe of reading, writing, arithmetick, and the Englifh grammar, are by no means difapproved. And whilft a careful attention is paid to the improvement of the children in neceffary needle-work and knitting, all that is thought merely ornamental, is uniformly difcouraged.

The girls make their own beds, fweep their own rooms, and take it in turns, by couples for a week, to wait at the fuperintendent's and girls tables; and fuch as are fet apart for that fervice, are fubject to be called upon in extraordinary cafes, to affift in preparing victuals, and other neceffary employments in the family.

N. B. Each girl pays at entrance fourteen guineas for learning, board and wafhing.

SOME

REMARKS

ON

CHRISTIAN DISCIPLINE,

AS IT RESPECTS THE

EDUCATION OF YOUTH.

THE Author of the Christian religion came to redeem and save from that spirit which opposed the coming of his kingdom. He has wonderfully displayed the efficacy of that good, by which evil is overcome, proving through the whole of his dispensations a coincidence of mercy with justice. And the operation of this benign principle appears to be in no case more necessary and profitable, than in the true support and discharge of the duties which we owe to those who are placed under our superintendence and care.

As

As there are difpofitions manifeft in children, after the knowledge of good and evil is contracted, which degrade the mind from that innocency wherein they were firft created, and which like an evil tree (if fuffered to grow,) will produce unwholefome fruit; fo there is alfo in the power of thofe who have rightly the care of them, a means which may, by the concurring operations of truth, be rendered effectual to the reduction thereof: and as both the diforder and the remedy lie deep in the heart, they muft be fought for there, without the love of fuperiority, a carnal judgment of good and evil, or the influence of felf-will.

To bring children to a true and profitable fenfe of their own ftates, and direct them to the fpiritual warfare in themfelves, is the main end of all religious labour on their account; and herein a fingle eye ought to be kept to the witnefs of truth in their minds, for that muft be vifited and raifed, before they can fo fee, as to repent and convert from evil. When this is the principal object in the view of thofe, who confider themfelves as delegated fhepherds, accountable for the prefervation of their flock, they are religioufly engaged to promote it by fuch means as are put into their power, under the influence of a chriftian fpirit; which preferves from a defire of occafioning fuffering, or more of it than is abfolutely neceffary for the obtaining of that end, gives patience to perfevere in labour without fainting, ftrength to bear and forbear in their waitings for the fpringing up of the good feed, and opens an eye of faith to look for, and depend only upon, the bleffing on their endeavours.

deavours. Hereby the conduct of such is deeply instructive to children; and may seal upon their minds the pious concern of their preceptors, and affectionately endear them in a friendship lastingly profitable, when they prove, through the influence of divine love upon their own understandings, the justice, mercy, and nobility of that christian discipline which has been exercised towards them, and whereby they have obtained sweet communion with, and an opening to, the fountain of good in themselves.

If in our passage through life, we are often brought to acknowledge that of ourselves, without divine assistance, we can do nothing, is it not abundantly obvious in the work of bestowing a religious education on youth? and should any wisdom preside over that " which cometh down from above, and is first pure, then peaceable, gentle, and easy to be intreated, full of mercy, and full of good fruits, without partiality, and without hypocrisy?" It is lamentable to see how people in general, and even some who seek the sense of truth on other occasions, seem to consider themselves, at any time, or in any disposition, qualified to instruct and correct children, without perceiving that their own wills require to be first subdued, before they can acceptably be instrumental in subduing the will of others. Though acts of indiscretion, or severities, may have a tendency to humble those who receive them (through whose sincerity all things work together for good, even as persecution has been blessed to thousands) yet the instruments are by no means acquitted thereby, their

conduct

conduct not being the produce of that faith, which worketh by love, to the purifying of the heart. It is not to be expected but that there is referved for fuch, a proportionate degree of fuffering, to that which, in their own wills, they have occafioned to others: though, by their natural underftanding only, their perception of divine recompenfe may not be clear enough to diftinguifh it, yet a righteous retribution, or receiving that meafure themfelves which they have meted to others, may await them.

" Provoke not your children to wrath," faid the apoftle. A conduct may be exercifed towards youth, which being under the influence of the paffions, has a natural tendency to raife a fimilar return. To punifh a child becaufe it has offended us, without the difcovery of an evil defign, is to act under an unchriftian fpirit, which revenges injuries. This is a difpofition which is apt to receive its gratifications from a flattering, cringing fpirit, and from fuch marks of refpect as originate in an impure fpring of action; and hence, teachers of children may, from a fuperficial judgment, approve and ftrengthen the little pharifees under their care; whilft the pure life that is ftruggling in the hearts of fome who refemble the publican, is crufhed and difregarded. Many and deep are the forrows of the childhood of fome, which proceed from different caufes: and doubtlefs that incapacity wherein they are placed for obtaining redrefs from real grievances, and the abufe of power being ftrengthened in thofe from whom they receive them, may be numbered among thefe affecting occafions.

casions. Many children, even in our society, have a loose unguarded education, and grow up as degenerate plants of a strange vine, having very little care exercised towards them, except to indulge their unruly appetites, and passionate desires: these require the yoke to be laid upon them with caution and true judgment, left more should be commanded than they possess abilities to perform, and so their deficiency be unjustly laid to their charge: yet the cultivation of their minds should be steadily pursued, under that holy assistance without which we can do nothing acceptably. Past experience does not appear to be a sufficient qualification for this, any more than for other religious services, even where it has been right, and much less so when it has not been strictly under the influence of that wisdom, which is pure and without partiality.

Wisdom and strength must be waited for, day by day, for the right performance of our duties, before Him who weighs our actions in the balance of pure justice, and only approves those which are wrought in the spirit. To educate children religiously, requires a quietude of mind, and sympathy in their guardians, with the state of the good seed in them, which will lead rightly to discriminate between good and evil; to discover the corrupt source of many seeming good actions; and to perceive that a real innocency is the root of others, which custom, and a superficial investigation, have rendered reprehensible. Here we see the necessity of true wisdom being renewed, and the insufficiency of that which is carnal, and boasts its own experience and strength. It is the humbled mind

mind to which is unfolded such mysteries of true godliness, for its own edification, and that of those under its care, as could not have been received in the support of a false consequence, and the love of superiority. If children are to be instructed in the ground work of true religion, ought they not to discover in those placed over them, a lively example thereof? or ought they to see any thing in the conduct of others, which would be condemnable in them, were they in similar circumstances? Of what importance then is it for guardians of children, to rule their own spirits; for when their tempers are irritable, their language impetuous, their voices excrted above what is necessary, their threatenings unguarded, or the execution of them rash, however children may for a time suffer under these things, they are not instructed thereby in the ground work of true religion; nor will the witness of truth, as their judgments mature, approve a conduct like this; though through the bias of self-will, it may be adopted in similar cafes, in a succeeding generation, by those who, instead of having gathered good seed, have, from the mixture of their education, preferred the bad, which meeting with a soil suitable to its nature, grows and becomes fruitful, to the corrupting of many more.

The love of power is so deeply implanted in the natural mind, that without we discover it, and its evil tendency, in the true light, we are not likely to consider it as an enemy of our own house, against which we are called to war with as much righteous zeal, as against the evil in others; yea
with

with more, because it is declared such are our greatest foes. Where this corrupt part is cherished it stains our actions; and having gained the ascendency over the pure, lowly seed, bribes and influences the judgment respecting good and evil, and establishes the mind in a self complacence, which, however productive of reproof, has seldom an ear open to that instruction by which itself stands condemned. The prodigal display and use of power is the very destruction of christian discipline. Power is necessary; not to be assumed in the will of the creature, but to stand subservient to the judgment of truth, under which it ought to be exerted; lying in ambush as a waiting, assisting force, ready to be called in cases of difficulty; when, if it step forth in true dignity, the appearance, rather than the use of it, may generally prove sufficient, and its wise retreat render it still more useful and reverenced. True love, clearness of judgment, and the meekness of wisdom, are the supporters of true dignity; and where these prevail in a mind under divine government and control, they give authority, firmness, and benevolence, in thought, word, and deed; which have a profitable and comfortable effect upon those who are placed under their influence, and open a door for undisguised familiarity, and affectionate intercourse, wherein children receive instruction more suitably and cordially, than under the arbitrary sway of a continually assumed power. Should we lay hold of christian discipline in all its branches, and return with it to its root, either among children or in the church, we shall always find it originates in a christian spirit, and that

that every plaufible appearance which is defective in this ground, is fo far no better than founding brafs, or a tinkling cymbal.

The right education of children, efpecially in boarding-fchools, is no doubt a clofe and arduous work; thofe, however, who are rightly engaged therein, and endeavour after their own refinement, and an increafing acquaintance with the Fountain of Purity in themfelves, need not have their eye outward for the eftablifhment of power and authority; for He who feeds the ravens and clothes the lilies, knows what they ftand in need of, and is able, out of his own treafury, to fupply all their wants; to be " mouth and wifdom, tongue and utterance;" and will not fail to help under their greateft difficulties, if they fupport a patient dependence upon Him alone, and profitably live under the perfuafion, that when He fhuts, no one fhould attempt to open, and when he opens, none can fhut.

EXTRACTS

EXTRACTS

FROM

LETTERS

WRITTEN BY

SARAH GRUBB.

SHEFFIELD 5th month 1772*—I cannot but wish to spend a few weeks with thee, either here or at York; but as I am sensible it is not good for any of us to have our inclinations gratified at all times, I am desirous to be easy, and resigned to every thing that may cross my natural propensities; that so, when affliction and probation may present themselves, which certainly will attend our pilgrimage through this uncertain stage of life, I may be the more strengthened to undergo these trying seasons with patience and fortitude. But I may conclude with the words which thou hast repeated before; " to will, is present with me, but to do, I know not:" for though this fortitude and resignation are things much to be desired, yet to be entirely given up to the will and disposal of a kind providence, is no easy attainment. Thou
mentioned

* In the 16th year of her age.

mentioned the difference of our fituations; and it would be ungrateful if I did not confider, and look upon my privileges, as favours from indulgent heaven, if I make a proper ufe of them. But it is the ftate of the mind that limits our happinefs; and alas! it is the want of a fufficient care in the cultivation of my mind, that is a means of obftructing that peace which it would be fweet to enjoy.

YORK, 7th month 1773—I often think our troubles are much augmented, by looking on thofe who are in a more advantageous ftation, according to our opinion; when, if we could but content ourfelves with putting their many mortifications, to balance the adverfe conditions of fome on whom external circumftances feem never to have fmiled, and whofe life has been a feries of afflidtion, it would amply compenfate for the labour. Due confideration would make our forrows appear greatly fhort of what providence might have allotted for us, and would frequently prove them to be the refult of paffion, or imaginary ills.

YORK, 4th month 1774—Thy Letter was falutary and grateful, arriving when my mind was anxioufly concerned on many accounts. The care of fo large a family, thou wilt readily own, muft engrofs a large fhare of my attention; it is a tafk to which I often think myfelf unequal, efpecially among children; but that I am willing to make the beft of, if I may but be enabled fo to condudt, as to give no real caufe of offence, nor to example in any thing that is contrary to the fimplicity of truth. Under thefe confiderations,

tions, I fee my own infufficiency, and how unable I am to act the part of an elder fifter, without a daily fupport from the Fountain of every good. What fhould we do, were there nothing to fly to but the inftruments, the publifhers of the gofpel? what aid can they lend us? what ftrength in weaknefs, in comparifon of that inward ftay, which, if enough looked unto, would be the ftaff of our lives! And with this gracious privilege, how mournful is it to confider the preference that is given to the foibles of this tranfitory life, before that true peace which flows from the Divine monitor, the teacher within!

York, 8th month 1775—And now permit me to tell thee how welcome a part of thine was; it led me, when I read it, to conclude, that after looking on all the frailties of human nature, and perplexing ourfelves with a view of the various and intricate fcenes of this life, the neceffary refult fhould be, " to be quiet, and mind our own bufinefs ;" or, as thou fayeft, to endeavour to feel ourfelves approved by Him who fees not as man fees. If we make welcome every obftacle that is prefented in the way to peace, we may juftly conclude that we fhall never arrive at the peaceful Jerufalem, the quiet habitation which cometh down from God out of heaven. The confideration of this enjoyment, fometimes prompts the mind to foar, or to afcend gradually to the holy mountain, where we may be taught the ways of righteoufnefs, and be inftructed in the paths of true peace: but how faft we defcend to the place from whence

we

we came! how precipitately do we drop into fome region of darknefs! for furely there are many degrees; but happy are they who are redeemed from its power. May we not juftly deem ourfelves, when under any entanglement, any fetter that prevents our deeds being brought to the true light, the light of the Lamb, as alienated, in part, from the Father of mercies, and eftranged from His celeftial fpring! how neceffary therefore is it for us to watch at all feafons, in times of peace, as well as in the fpiritual warfare; for we know not when the hour of temptation cometh, and our fortification may prevent the engagement. How preferving is that language; " I will get me to my watch tower;" and what a favour it is, our not being ignorant, that the name of the Lord is a tower to the righteous.

10th month 1777—I expect this will find thee at ———, where I wifh thy vifit to be attended with more folid fatisfaction than thou looked for; if not, it may be no lefs profitable. My very fmall experience has taught me, that endeavouring to keep near to the Fountain of life, in company where its arifings are evidently fuppreffed, often tends more to our real growth in the root of true religion, than the eafy enjoyment of valuable friends company, with whom we are not driven to our refuge.

12th month 1777—I doubt not but thou haft thought, with myfelf, the conduct of the generality of young men to be painful; for what numbers do we fee of thefe, who, prompted by the

irregularity

irregularity of youthful fervour, fuffer their minds to be entangled with every fluttering object of vanity; little confidering that they are expofing themfelves to innumerable forrows, and inconfiderately and rapidly purfuing an Ignis-fatuus, which will lead them into a labyrinth of perplexities. Oh! could they, inftead of this, centre and retire to that reverent fear in themfelves, which would prove a fountain of life, preferving from the fnares of death, there is no reafon to doubt that the inexhauftible Fountain, would not only turn their feet into the path of peace, but fo far eftablifh their goings therein, that every important concern of their lives would be favoured with divine direction; and in that very momentous one of marriage, the language of truth would be fo intelligible as to direct them to the right object; and then, with what holy confidence might they propofe thefe connections, while our fex, with an humble awful diffidence, wait alfo for counfel from on high, and to feel the fame affurance of divine approbation : thus all would be confummated to the praife of Him whofe favour they had fought and implored. Much do I wifh that my heart may ever be favoured to poffefs a degree of this primitive purity, though no matrimonial confiderations require it; the faying of the Apoftle often occurs to my mind; " that godlinefs is profitable unto all things."

7th month 1778—We are now again left with the care of a family that requires fome attention and circumfpection. I never felt more unfit for the tafk, nor more ready to query, who is equal to it, and to conclude, furely not I. A difcreet conduct, an affectionate behaviour, attempered with juft fo much fteady authority as to excite refpect united to an unavoidable love, and thefe not to fluctuate with the fituation of the mind, is an attainment which I fear will never be mine, and which indeed will be unneceffary in a very few years with refpect to my fifters; but yet it does appear, at leaft in my eyes, abfolutely requifite for thofe on whom the education of children devolves. Where people are thus qualified, and difcharge their duty, they will find a pleafure with the important charge; " for in it there is a happinefs as well as care." There is certainly fomething in the affectionate part of us, which tends rather to defeat, than promote the growth of true religion, except it be fanctified under the operation of the divine hand; when that is happily experienced, fome of the natural propenfities become bleffings, and very laudably heighten the enjoyment of fpiritual ones.

11th month 1778—Thou haft, I doubt not, already heard of the unfettled ftate we have lately been in, occafioned by a forrowful and affecting event, the death of our dear friend ———. She feemed but juft arrived at the fummit of earthly happinefs, and to have conferred the fame enjoyment upon her beloved partner; yet alas! how tranfient was the duration of this ftate; and indeed, how unfit is it for minds who are too apt to rejoice in profperity without trembling, and whofe affections are centred only in focial comforts! We cannot but conclude that, by thefe
inftructive

inftructive leffons of mortality, the divine intention is to refine and purify, and to fhew all who behold them the neceffity, the great neceffity, of having our minds centred where fluctuating things can never come. This was, beyond a doubt, the happy fituation that her mind was in fometime before her departure; for about a week before her death, fhe told her hufband, " that her mind was fteadily fixed upon the joys to come;" and added, " I am fenfible I fhall not recover; and I have now been where they were finging Hallelujah's to the Higheft, and it was pleafant in my ears. I have feen the beautiful fituation of the inhabitants of the new Jerufalem:" with many fimilar expreffions, which I have hardly either leifure or room to infert; but the foregoing will give thee an idea of the comfortable ftate her mind was in, which fhe appeared to preferve to the laft.

The two following pieces of religious poetry appear to have been compofed, the firft, in the year 1778, foon after her return from a vifit to fome of her friends, and the latter, fome confiderable time afterwards; and as they are folemn and inftructive lines, and defcribe the pious and exercifed frame of her fpirit, they claim a place in this collection. Though fhe poffeffed a confiderable talent for this fort of compofition, yet fhe cultivated it but little, and very rarely indulged herfelf therein; this may have proceeded from an apprehenfion, that it too often tends to draw out, and habituate the mind to a difplay of unfelt fentiments; a too high colouring, if not a falfe
reprefentation,

representation, of things; and a decoration of language inconsistent with the simplicity of truth. It is, indeed, a talent which, in its exercise, requires very great circumspection; and, in the reading to which it leads, a religious guard and limitation.

 Though clothed now with ease, tho' the pure stream
Of social converse and congenial love
Now offers me its balm, yet doth my soul,
In retrospect, far other scenes survey,
Far other sources for energic pow'rs.
How can my pen pourtray the deep distress,
How paint the anguish of a heart that bled,
Or how describe the current as it flow'd
From sorrow's briny deeps! It fails; and lost
In recollection's maze, the mind that felt,
Can only now explore the ambient main,
Which, with impet'ous haste, my little bark
O'erflow'd, and seem'd to sink it in th' abyss.
But say, why sunk it not? by what kind hand
Was it sustain'd? or why was it not driv'n
Against that rock, on which so many split,
And pour their mournful accents to the waves?
'Twas not thyself that did support; 'twas not
Thy strength bore up: thou canst not thus convert
Th' o'erwhelming surge of mourning into joy.
Then who? that great I AM, that Majesty
Who made the bush his temple, and whose flames
Consum'd it not; who breaketh by his word,
And with consolatory bands binds up;
Did he not condescend to intervene?

Did he not fay ? " be ftill, it is enough,"
Yea, with compaffionate regard, pour'd in
The wine and oil. Forget it not, my foul !
Nor feek a greater joy : yet patient be
In fuffering ; in feafons of diftrefs,
When nature pours her bitters in thy heart,
When heav'n feems brafs, and earth with iron bars
Doth hold its cheering goodlinefs from thee ;
Then with a calm refigned mind give up,
Freely furrender all thou calleft thine ;
No longer reft on Jordan's banks, but with
Stability ftep in, and learn to know
That ftones there are which for memorials ferve ;
Then bring them up from thence, as proofs where
    thou
Haft been, and therewith raife thine Ebenezer.
But ah ! how thoughtlefs in this profp'rous ftate,
Which now I view, but not with equal eye ;
Yet humbled in the duft, implore thy aid,
Thy care, thou benefactor kind ! or how
Can I, amidft each fmiling fcene, felect
And cull the chiefeft and the beft of all
That's offered ? How render thee thy due
For benefits, " thy mercy and thy truth ?
Through ev'ry difpenfation of thy love,
Through ev'ry min'ftration of thy judgments,
Grant, ah ! grant, a felf-abafed fpirit ;
That fo, thy great fupreme commands, thy will
May be obey'd, and mine as clay be form'd.

And ye, my friends ! who lately were and are
The fweet endear'd companions of my life,
Ah ! may we long each others bleffings fhare ;
Soften each forrow, intermix each joy,

With unity of spirit soar above
These transitory things, and as we rise,
Together drink the well refined wine;
And in that pure and purifying stream,
Which from the throne of the most High proceeds,
Witness our minds repeatedly baptiz'd.

My soul ascends in humble flight
　Above these transient woes,
And fill'd with songs as in the night,
　She to the mountain goes

With harp and pipe, to celebrate
　The praise of Zion's King,
And with a weaned mind prostrate,
　An humble off'ring bring.

Prepare the off'ring, sacred flame,
　And consecrate my ground,
That, by the virtue of thy name,
　Acceptance may be found.

Thy gracious majesty that deigns
　The contrite soul to hear,
Thy wisdom that forever reigns,
　Bid humbled minds draw near.

Shall I repine then to present
　The off'ring of my will,
Shall I ungratefully consent
　Th' immortal birth to kill?

Forbid it Lord! and aid my foul
　The conflicts to endure,
Which, thro' thy merciful control,
　Make all things new and pure.

O grant thy all-fuftaining arm
　My drooping mind to bear,
And with thy confolations warm
　Preferve me from defpair.

Thou know'ft the tribulated path,
　Which leads from death to life,
Thou know'ft the baneful dragon's wrath,
　His enmity and ftrife.

Thy light and truth, moft gracious God,
　Withhold not from my foul;
Nor yet thy wife chaftifing rod,
　Nor David's wafhing pool.

In faith and patience, centre deep
　The my'fteries thou reveals;
And, with an everlafting fleep,
　And thy immortal feals,

Envelope each unworthy view;
　That fanctified aright,
Thy glorious caufe I may purfue,
　And witnefs to the light.

Thus thro' the few fucceeding fteps
　Appointed me to run,
Thy honour may be all in all,
　Thy praife alone be fung.

1st month 1779—The re-establishment of our own, or our friends health, from the verge of that eternity to which we are hastening, ought to excite deep gratitude of mind, and lead to a still greater degree of obedience and preparation for the final call. The seasons which I passed, and the meditations with which my mind was supported, when watching over my departing friends, are, I think I may say, continually before me. How low and how grovelling appeared every mundane thing! How insignificant the most desirable connections in life, when compared with that certain portion of happiness, that unbounded sphere of felicity, which is reserved for the pure in heart! even the strong ties of friendship and love were subservient to these feelings; insomuch that I have queried, when reflecting how these fetters to our dissolution were removed, whilst those important prospects were before me, "what ailed thee, oh thou sea, that thou fleddest, thou Jordan, that thou wast driven back, ye mountains, that ye skipped like rams, and ye little hills, like lambs!" But alas! this lasted not long; for when the solemn, awful messenger had proclaimed liberty to a captive spirit, and translated it to where mine could not ascend, then arose every natural emotion, and instructed me, that in a continual warfare consisted my peace. But what can I now say? for on these things, as on the manna that was gathered yesterday, am I too apt to live, without enough seeking the fresh descendings of celestial food, and patiently submitting to that creative power, which would form us into the state of a little child. The aptitude of my disposition to rise above the humbling principle of truth, and form

form to myself a likeness which may be compared to a marble statue, or an image of substantial good, often leads my mind into deep lamentation and mourning; with a painful fear, that I shall never be intitled to the handing forth of the royal scepter, the mark of divine approbation; but to that sentence of *depart*, and being set as on the left hand: yet when we survey these fleeting moments, or rather look over them to the endless ages that ensue, we cannot but conclude, that nothing short of a state of infatuation would lead us to exchange, or even risque our everlasting well-being, for the very best things of this world.

4th month 1779—Alas! how is a large degree of truth, inward excellence, and whatever constitutes true loveliness, removed! how is the beauty fallen! Affecting instance to us her friends; but to that immortal spirit in her which has long, in prospect of a future glorious admission into the celestial regions of light, been willing to descend into the deeps, and there behold the marvellous works of Him whom she served, it is a happy lot. Though she suffered much, though sorrow came in the night, in the close of a world wherein she had many troubles, yet joy has, I doubt not, sprung in the morning, in the opening of an endless day. How justly may we rejoice on her account, who was counted worthy of so early an entrance to where the aged can but hope to be, and whose work is done: a circumstance which the impatient mind, I believe, often wishes for. A lamentation for those who knew her worth, and who hoped for a future uniting with her in the covenant of life, and of that wisdom which is from above, may, with unfeigned propriety, be adopted. For my own part, all that was within me, (when I found what thy intelligence was) feemed ftruck with amazement, and was loft for a time in reflection on her great and awful change; but when I recollected myfelf, that fhe was forever removed; and that, through the intricacies of life, I was left to move without her friendly affiftances, and fellow-feeling mind, a deep fenfe of mourning enfued: for from fo fhort, and even from a long intercourfe, I think I never reaped fo much folid benefit with any. And alas! fhort fighted as I was, I imagined it an earneft of fome future fellowfhip in this life; and that through the various trials that attended it, a providential help might be difpenfed us through each other. But now, I find it was the fulnefs allotted us, and that, like Jonah's gourd, it fprung to me in a night, and has withered before the brightnefs of the day; withered in a time wherein my weaknefs leads me too much to lean on fuch helps. But this fhock relaxes the defire, and points to the ftrong tower, the refuge of the righteous, where alone is true fafety; and oh! may we flee thither, for the habitation is quiet and fure. I very much fympathize with you in the prefent trial, the lofs of fo near and valuable a friend. Your attachment I believe was ftrong, and the feparation hard; but how much more profitable, if, inftead of an unavailing forrow, we confider the church's lofs; that one who filled an ufeful fphere is removed, and confequently, that that fhare is left to devolve upon the fhoulders of fome; I fay, if we confider and look fufficiently at this, being willing to ftep, if required, into her path,

path, (which I know was fecretly exercifed, not only for herfelf, but for the profperity of the great and noble caufe,) and thereby redeem the lofs, how acceptable muft that tribute be, in the fight of Him who fees not as man fees; and, if it fpring from a heart devoted to the work rather than the reward, how truly profitable to ourfelves ! The end of the righteous is defirable, in whatever ftage of life it arrives; but for my own part, if I could hope mine would be fuch, I own I cannot help feeling a wifh, that its approach might be in the early or middle part: in what the defire originates, I cannot pretend to fay, but it is, perhaps, in fome unjuftifiable part of felf-love.

6th month 1779—How acceptable was thy account of the latter, and laft end of our beloved friend ! My mind often recurs to it for hope, and for ftrength to perfevere and to obtain; but there appears fo much to conftitute our claim to the peaceful abode, into which the righteous only can enter, that my mind enjoys but a fmall portion of faith to believe it will ever reach its confines; yet I am fometimes led to confider, whether our refearches after happinefs, are not too much actuated by principles of felf-love; and whether it is confiftent with the benevolence which the gofpel inculcates, that in all our concerns, and the exercife of our greateft virtues, we fhould be continually inquiring after the reward: does it not, my friend, (for I really do not know) indicate a littlenefs of mind, and a want of confidence in Him who is, " juft and equal in all his ways ?" for in our works there is no merit to the creature; if we truft not, where is our faith ? if we perfevere not, where is our patience ? and if in this life, we partake of the fulnefs of that joy which is fown for the upright, where is the glorious referve for futurity? Should we not then, if our minds were clothed with the nobility of the fpirit in which we believe, refign all things? and being humble, fuffer all things? and do all things in pure love, exclufive of any felfifh view?

In your county as well as ours, there are a few who have not bowed the knee, nor facrificed to the workmanfhip of men's hands, yet the general depravity does fo often obftruct the current of life, and thereby ftagger the feeble mind, that I believe you often experience, a feeking water and finding none; but fear not, for He in whom is the fulnefs of ftrength, is your refuge.

8th month 1779—Though I am firm in the belief, that if we experience the work of true regeneration, all our attachments muft be tried in a furnace, which the natural underftanding cannot of itfelf comprehend, and that the precious muft be feparated from the vile, by the myfterious operations of the divine hand; yet I do alfo hope, that ours will be permitted to ftand, and that, if we live to furvive the ftrength of that youthful ardour with which our prefent union is heightened, there will be enjoyed a fellowfhip, better and more pure than any we have yet experienced, and againft which, all the fiery darts of the enemy will never be able to prevail. This, and fimilar to this, is, next to the immediate influence of of the divine prefence, what I ftrongly covet to partake of, in this viciffitude and vale of tears; wherein a cup is fometimes handed, which is fo repugnant to our nature, that we cannot help entreating, let it, I pray thee, pafs from me. But oh! that we may be found worthy to enjoy the celeftial bleffings difpenfed to the faithful, by obedience to that power, which in all its workings, tends to crucify felf, and prepare the mind to adopt that refined language of, " not my will, but thine be done." The more a mind poffeffes of that wifdom and nature, which act in oppofition to the true fimplicity of a little child, the greater muft be the exercife; and if it has long refufed the clear manifeftations of duty, it is no wonder if a feafon of painful uncertainty enfues.

9th month 1779—Art thou in health? art thou ftrong in Him who goeth before thee, and who hath promifed that His glory fhall be the rere-ward of the number that deal prudently, and go not by flight? Ifaiah lii. 12, 13. How fafe do the fteps of fuch appear, who have this glory for a light to their feet, and the divinely illuminated lamp to attend their path! It is no wonder that a way fhould often open, where the human underftanding (which is dark and comprehends not the things of the fpirit) can fee no way; and that every neceffary refrefhment fhould be interfperfed therein. I fometimes think it is a favour, that an eye is opened into this path, and that though the advancement in it is fmall, if there be any, yet thus feeing, and preffing forward, we may obtain. I hope thou art treading this fure ground, and

and that thy memorials, which are brought from the bottom of the purifying waters of Jordan, are not hid; or if they be, that it is only for their refinement. But perhaps they are like the fling ſtones which David had ready in his bag, until the appointed time of meeting the defier of Iſrael was come, and are to be alike powerful in prevailing againſt the enemies of the poor, and the afflicted people, which may be ſpared in the day of general calamity. But be this as it may, obedience is ſtill to be attended to, and the prophet's advice remembered, of not ſeeking to ourſelves great things, but to be content with every diſpenſation, whether of want or of plenty. When this ſituation is in any degree attained, how thankful do we feel for even a ſmall appearance of good; for if the divine preſence is no more beheld, than by the putting forth of His hand through the hole of the door, it ſtill ſuſtains and refreſhes, and ſerves as food for many days.

10th month 1779—Poor ——— I feel for her frequently, and have often thought of writing to her; but it has as often occurred, that except the great Shepherd of Iſrael aſſiſt her, whence ſhall another do it? As his voice, his crook, and his protection, are undoubtedly offered, it is ſurely weak to ſuppoſe that the language of the creature can equal the voice of this Charmer; if indeed it do not derogate, (as I am inclined to think it does) from the omnipotence and wiſdom of our holy head: and I ſometimes think, that nothing more proves the deep rooted depravity of the human mind, even when meaſurably illumined with the brightneſs brightnefs and glory of the eternal excellency, than looking at the members for help, and craving it from that often poor, benumbed quarter, when, at the fame time, it might be faid, " you have an unction from the holy one, and you know thefe things."

1ft month 1780—There appears to me, no joy like the joy of the righteous, nor any unity like theirs; and next to the immediate influences of the divine Spirit, it is to me defirable. But obedience being the terms of this great and valuable pof- feffion, what numbers, for want of this, are de- prived of it! Yet he who is infinite in condefcen- fion, and whofe love is unutterable, deigns to re- ward for every little fervice, and grants, at times, a facred view of the myftery of his own church, and his marvellous work therein. My friend is, I doubt not, well inftructed in thefe things, and though I alfo believe it is a time of fuffering like Jacob's, when the fun confumed by day, and the froft by night, yet He who knows our neceffary refinements, is able to limit the waters, that they do not overflow us, and, in his own time, will fay to the operation of the furnace, " it is enough." Until then, I truft deep will " utter unto deep," and with an increafe of fuffering, we fhall ex- perience an increafe of holy fellowfhip.

3d month 1780—My dear friend's letter was too acceptable to lie long unacknowledged ; becaufe it revived in the breaft of her friend all the cordiality of an union and fellow-feeling, which I truft do not originate in the part appointed for deftruction ;

but

but are rather the offspring of minds engaged, (though feebly) to travail on as in great weaknefs and fear, and fometimes having no language to exprefs, either to the Fountain of good, or to one another, but " fighs unutterable." How infinite is the condefcenfion of that precious influence, which helpeth thefe our infirmities, and is touched with a feeling of them; aiding the mind, with a degree of holy confidence, after all its apparent exclufions from the participation of divine good, once more to look towards his holy habitation. And as it is through fufferings that our natures are refined and fanctified, they muft not be of our own choofing, becaufe the fuffering might then, in a great meafure, ceafe, and that neceffary heat which attends the furnace of affliction, and which purifies the mineral, get quenched; for fo depraved are our ideas of things, that I have thought, and in fome meafure felt, that even in our baptifms of fpirit, we would wifh to have a choice; fo active is felf, that it cannot be fatisfied without a fphere to move in. Think not, my beloved friend, that I confider this as a peculiar propenfity of thine: for it rather occurred as a degree of painful experience. I have often viewed your fituation, (and particularly fince the receipt of thine this morning) as almoft too trying for flefh and blood, but He who placeth the members of his church, and appoints them their lots, does not leave their fupports to flow through thefe corrupt fources; but marketh their fteps, and, perhaps quite hiddenly, confirms the feeble knees, and leadeth them in a way they know not. My mind is frequently too much depreffed, and fometimes toffed with tempefts, to

admit

admit a confolatory fentiment, much lefs to offer my friend the language of encouragement; neverthelefs I cannot help expreffing my firm belief, that all your troubles will work together for good, and that the deeper they are, the greater will be the preparation for a glorious reward in the houfe of the one Father, with whom a book of remembrance is written.

4th month 1780—I want to hear how you feel yourfelves at your new habitation, and whether it proves a Gofhen to————, whofe mind has often felt to me to be fecretly clad with fackcloth, even when perhaps obeying the command, " to wafh and to anoint, rather than appear to men as if fafting:" and as this is a fituation neceffary for us, its continuance adminifters no caufe of difcontent, if we have but an evidence that we have not ftepped out of the holy inclofure; finding the fence of divine appointment to be about us, no matter what we fuffer. It is not for our rejoicings, and what feels comfortable to ourfelves, that we can expect a reward; but rather for our trials and probations, if we endure them with patience; and even for thefe we have no reafon to expect a full reward; for if that were the cafe, where would be the referve for the fruition of joy in the life to come? Neverthelefs, we do fometimes get favoured, in our wildernefs journey, with a little bread handed in fecret, and with an opening of the brook by the way; and the remembrance of our partaking of this together, refrefhes and ftrengthens in fome gloomy feafons. I have often reafon to number your friendly regard to me among the bleffings of my my life, and I sometimes think, in the feeling of a nearness I cannot describe, that my affection to you is not less than filial. May I be preserved worthy this fellowship, and, by an increase of purity, find an increase of that union of spirit which lives beyond the grave! I think nothing has more conduced to my confidence in, and fellow-feeling with you, than the belief that your reproof and plain dealing would be as readily administered to me, as your encouragement : and I beseech you, never lose sight of this openness, for I am surely one of the weakest and most frail of the whole flock and family, if I am worthy to be included in the number: and yet if I know my own heart, it is not myself, but the cause which I have in view ; and I wish for still more of that disposition which can enable us to say, " let the righteous smite me, and it shall be a kindness; let him reprove me, and it shall be an excellent oil."

5th month 1780.—How truly valuable is this precious unity which, like the oil that was poured upon the head of Aaron, remains to anoint the very skirts of the garments of those who have obtained the mark of discipleship, to love one another! In the renewal of it, I feel greater consolation than is usually bestowed upon me from causes of this kind, because there are few indeed with whom I find myself nearly united, or whose regard affords me relief in the time of want, although I know them to be far superior to myself; insomuch that I conclude the command is certainly to me, " salute no one by the way." But glad I am that there is an exception to this, and that I hope I can

in

in the right line falute my friend by the way, and vifit him in the wildernefs, where all who are united to the true church muft chiefly dwell, and wait for its redemption: and if this is not found in our time, we have yet reafon to hope, that having partaken in fome meafure of its fufferings, whether principally for ourfelves as members, or for the whole body, this offering will be acceptable to the Searcher of hearts; and, then if in His wifdom fome of our days fhould prove to be few and full of forrow, may we not look towards the morning of a better day, and an inheritance in that country whofe inhabitants never fay, they are fick! Were it not, now and then, for a little of this hope which lives within the vail, I know not how things would be got through; fo felfifh am I that I fear the reward is too much an object, and not that perfect love which cafteth out fear, and is ready to obey and fuffer all things for the work's fake.

9th month 1780—I have felt a more than ufual impulfe to falute thee, my much beloved friend, and, according to my little ability, to ftrengthen thee in repeating the efforts which I truft thou art, at times, concerned to ufe for thy own everlafting welfare, by turning a deaf ear to the fubtil infinuations of the adverfary, who is evidently feeking thy deftruction. I am well convinced that no language I can ufe, except it be bleffed with the efficacy, as well as appearance, of indifputable truth, will ever be acceptable to thee, or prove profitable; and it is, I may truly fay, at this time particularly, the fervent engagement of my mind, that

that thou mayest come to a settlement in that power which is unchangeable, and which would, if thy anxieties and destructive heat of spirit were more damped, instruct thee still further in the mystery of thyself, and that of godliness which is profitable for thee. With what manner of love hath the Father loved thee? hath often in effect been the query and exclamation of my mind, when the wonders of thy deliverance from Egyptian bondage have occurred, with an evidence of the Hand that wrought them, and of that mighty power which hath caused the bush to burn before thee, and convinced thee that the ground whereon thou stood was holy. As sure as ever he was with Israel, and with Moses their leader, he is with thee; and thy trust in him, and seeking for a passive state of mind in that wilderness travel which may be assigned, will, I believe, effect thy arrival at the Land of Promise. But think not, my beloved friend, when there is a want of water, and of that refreshment which the unmortified will is eagerly thirsting after, to use the means whereby the meekness of Moses was overcome, to strike the rock, and thereby offend that holy providential care, which will never have thee to suffer for want of true knowledge, but will be found to provide thee with food in due season; and though it may not always be pleasant, but, at times, may resemble Mara's waters for bitterness, yet the spiritual Canaan being in view, and not expected on this side Jordan, the river of true judgment, it will animate to still greater degrees of virtue, such as patience, fortitude, and strength, in this holy travail. Under a renewed belief that thou art in the place allotted by divine wisdom, I feel an earneft folicitude, that thou mayeft be ftrengthened to difcharge thy duty in every good word and work; and that He who hath plucked thy feet out of much mire and clay, may not only fet thee upon the immovable Rock, and eftablifh thy goings, but, in His own time, put fuch a fong of deliverance into thy mouth, as will laft to all eternity. It is, my dear friend, with a love which I truft is more than natural, that I re-falute thee, and bid thee be of good cheer, and labour to detect every delufion, for truly there is light enough for it.

10th month 1780—Animated with the effufions of much love and near fellowfhip, I have many times fecretly faluted you fince my abrupt departure from ———; where I was thankful to feel, after a long faft from fenfible enjoyments, either religious or focial, that there is yet an union to be attained with the fpirit of pure love, and that we can in a ftate of mutability, in proportion to our faithfulnefs, partake together of its binding influence. A revival of this fenfe, I was and am, I hope grateful for, and glad to find a fimilar fentiment in my companion. I neither received, nor expected any great peace and reward for the offering of paying you a vifit, which was not completely of the free-will fort; but thus much I may fay, that a degree of comfortable ferenity attended my returning mind.——My throwing myfelf in the way of meetings, in which my attendance has not appeared to be in the movings of light, is not, in my idea, without danger : for if we depend, though in ever fo fmall a matter upon a putting forth which

which has not a little clearnefs for its evidence, we may likewife conclude it to be equally fafe to offer our fervice from as doubtful an impulfe; and thus, I am apprehenfive, a clouded ftate may enfue. And having been accuftomed to adopt things through perhaps a willingnefs to do good, which have not borne the royal impreffion, our diftinguifhing feelings may gradually become fo weakened, that the pure unmixed word may get fullied, and the powerful demonftration thereof decreafe. This is a fentiment which I offer by way of apology for myfelf; and yet I would not have my friends to conclude, that I believe great openings are to be looked for, in every little fervice. If the token of rain be ever fo fmall, yet if it be fo fure as to bear the comparifon of the cloud of the fize of a man's hand, I am of opinion, (though not always willing to accept it) that it is as much to be depended upon, as if the clouds were opened, and we felt the fhowers from thence. It is certainty, though ever fo little in appearance, that I wifh to follow.

1ft month 1781—The trials which I believe are in infinite wifdom allotted to the rightly concerned, are many; of which, I truft, we have been favoured to fhare; yet we have no need to make our way harder, by adding fo continually our own judgments, and difcouragements upon them; making comparifons which we have no right to do, and weighing things which can only be tried in the balance of the fanctuary: for we know fo little of things above us, that we are very incompetent judges who ftand moft in divine approbation. I

cannot

cannot but much wish that ——— would grow wifer refpecting thefe things, and endeavour to shut out difcouragements which do not come in the line of wifdom; and then, I am fatisfied, fhe would find her way to be as eafy as fhe thinks mine is, and would be convinced that her labours have been more acceptable to him who put her forth, than fhe will often allow.

1ft month 1781—Does not Solomon fay, that a few words fitly fpoken are like apples of gold in pictures of filver? I think he does; but whether or not, it is fo in the fcripture of my heart, and your lines prove the juftnefs of it. Feeling has no fellow, and if the addrefs be but felt by the receiver in the covenant of true love, it is fomething like fuch a miniftry as I covet, where words are loft in power. Deceitful as I know my own heart to be, I will not allow that my remembrance of you arifes wholly from " an imbibed favourable impreffion in times paft," and that a perfonal abfence revives it. I fhould conclude that to be a formal attachment which hath nothing but age for its origin, and is not fupported with repeated renewals of life. Is this the inward tie that no change can break? the love that many waters cannot quench, or the floods of affliction deftroy? Surely it is not of that nature which can endure the fire, and be refined by it; it is more like the bafe metal which would rife as the fcum and be loft, than the folid gold that appears afterwards, and is able to endure even the feventh purification.

3d month 1781—I think I have entered into my domeftick ftation, with a degree of awfulnefs and fear

fear, and not without an humble fenfe of the unmerited favours I received from divine condefcenfion, and from my friends during the ceffation of it. And notwithftanding many deep trials attend our leaving home, when under an apprehenfion of duty, and many painful jealoufies neceffarily arife, left the moft important of caufes fhould fuffer, yet when we are in a fettled fatisfaction, or under the cares of a family, by not being fo frequently put upon a fenfe of our danger, and of our own unfitnefs to do good of ourfelves, our minds are apt to lofe their centre, by getting off the watch, and fo become diffipated and carried away with trifling things; at leaft with things fhort of that certain treafure which is fecured out of the reach of either moth or ruft; and then they become to us (however plaufible to that wifdom which cannot comprehend the myftery of godlinefs) unfubftantial trifles. Thus we fee the neceffity of having a foundation of our own; and we need not that another fhould build upon us, but by that fame power which directed the firft ftone, fimilar to what was and is laid in Zion, tried, elect and precious, whereby we may be built up in the moft holy faith. I often find it my duty, ftrictly to fcrutinize into the moving caufe of my fteppings in various refpects; and notwithftanding the greateft abafednefs is my due, on viewing my own innumerable frailties and inability often to turn my mind availingly to the invincible fortrefs, even in times of deep probation; yet if there was not a fecret teftimony in my heart, that it is much my lot to know an abftraction from human dependancies, my feelings would be infupportable, becaufe

I could

I could not look for that peace which is preferved from human mixtures and interruptions.

4th month 1781—Weary indeed I have felt myfelf of this changeable world for a few days paft: perhaps it proceeds from too great an indulgence to that eye, which is viewing the difcouragements of the prefent day, and which has caufe to run down with water, for the flain of the daughter of Zion. How are the Aarons removed, and removing, and fuch as might feem likely to receive the garments, have the work cut fhort in righteoufnefs! how do the ftandard-bearers faint, and how doth the enemy prevail in his transformations, in deceiving and drawing down even of the priefthood! In contemplating thefe things, I think I may fay, that I never felt my mind fimilarly clad with a ftate of fecret mourning and fackcloth, as fince you left us; infomuch that I am ready to inquire, who fhall ftand? or from whence can the watchers come, that will faithfully difcharge their truft upon our walls in a future day? I am daily convinced of the great need there is for me frequently to be taken throughout in pieces, that no comelinefs may remain to felf, nor manna be preferved from one day to another; that my own ftate, and the wildernefs ftate of the church, may be (though not fully yet) clearly feen.

6th month 1781—I have, after contending my ground by inches, ventured to fet off towards a place which I have often looked at with a kind of dread and difmay; from an apprehenfion that it ftrongly refembles that great city Babylon, in which it is hard to be preferved from tafting of the cup, either in a greater or lefs degree; and where, if there even be prefervation from this, deep fuffering muft be the confequence; a ftate not likely for flefh and blood readily to enter into. I can truly fay it is in great fear and abafement of mind, that I advance towards it; earneftly defiring to be kept to that power which difcovereth the hidden things of darknefs, and fhews us the different fources of felf-love.

11th month 1781—We are fometimes at a lofs to account for our own actions, becaufe they proceed from caufes unfearchable to us, and which we are led infenfibly to comply with for our own good, that *that* part in us which is appointed for death, and which by means of the flaming fword, is totally feparated from the tree of life, may receive no food nor vigour to fupport it. Since I faw thee, many and complicated have been the concerns and feelings of my mind; new caufes and new anxieties have occurred, from which I have feen great need to procure a fecret dwelling in a quiet habitation, and to crave daily affiftance to abide therein, that my own root might not be more impoverifhed; but that by an inward attention to the voice of the true Shepherd, a more intimate acquaintance with him might be cultivated, and a greater fubjection of fpirit experienced; whereby I fhould be more clothed with that true humility and pure fimplicity which are effential to the caufe of righteoufnefs, and neceffary for the prefervation of our minds in a ftate of acceptance with Him, who fees not as man fees, but who knows what His wifdom has prohibited to us, and marks our obedience.

How

How affecting was the removal of our beloved
————! Silent aftonishment, and fecret mourning, for an individual and general lofs, was all the language I could use. My heart was indeed affected, and is not lefs fo in the frefh feeling of a diffolved affectionate tie, and of the uncertainty of all our comforts and attachments, notwithftanding they may in profpect appear durable; but as we do believe there is an union which exifts beyond the grave, a fellowfhip unconfined to thefe mortal bodies, how ftrong an incentive is it to purchafe this permanent inheritance, though at the expenfe of our own fervour, and that friendfhip which is conceived in the falfe refinements of the human imagination; and which being tinctured with the gilded impurities and dregs of nature, becomes of that kind which is at enmity with God, becaufe not fubject to the power of His crofs. To be ftripped of ourfelves, to be fimple, to be fools in our own eyes, and in the eyes of others, are experiences not pointed to by our own difpofitions, but are indifputably the way to that kingdom which flefh and blood cannot inherit. By yielding to this way, how humbly may we commemorate that power which gives according to our advancement, the victory over a hoft of oppofition, and dims that eye in us in which our enemies are magnified; giving a holy confidence that binds up the mind, humbly exalts it above thefe momentary things, and, by meafurably uniting us to itfelf, enables to difcern the origin of our feelings, and what proceeds from them, by tracing them to their fpring, and proving them in the light. Our experience is fmall, but, I truft we mutually long for that which

is good; may we each be, more and more, drawn from every mixture of felf, and become as a weaned child!

12th month 1781—If I had known your plan of proceedings, it is likely I fhould have met thee with a few lines fomewhere; but a morfel of friendly converfe, or a token of true regard, may, perhaps, be as acceptable now thou art returned to a more homely fare, and feeling a little more defcent to fome inferior fervice in the houfe, than was then allotted. Notwithftanding thofe that vifit the true feed in this declining day, feldom find themfelves, either fecretly or publickly, mounted on the king's horfe, but rather have to experience a baptifm into its fufferings, and a fellowfhip therewith; yet even in this ftate, if our minds are kept low enough, and in a fituation ready to receive and dwell under the divine allotment, there is a ftrength attends it, of which the moft favoured fervants, we have caufe to believe, are often ftripped on their return. No wonder then, if we, who are infants in this fervice, fhould be fuffered to feel ourfelves, as the dry bones in the open valley. Under this ftate of humiliation before Him who knows all things, and who wifely ftrips us of our judgment, in order to refine it; how beautiful that reply to the query, " can thefe bones live?" thou knoweft oh Lord: in this humble fituation, how ready are we to receive the refurrection of life, or to wait for it the appointed time until all unprofitable moifture is exhaufted, and the feafons have paffed over us!———A moft affecting circumftance it is, that a man, and indeed a family,

ftanding

standing in apparent approbation as ——— did, should bring such dishonour to the cause, and themselves be plunged in such deep distress! It is, however, a proof how we ought, in whatever we do, to fix our eye upon the right object, and to prefer a consistency with the truth, to our appearance in the eyes of men; for certainly if this had been more the engagement of many minds, there would have been preservation experienced from many of these painful and dishonourable circumstances.

1st month 1782—My remembrance of thee was tenderly affectionate, and a solicitude accompanied it, that we may live so near the pure life of truth, having our minds frequently stripped of whatsoever is tinctured with the gilded impurities of nature, as to feel an increase of unity therein. When I am led to consider my own aptness to get from under the power of the cross, a fear is ready to enter, that the garments, the coverings of my mind, which may, in some small degree, have been washed, will again gather their spots, and I become more and more reconciled to them; so that the consequence may be an inability to distinguish betwixt the clean and the unclean. In this necessary perspective of myself, the means of preservation have, in infinite condescension, been discovered; and a willingness frequently to descend to the washing pool, has proved the request of my heart, that He in whose hand I wish to feel myself, may not only be the reprover, but the remover of every opposer of His work. Discouragements arise from without, for on every hand there is cause of mourning, and the few stakes that can be perceived among us are ready to fail with weaknefs; wherefore we fee the greater need, with all the vigilance we poffefs, to repair to that foundation which ftands fure; and truly thofe who are eftablifhed thereon have engraven upon them that indifputable feal, and moft defirable evidence, of divine acknowledgment. Our pilgrimage here feems, and will prove, of fo fhort duration, that the fufferings which attend it for our refinement, are bleffings demanding our humble acknowledgment. I have often reflected upon your fituation with a fympathy which I truft is meafurably of the right kind; and have felt the arduoufnefs of your path, the ftability that is required for it, and patient refignation of the caufe to Him whofe own works alone, or thofe of His own pure fpirit can praife Him and effect true and profitable deliverance to his dependant children. " What can the wrath and envy of man (if we are tried with it) do unto thofe that are hid in the fecret places of the Almighty, and gathered under the healing wings of the Prince of Peace? fince by his armour of light they fhall be able to ftand in the day of trial."

12th month 1782—I place little dependance on dreams; they are often a mafs of confufion; but we are bound to acknowledge that they fometimes contain clear intelligent information or caution. I believe however, it is always fafe to attend to the hint, " let him that hath a dream tell [it as] a dream," but the pure word fhould be fpoken more freely, for what is the chaff to the wheat? Thine was expreffive of a union with thy friend which is comfortable to her, and from which it is

the

the fervent defire of my mind we may receive ftrength and inftruction in the future movements of our lives; wherein perhaps, if we are favoured to be of any fervice at all, it may go hand in hand; but what are all the emblems of this fellowfhip to the thing itfelf? what are the branches without the Root that bears them? I often wifh the great objects in my eye may be folid and permanent; that vifionary and delufive gratifications may be proved, by being brought in their infancy to the balance of the fanctuary; and that nothing may refift the fire in doing its office upon that which is light, and which has not been formed and tried in the hand of the Potter and Purifier of his people; but watchfulnefs is our beft retreat, and I find that without it, in this land as well as in our own there is continual danger of being warped afide, and lofing our attention to the fecret reproofs and dictates of wifdom.

3d month 1782—I felt a fatisfaction in hearing from thee, and finding that the exercifes which had attended, were productive of that peace which never fucceeds our moving out of the line of pure wifdom, and is therefore an evidence of the Mafter's approbation; and what more do we wifh for; for if that is experienced when we have broken the morfel of bread given to our charge, it is enough for us, and the bleffing muft be left to that bountiful hand, which owns only its own works. Though poverty was the covering of my mind on my return home, yet I felt no uneafinefs from an apprehenfion of having left thee too foon, but rather a belief that it was right for thee to feel that thou waft ftronger than thou apprehended: and I now hope, that as thou haft afrefh found the divine ability allotted thee, to be fufficient for the work of the day, that thou wilt be more devoted to move alone in future, and become lefs dependant upon reeds fhaken with the wind. It is an excellent thing fimply to mind our own bufinefs, to attend to the path cut out for us individually, and let it be what it may, to be content therewith; becaufe it is only by the members of the body thus keeping their places, that they can be made truly ufeful to one another, and profperous in the caufe wherein they are engaged.

3d month 1782—I can feelingly fympathize with my dear friend in her prefent fituation of mind, and under fome difficulties, which may be increafed by the want of feeling, baptized elders, fuch as live near the fpring of life themfelves, and whofe deep can call unto the deep in thofe whofe line of fervice varies from their own. Where there are fuch as thefe, they are felt to be ftakes in the divine enclofure about thofe I call the moft tried of the flock, the poor meffengers that blow the trumpet on the holy hill, and have to defcend from thence into the deeps, and awfully to dwell there, humbled under a fenfe of themfelves and *what they are:* and though in this day of weaknefs, each member does not keep in its own function, but numbnefs and infenfibility have feized many, let us truft that our holy Head will not fuffer us alfo to become caftaways, if we attend to his direction. ——A fecret dwelling as in deep waters we know to be fafe; and, my beloved friend, may we keep
there,

there, grow more and more united to the truth itself, and support one another in the fellowship thereof!

9th month 1782—When an unavailing anxiety has possessed my mind, about the situation of things among us, and the wilderness state of the church; I have been led to conclude that it is not consistent with the divine will, that we should be ever impatiently inquiring, " what wilt thou do for thy great name? but that we should rather centre deep in our own minds, and resignedly and faithfully co-operate with his work in the earth; feeling our minds so reduced as only to pray for that which is the mind of the spirit, even if it required the petition, " feed thy people with thy rod! In our late visit, we deeply felt, at times, our weakness, and when most baptized thereinto, with our eye single to divine help, we had humbly to observe, that then His strength was manifest in our weakness; and that it was only as we descended to the spiritual brook, and there received with simplicity the heavenly armour, that the battle was blessed, our heads covered therein, and ability found to discover the little ones on whom the purifying hand is turned. I believe I may say we returned under the humbling impression of being unprofitable servants, begging to be enabled to continue suppliants at the gate of wisdom, and to attend in future to the smallest of its pointings. I need not tell thee how agreeable it was to meet my husband at my return home. On our separation, the passage feelingly occurred to, and refreshed my mind; " Lord I have left all to follow thee." To be employed in the cause of truth, and to have the spirit thereof for my companion, appeared when nature was fubordinate, far to furpafs every felfifh enjoyment in this life, notwithftanding I might prove a veffel of leaft honour in the family, and on our meeting again, I found there was need of a renewed engraving of thefe impreffions, in order to preferve a preference to the truth, and to keep in our remembrance that we have no continuing city here.

10th month 1782—It is an unfpeakable favour, through all, to believe that, if we dwell in the pure life and onenefs of the truth, many waters without, or floods of temptation within, will never be able to quench our love, though for a time, when they rife high, they may veil it. The prayer of my fpirit is, that my dwelling may be in this hidden life, that I may prefer its fubftantial operations to either fpiritual or temporal enjoyments, and that by it my body and mind may be preferved from running to and fro in the earth, with any blaft from the wildernefs. But oh the need of " ftanding ftill in the watch," the infirmities of our nature are fo many and great! Remember me and crave my prefervation, that my life at leaft may be given me for a prey; and may you and I farewel, and increafe in that life and love which change not, nor end.

—————— 1782 — I received thy affectionate letter in due courfe: it was truly acceptable; and though thou waft far from being forgotten by me, it tended to revive that near fympathy with thy fecret fpiritual travail, which particularly accompanied my mind when near thee in perfon, and which I truft proceeded from the cementing influence of divine love, and gofpel fellowfhip.

We

We meet with but few in this pilgrimage and state of probation, who are dipped in sympathy with us, and know what it is to be destitute of all comeliness. There are many who, were we clad in royal apparel, and had the King's signet always unveiled upon us, would no doubt acknowledge us in the gate; and, in the victory of the heavenly cause, cry, Hosanna! with us in triumph. But what was the path of the Master? Was it not the path for his servants, that they might be encouraged, and have a steadfast example therein? He trod it before them, and endured the several gradations and dispensations of the spiritual warfare; he fasted in the wilderness, until he was an hungred. Let us not then think it strange that the servant is not greater than his Master. Our safety depends upon our watchful attention, that when we are tempted we yield not; but oh! how near does the impatience of our dispositions border upon that language, " command these stones that they be made bread;" forgetting that it is not by bread alone that our hidden life is preserved, but by every word that proceedeth out of the mouth of God, and by every turning of his divine hand upon us; whereby, in his wisdom, we grow from stature to stature, which by taking thought for ourselves we cannot do. If we are found worthy to stand as pillars in the Lord's house, in this day when there are many heavy burdens to bear, we must be first upon a sure foundation, our dispositions, like those of the disciples that discovered the love of their Master's glory on the mount, must be subservient to divine control; and we must not only learn to descend from the vision of light, but to keep the charge,.

charge, and tell it to no man until the life of power arife. How hewing and forming are thefe things! and what inftructive traces do they leave of the Mafter's work, becaufe they reduce felf, and convince that no confidence muft be placed therein! May it be our experience, dear friend, in the few fucceeding fteps of our lives, patiently to fuffer, and fervently to wreftle for the blefling of prefervation.

1ft month 1783—What has felt very defirable to me is, that in thefe outward feparations, we may increafe in that which is good, and that whatever befals us may tend to fettle us the more in the ground-work of true religion, that therein we may ftand, and therein grow; then will the fluctuations of this uncertain ftate become fanctified to us, and being inftructed in the fchool of Chrift, our fpirits and conduct will become more conformable to the purity of the Pattern. My fear of myfelf daily increafes, and I am alfo apt to think that by looking too much at any evil, we may infenfibly be almoft drawn into it. It is neverthelefs good to furvey our ftandings, to prove our own infirmities, and repair to the place of help. The multiplied diftreffes, both fpiritual and temporal, that have been permitted to befal us in this land, or fince I left my own, have often occafioned a fecret cry for the continuance of divine prefervation; and a little ray of hope that the Lord hath not forfaken us, is all the fuccour that my poor toffed mind has often felt. There is great need in time of outward perplexity, impartially to examine the caufe, to fearch what there is in us

that

that requires thefe things; by fo doing we may often fee couched under them the wifdom of a divine Hand, and that to remove the caufe in ourfelves, is to go to the root of the matter.

1ft month 1783—I feel now, as at many other times, my mind drawn into near affection, and, I truft I may fay, that true fellowfhip with thee, which fprings when I am capable of experiencing any better enjoyment than what is natural; but as that only arifes from the renewings of life, I am often afraid to fpeak of it, left it fhould fall fhort of its character in the time of trial: however, I may fay I feel that love which many waters and feafons of deep and fecret diftrefs, have not quenched nor diminifhed. A degree of this mark of difciplefhip reviving in my mind, has fometimes been as a temporary cordial, tending to difpel the gloom of many difcouragements, and opening the view to a little pure ferene fatisfaction. My dear friend, many are the trials of the enemy of our peace to overfet us, many have been the affaults which I have met with fince I faw thee, far exceeding what I ever knew before. If divine help will condefcend to be near, and preferve me from finking in the pit of difcouragement, juft keep my fpirit alive to confide in his name, and dwell under his power, my heart, I truft, will bow in humble gratitude before him, and acknowledge his might. Our eye is now much fixed upon Yorkfhire; oh! that we may there experience the evidence of divine acceptance, and that, in our movements, or not moving at all, the bleffing of prefervation may attend us. Outward enjoyments, domeftick tranquillity,

quillity, and the affectionate regard of our friends, are all in themselves defirable objects, but without this bleffing, what are they? infipid, or fruitlefs delights.

1ft month 1783—As, (in infinite wifdom no doubt) our minds are at times drawn into folitude, fo as to refemble the Pelican in the wildernefs, having no accefs to the habitable parts of the earth, nor fubject to human obfervation, fo it appears confiftent with godly jealoufy that human confolation fhould be forbidden, and that, having our dependance only on a gracious and merciful Father, who deals with us as children who require his chaftifing hand, his rod and his ftaff, we may procure to ourfelves a fafe foundation, with a quiet habitation thereon, out of the reach of human interruptions. Surely there are none fo tried as the poor weak inftruments, that are ufed for the divine will to be communicated through.. Thefe require not only the forming of the Potter's hand, but higher degrees of drying, and greater heat in the furnace to prepare them, than almoft any other veffel; nay (if I may be allowed the comparifon) they are like difhes that have to pafs through the oven for every fervice, and which, after they are emptied, and the company has enjoyed them, need more wafhing and care than any other utenfil at the table; and great danger there is that, by indifcretion of fome fort or other, they will get cracked or broken. I look with dread, I am bowed down and difmayed, at the fight of the precarious ftanding of fuch, but efpecially of my own: the confideration of human weaknefs, and " how frail I am," am," is almost my meat and drink. How excellent is the privilege of having a monitor at home, an impartial Friend in our bosom, who, if we enough attend to Him, is able to make us as wise even as our teachers ! the reproofs and wounds of this Friend are better than the kisses of an enemy.

1st month 1783—I have now continued about two weeks longer in this place, and have received very affectionate kindness, and great hospitality from my friends. Were there not something in our minds that is panting after superior, more extensive, and secret enjoyments, I have thought myself placed among the cordials of life : but without the seasoning virtue of truth, and an evidence (though ever so small) of divine approbation marking, or resting upon, our dwelling place, they are tasteless and insipid enjoyments. Perhaps I have deprived myself of that which is good, and am now too ready to let others share the same ; a disposition which I wish not to cultivate, it being highly inconsistent with the benevolence of the gospel, which breathes no language inferior to that of, " Glory to God in the highest, peace on earth, and good will towards men." But how to distinguish, at times, the grand cause among a multiplicity of causes, requires wisdom, undefiled wisdom, that the immortal birth may be surrendered to the breast and care of its true mother, and that nothing hurt it, or diminish its strength ; but that, under all turnings and overturnings, divisions and subdivisions, it may gradually and steadily grow in stature, in wisdom and pure understanding, and take to itself an everlasting dominion in us. It is

the

the "deep that calleth unto deep." I thought I felt, on reading thy laſt, ſomething of the mind of truth in reviving a little my drooping ſpirits; a degree of thankfulneſs covered my mind, and I was encouraged to wait the paſſing away of this gloomy night, in comfortable hope of the dawning of a better day, wherein the former and the latter rain may deſcend, to add ſap to the root, and to refreſh the branches. What is it in us that flinches ſo much at ſuffering? It muſt be that fleſh and blood which can never inherit the kingdom. I have beſtowed ſome pains to ſilence it with reaſoning, and arguing the nature of things; but alas! I have ſorrowfully found it fed thereby, and perceived that it is only in humbly abiding under the divine operations, that ſubjection is wrought, and the moſt ſo, when the cauſe was not fully diſcovered; for then the lowly petition aſcends, which at this time covers my ſpirit, Grant me a grain of the precious gift of faith, that I may live and walk thereby.

1ſt month 1783— O this root of ſelf, when will it be ſubjected! It perhaps appears more to oppoſe thy ſervice, but I believe it more ſecretly prevails in me, and is not under that control and ſubordination which thou haſt it in more minute things. But let us not weigh ourſelves by one another; let us rather bring our ſpirits to the balance of the ſanctuary, and if there we want chipping and hewing, not think hard of the inſtruments that are to do it; but paſſively and patiently endure all things, in hope to enjoy that little which is our own in the end, having it pure and ſeparated from the vile. My mind has been drawn into great

nearneſs

nearnefs to you many times fince we parted. I have feelingly remembered the feafons when, though befet with many fecret probations, we might fay, We took fweet counfel, and our fpirits were baptized together, and prepared thereby to go up as to the mountain of the Lord, and to the houfe of the God of Jacob, where He has gracioufly condefcended to teach us more and more of his ways, and begotten frefh refolutions in us to walk in His paths. Let us not faint, my beloved friends, but wreftle with Him for the renewal of this bleffing; that though it may be our lot often to be feparated, our fpirits may unite together in holy fellowfhip, and that pure love which many waters cannot quench, nor all the changes of this uncertain ftate of being ever diminifh.

6th month 1783—My mind is much with you, and I truft it is in that fellowfhip which can unite with the abfent though in fuffering, and breathe for the profperity of the precious truth. I beg to be more and more bound to that, let its appearance among men be ever fo mean and contemptible ; for it is here that we are not afraid of human wifdom and difpleafure. But is there not, fometimes, too much fear of this fort, when under that power, and the burthen of that word which, if it met with no obftruction in the inftrument, would oftener break the rocks, and be a confuming fire among the cedars of Lebanon ? May this your feafon of fuffering be blefled to you and the church ! and oh! may your hands be ftrong in the faith, and hold out to the end in patience, that with the church coming out of the wildernefs, you may repofe on

the

the breaft of the Beloved of fouls, and your caufe centre with Him.

7th month 1783—My beft wifhes accompany thee, in this ftepping out into the awful fervice of vifiting the few fcattered profeffors under our name, and perhaps of unfolding in the frefh openings of life, further manifeftations of gofpel light to fuch as are not yet of our fold, particularly in Scotland. I remember that before we entered the borders of that land, and indeed whenever I viewed it in profpect, it was clearly impreffed upon my mind, that there was no track for us to go in, nor any footfteps to be depended upon in that journey; but that our attention would be continually required to the frefh pointings and qualifications for fervice: and on our leaving Scotland, we had greatly to lament a deviation from this pure indwelling of fpirit, and unfaithfulnefs to fome manifeftations of duty. When the mind, after being engaged in fervice, has got a little liberty, and feels itfelf as a bow unftrung, it is too apt to rejoice, and evade the next bending for fervice; whereby half our commiffion may be neglected, when we are peculiarly called to watch, to try and to feel every ftep that we take. Here fimplicity and humility are our companions, and if a pure holy zeal covers us, in a ftate of true dependance, the wifdom of the creature has no part; but the life rifing into dominion, and being taken for our guide in every ftep under the exercife of the gift, we have no need to be anxious for doctrinal arguments to prove what we affert to the people; becaufe this life anfwering the life in thofe that hear, can expound and unfold fuch myfteries as have been

hid

hid from ages; and it is only by our single attention to the purity of the gift, and the milk of the word, that we can be preserved in that simplicity which confounds the wisdom of the wise, brings to nought the understanding of the prudent, and exalts the seed of the kingdom. Thus I apprehend the ministers of the gospel are led, not only to teach all nations whither they are sent, but to baptize them into the power of the gospel, however few the number of their words may be. I feel a strong desire for your faithfulness in this journey, and that as you pass through little villages and towns, it may not be without feeling for service, for in this respect we were deficient. Look not too much at your own weakness, but consider the strength of that almighty Arm which works marvellously for those that rely upon it, and gives them faith for their victory. I know there is something in us, when we occasion many people to be called together, that fears for ourselves, and for the truth; it is well, in these times of trial, to consider our own inability, and in whom help and power dwells; for then a calm sometimes allays these anxieties, and spreads upon our minds the beauty and convincing influence of a lively, awful, silent worship, which stands in need of no addition, but which, at times, is accompanied with words in the demonstration and power of the same spirit.

7th month 1783—I think I was scarcely ever sensible of more death and darkness than since I came here: if a little life and light should spring in our future sittings, it may have some reviving effects, for really my spirits are in a drooping way, and my

strength

strength also. I expected nothing but suffering on coming here, and thus far it is my portion; this satisfaction, however, attends me, that it is but for a day or two, and I endeavour to lift up my head above sinking too much; but oh for the cause! the testimony of truth seems nearly laid waste, and the pure life crucified. Here are, indeed, many valiants, but what can they do? it is not the servants of themselves, that can make the dry bones live. The little strength I feel, seems to be in endeavouring after a settled retirement of mind out of meetings, and being willing to appear foolish as I am.

7th month 1783—There is a beautiful order in the growth of the spiritual, as well as natural man: he is at first carried and fondled, and it is then generally right to give him what he cries for; in a little time, he makes some efforts to go by himself, which, sooner or later, mostly prove effectual. Presuming now on his own ability, he assumes the air and carriage of a man, and in this confidence goes forward, until his stumblings, his falls, and his wounds, have sufficiently convinced him, that he is but a child, and that his will is no more to be depended upon than his strength. As it was right to indulge the simplicity of his first desires, so now, these becoming mixed with evil instigations, either in the appearance of a friend or an enemy, it becomes necessary, in order to preserve this simplicity, and the divine impressions which may renewedly descend upon it, industriously to repel and guard against the powerful influence of self-love and self-seeking, which is the beginning of our continual warfare. I at times thankfully view some of the exercises of my mind,

mind, as a probationary childhood, frequently occasioned by indifcretion, and increafed by the growth of the corrupt will with a growing knowledge in divine things; fo that I have been and am frequently ready to conclude, I fhall one day fall by the hand of this enemy : but oh! may we fupport the warfare which is mercifully begun ! and by depending folely on that Arm, which cut Rahab, and wounded the Dragon, be no ways inftrumental ourfelves in preventing a maturity in the pure life, and preaching by good works. I hope my dear thou continueft, and will continue to feel thy habitation like the houfe of Obed-edom. It is indeed diftant from us; but of how little confequence is that, when there is fellowfhip in the circulating life of truth, wherein we are as epiftles written in one anothers hearts, which are meditated in, at times, to the refrefhment of our fpirits when drooping and feeble.—It is a blefling not to be lightly efteemed, to be married to thofe of lively fpirits, and clean conduct ; not drawing back, but helping forward, that work to which there is a divine calling : and as ——— is among thofe who are thus bleffed, it will, I have no doubt, fweeten many unpalatable cups, and render moderate fome blafts from the wildernefs of this world, and its corrupt fluctuating fpirit.

1ft month 1784—Oh the need there is, when we feel a fecret divine approbation for fome little faithful fervices, as the anfwer of well done, carefully to centre this treafure, and leave it in the hands of our great benefactor ! for how unfit are our earthly hearts to be entrufted with riches fo weighty, and fo different in their nature ! they are indeed found to be be as bags with holes, which lose the precious gift among the rubbish of the house. Under these considerations, I am led at times to prefer poverty, and nakedness, and want, to an appearance of wealth, and spending my spiritual substance in riotous living: and to be preserved chaste and faithful in this state, is one of my strongest desires, yet attended, in some degree, with the certain knowledge of how frail I am.

1st month 1784—We have great need, in this day, for clean-handed, single-eyed instruments, in the work of reformation; such as demonstrate, in the particular parts, and general tenour of their conduct, that they truly fear God, and hate covetousness: for, of such only is the pure spiritual building composed; the church, against which, Satan and his agents can never prevail; whereto the nations may gather, behold its purity, and be invited to become living members thereof. But, oh how defiled is our camp! how temporizing are the spirits of those who ought to stand, as valiant soldiers, against spiritual wickedness in high places, and fight manfully under the banner of the Lamb! The world, with its gilded baits, has allured their attention, and attracted their sight, from the example of our holy pattern; it is therefore no wonder, if the work they undertake is superficially done; and that which has been their snare, passes unobserved for want of purification. From a view of these things, I have been led to prefer, and even to request tribulation, mortification, and what may be called evil things, in this life, to an unsubjected mind, being an unsound

member

member in the church, and feeking to be heir of two kingdoms. Whether I am thus preferved or not, I believe that now, as formerly, the lame, the blind, and the dwarfs, will not be accepted to minifter of the moft holy things, and carry forward the caufe of righteoufnefs in the earth, until their application is uprightly, and humbly made to Him, who is the healer of all difeafes, and the reftorer of ancient paths to walk in.

2d month 1784—Thou haft often been in my remembrance fince we parted, and both when hoping and doubting, I have wifhed to addrefs thee in this way, believing it warrantable now, as in the captivity of the Jews, for thofe who are uprightly, though feebly, concerned for the profperity of truth, to fpeak often one to another; and the trufting that a book of remembrance is written, cafts, in fome depreffing feafons, something of a ray of fpiritual funfhine upon the fpirits in prifon; which, though not a promife of freedom, yet cheers a little, and renders tolerable our unavoidable fituation of mind. A multiplicity of concurring circumftances, paft and in profpect, have of late deeply affected me: the fpirit of Goliath rages from every quarter: its power I feel, the low ftate of the church is evident, and my own weaknefs ftares me in the face. I would be glad to dwell in obfcurity, and have my name blotted out of remembrance. There are many called foldiers among us, but oh! how few of fuch as are loyal to the King of kings, and whofe work is diligently to eftablifh his government; infomuch that fuch children as I am are ready to conclude,

that

that if we move at all, our hand muft be againſt every one, and every ones hand againſt us: for though retirement is what above all things I would choofe for myfelf, yet if I apprehend myfelf called to fervice at all, it is the fervent prayer of my fpirit to be preferved therein from the fear of any man, and from doing the work deceitfully: neverthelefs, the fecret feelings of my mind feem to fay unto the feed, that " bonds await you." May we then poffefs our fouls in patience, and not fear in feafons appointed to contend for our faith!

2d month 1784—Being affected with the general caufes of difcouragement, and fo much afflicted with fome particulars, I am ready at times to conclude, I cannot hold faft my faith without wavering in this time of trial. You, my beloved friends, have your fhare of exercife; and whatever others do, be you faithful unto death, fpiritually and naturally, and then will your fervices be crowned with that life which cannot be gainfayed. We have much difloyalty among us to the King of kings, and fome who are his fubjects want to take from him an improper fhare of rule. Seeing thefe things, let us be lowly, and fhelter ourfelves under the fpirit of the Lamb, that the prevalence of this alone may be the weapons of our warfare: though we experience him to be flain as from the foundations of the world, and have to go down into fuffering with him, and our faith deeply tried, yet let us remember that He lives and reigns for ever, and that, notwithftanding the combined powers of darknefs, of the increafe of His government there fhall not be an end.

Our

Our paffage through life is like a journey wherein are difficulties and fnares; and wherein we find many who fay they are going to the fame port, and who think they have found out, from longer experience and fuperior wifdom, a better and fomewhat different road; but when we believe them, and make a little trial of their path, how have we, with painful fteppings, to return to our tribulated pilgrimage? I feel deeply engaged in my fpirit, that I may, and that we all may, look to our own ftandings not even to the moft approved inftruments for inftruction, when our application ought to be to the Spirit and example of our Holy Head and High Prieft.

11th month 1784—I am really very poor, but whether enough fo I cannot tell. I am however rather more contented than when thou faw me laft, having been a fhort time with ———, and fecretly comparing trials a little has done me good : indeed I think it is a wife way, when we imagine ourfelves under fuffering, to look into the pages of another's book, and meditate in their probations. Here we number our own bleffings, and a language fometimes unexpectedly arifes, " what fhall I render unto Thee for all thy benefits?"

1ft month 1785—Though outward feparation, and other circumftances inherent to our peculiar ftations, may fometimes blunt the continual keennefs of natural affection; yet the pure cement of true religious union being more durable in its nature, and of a more preferving quality, it can never be diminifhed, as our fpirits become more and more influenced thereby, and we fo transformed by the renewings of the mind, as not only to prove what is the divine will concerning us, but to yield obedience to all its requirings. Under this holy and spiritual canopy is preservation and peace; and while the carnal mind, and the wisdom thereof is perplexed, and exposed to almost continual fluctuation and disturbance, they that are gathered here (not from speculation, or the line of another's experience) but from a living and heart-felt sense of the certainty of divine truth, can acknowledge, " we have a strong city and that salvation is appointed for walls and bulwarks." Oh! that we may more and more know our dwellings to be within this holy enclosure; for the incorruptible inheritance is no where else to be found, than in knowing the divine will, and doing it.

7th month 1785—There is a love which I trust is ours, independent of visible signs, and distinguished by that freedom which the truth gives, whether it be in speaking or in being silent. The substance of true friendship is hidden; and it is not of a corruptible nature, if we keep it in its right soil. Though its branches are often cut down by the good Husbandman, yet the stump is fastened, like that we read of, with a band of iron and brass in the tender grass of the field; and when we renewedly experience that the Most High reigneth, it puts forth again, and excellent dignity is added unto it. I feel as I write an affectionate nearness to you, and oh! may we all so dwell under the dew of heaven, and the times and dispensations appointed to pass over us, as that the joy of the Lord may fully become our strength!

8th month 1785—Perhaps this may find thee in some desolate place, where my spirit salutes thee in the

the renewed feeling of sympathetic affection, and comfortable hope that, through the multiplied trials of thy day, and of the present journey, thou wilt be secretly supported with the arm of Omnipotence, and refreshed after many weary steps, with the streams of divine consolation; so that thou wilt still be able to do all things, through Him that strengtheneth thee.

My mind is much with thee and thy valuable companions, and sometimes I think I feel a fellowship in some of your sufferings, not doubting but a measure of them is mingled in the cup of your present service: and why should it not be so, when we consider the tribulated path of the great Master, and that it is enough for the servant to be as his Master, and the disciple as his Lord. The wise purposes of the great Potter are not always seen; there are many things in the process of forming the clay, or a people to His praise, the necessity whereof is not always manifest to those that stand by; and I have thought that in the line you are, have been, or may be led in, some among you may find openings to services, which not being found in the pages of past experience, may occasion doubts and dismay, and perhaps a profitable query, hath the Lord done this? yet it is also profitable to remember, that it is not for the instrument to say to him that useth it, " what doest thou?" I do not wonder at your feelings in being so separated in person from the visible church. I remember, though in a less degree, similar impressions which have never left me; and indeed my mind is comforted in finding an increasing attachment to, and value for the precious fellowship of the brotherhood, though it is not always found in an entire

similarity

similarity of prospects, and of ways and means of prosecuting good, so much as in an uniform, upright concern for the prosperity of the cause, which under the shadow of heavenly instruction, is one of the best cements that fellow travellers can experience. We should be glad, in our passing along, to find more of it; and were this united engagement to appear in an honest search into the real state of individuals, of families, and of meetings, some of Jericho's walls might fall in the contest, and people's attention get turned to desolated Jerusalem. But it is a land of mists and fogs, yea, in some places, of clouds and of thick darkness: may that over-ruling power which has its ways in the deeps, dispel these temporary things, and usher in a greater display of pure light, that they who are engaged to work, and are appointed for it, may work in the light, and fully approve themselves children thereof.

11th month 1785—I feel for ———, and wish her an increase of faith, or a more free exercise of that which she has, that so, it may fully be accompanied with such works as the great Father of the family has assigned her; perhaps both she and I would fare better, did we look more inward and less outward in our reflections upon ourselves, and for every future supply of wisdom and strength. It is surely a wonderful attainment to live by faith; it is deep beyond human penetration, and seems to comprehend all that is needful for a follower of Christ to experience: but the trial of it remains to be more precious than that of gold, and preferable to the best of our faculties that we can substitute for it. Poor ———, she has often felt near to my life. It is the poor that can most feelingly salute the

the poor, and dip with them in their afflictions; go with them to the houfe of mourning; and, when the holy anointing is poured forth, rejoice together in hope.

1ft month 1786—I hope that county is by this time profitably vifited, or rather the feed therein, a place where I once thought it was the hardeft to find (however in myfelf) of any I was ever in. But places and perfons alter; and where death moft reigned, perhaps life may now moft eminently abound; and life is never more acceptable than when it fucceeds a total death, nor light, than when it fprings out of the greateft obfcurity. To dwell with that which teaches to die daily, and to be preferved from the fleep of carnal death, is an attainment I fometimes covet; but flefh and blood had rather be fuftained with a little of yefterday's manna, and retain a former evidence of life, than undergo, from day to day, in religious fervices, the conflicting exercife of being buried in baptifm, though it is bleffed with the refurrection of divine virtue and power: and the reafon I apprehend is, becaufe no flefh can glory herein; it therefore oppofes this work, and the refifting of this oppofition with the little ftrength we have, truly occafions a continual warfare to the chriftian traveller.———
The prefent is a fcene of conflict and probation; but when we are ftrengthened to look over it, to that glorious habitation, whofe walls are falvation, whofe gates are praife, and whofe inhabitants no more fay they are fick; there is fomething fo animating in the profpect, that we are willing to endure all things to attain it. Let us then take courage in hope, and faithfully endeavour to do our prefent beft.

4th month 1786—We have often converſed about friends in Ireland, and felt the glow of true love therein; which, though not much expreſſed to themſelves, is yet a living ſpark in all our breaſts, which many waters cannot quench; nor will long ſeparation be able to eraſe thoſe epiſtles which are written by the finger thereof, and in which there is a liberty ſometimes allowed for the ſpirit to meditate, with a degree of ſtrengthening conſolation, eſpecially when, by the clearneſs of the characters, we find one another as fellow pilgrims, travelling after the reſurrection of pure life, and making ſteady advances towards that city which hath foundations. Upon this object I ſometimes fix my eye, with renewed reſolutions, through holy help, to preſs forward through the difficulties of the preſent ſcene, and to count all things but as droſs and dung that I may win Chriſt, and be found in him; not having on my own righteouſneſs, but the righteouſneſs of faith in Chriſt, that thereby I may attain the reſurrection of His power, the fellowſhip of His ſufferings, and be made conformable to His death. The ſpirit is willing thus to endure, but the fleſh and its inherent propenſity to eaſe, creates a warfare, wherein I ſometimes fear, the natural and beſt life will entirely fall.

5th month 1786—We are ſometimes like pilgrims whoſe faith and patience are at a low ebb; and were it not for the gracious condeſcenſion of Him who regardeth even the ſparrows, and whoſe arm of everlaſting ſtrength is underneath in ſeaſons of drooping and diſmay, we ſhould be ready at times to faint; but it is the renewings of holy help that become ſtrength in weakneſs to thoſe that
put

put their truft in it; and is a prefent fufficiency when we are not able to provide for ourfelves. May thou be fully grounded in this truft, that thereby, in times of difcouragement and fifting, thy ftability may endure, and thy experience increafe in the knowledge that all things work together for good, to thofe that truly love the appearances or manifeftations of the divine will. I believe thou knoweft that I dearly love thee, and, I may add, have felt fweet unity with thy fpirit; and therefore hope ever freely to pour into thy mind any little hints which may in that love revive towards thee. And now, as thou haft put thy hand to a good work, let me fay, look not back; and when the certainty of thy being rightly anointed for it is withdrawn, which is no uncommon trial, look not then to the fentiments of others for fupport and encouragement; but labour after true quietude and patience of foul, whereby thou mayeft, with comfortable affurance, in the right time, have thy head raifed in hope, and thy growth in religious experiences be lefs fuperficial, than I fear is often the cafe even with thofe who have been put forth by the heavenly fhepherd. There is no confolation, no confidence, wifdom, or ftrength, like that which proceeds from the deep and hidden fpring, whereunto we muft learn to dig, if ever we are rightly grounded in the work of fanctification: and as the divine will is our fanctification, if we obey it; be not flack in furrendering thyfelf thereto. I write not thefe things from an apprehenfion that thou needs them more than others, for my fentiments of thee are very different; but I wifh thee to fet out independent of any inftrumental help, except that which is sent from the fountain of purity; and to look to no example further than it is confistent with the holy pattern.

7th month 1786—I remember it is said, that even " when the sons of God met together, Satan came also among them;" so that if he did so again, it was no new thing; and we are instructed by the angel how to deal even with him; not to bring a railing accusation, but patiently, and with christian fortitude, to commit the great cause to that power which can protect it, and rebuke the adversary, but not in our way, and in our time; for it is in general most eminently displayed when the creature is reduced, and nothing left in us that can boastingly exult even over Satan himself. To behave ourselves wisely in the church, humbly and watchfully to fear meddling with things too high for us, things into which our minds are not renewedly baptized, is a care which I wish we may ever preserve; for herein a godly jealousy over ourselves and our own spirits, will help to centre us in that meekness for which the paths of true judgment are appointed, will give a right feeling of what is opposition to the truth, and what is not, and how to use the armour of light; which, when rightly put on in meetings for discipline, unfolds the simplicity of truth, and discovers the pure disinterested foundation of those who are engaged to contend for the faith. It is becoming the nobility of the cause of righteousness, to see its warriors so unfeeling of personal opposition, as to return good for evil, and patiently to endure all things, seeking an opportunity to bless, by candidly opening each others understandings, and then generously forgiving. There
is

is no doubt, but that, in our society, if the root and ground of chriftian difcipline in ourfelves were attained to, and abode with, meetings for the promulgation of it in the general, would be more owned by their members being baptized by one fpirit into one body, and more crowned with that life which is peculiarly in referve for thofe, who have been faithful to the death of the crofs in themfelves. I am often humblingly convinced, that whatever I do in the facred offices of the church, if it be the fruit of fpeculation, a lively imagination, or only a defire to render myfelf ufeful, however fuitable it may feem, yet not proceeding from fome little influence of the holy anointing, which lets me fee myfelf with others, it is fure to leave a painful corroding fenfe upon my own mind, which I am afraid I have fometimes charged others with being the caufe of rather than myfelf. Thus danger appears on every hand, except we are watchful and humble; but " the humble the Lord teacheth of his ways, and the meek he guides in the paths of judgment: " thy gentlenefs (faid David) hath made me great."

8th month 1786—I fee abundant occafion to watch the fpring in myfelf from whence my rejoicings and depreffions come. Self is a fubtil enemy, infinuating itfelf into the company of the pureft intentions, and approved fervices, claiming a fhare of their peace, and of the fpoil of the moft righteous victories over every enemy but itfelf. A furnace, however, is wifely prepared for gold, where this drofs difcovers itfelf by feparation; fo that if we are zealous enough to get rid of it, we muft frequently retire to the teft, fubmit to whatever degree

gree of purification the great Refiner fees meet, and cheerfully endure hardnefs under His gracious protecting power; for, according to my experience, I take this redemption of the pure life from all felf-feekings, to require the clofeft combat, and moft intrepid perfeverance of a chriftian, in order to gain accefs to that river which makes glad the city of God, and to inherit the promifes of the gofpel in their own purity; where the edge of many forrows and trials is blunted, when they have nothing to ftrike at but holy humility. O it is a bleffed experience which my foul fervently craves! I fometimes think I gain a little ground towards it, when a difcovery of its animating glory, fubftantial feeding, and impregnable defence, is made to my underftanding; but, on finding how little capacity I have to receive things genuinely divine, the acknowledgment is readily made, that I know nothing as I ought to know, which is only attained by an experimental growth and eftablifhment therein; and yet fhort of this I fometimes defire to find no reft.

10th month 1786—Experience teaches us, that it is not always we are capable of even enjoying that good and profitable communion which, by virtue of the key of David, is fometimes opened for our prefent refrefhment and encouragement, in our path of deep proving and frequent difmay; much lefs of fo refting in it, as always to be ready for the expreffion of thofe things which are not at our command. I conclude thou knoweft that——— has been fometime in a low depreffed fituation of mind, but her company had a favour in it, of which fhe herfelf was not fenfible, as is generally

the

the cafe with thofe who are under the moft unmixed difpenfations of purifying virtue. That ftate wherein all fenfe of comelinefs is taken away, and under which we are clothed, as the prophet Daniel thought himfelf, with corruption, is that which appears to me the moft acceptable, and no doubt is the beft prepared to receive the language of, " arife, thou art greatly beloved of the Lord ;" the chaftening of thefe having been feen, and their many mournings heard, by the gracious ear of the Lord of Sabaoth. How different would things be among us as a people, if all thofe who wifh to be confidered as under the divine forming hand, and who are ready to ftep into fervice, were but enough emptied, and their beauty ftained in their own eyes ! many fpacious buildings on a fandy foundation would then be thrown down, and there would be more exercife and care in fearch of the immovable Rock of ages, which really in many places feems grievoufly neglected. My profpects are often mournful when I look at myfelf, there weaknefs and inexperience in fome neceffary refinements are forrowfully manifeft; and on taking a view of the ftate of the vifible church, we fee many of its members fo difeafed that they cannot perform their allotted functions, nor edify the body, though they retain their places there : the redeemed fanctified church how fmall ! and in what a wildernefs ftate ! So that to look at ourfelves, at the degenerate, or at the preferved church, minifters difcouragement, and fhews us the neceffity of turning our attention another way; inward, inftead of outward, and there waiting for the renewings of that power by which the worlds were made, and receiving fupplies for fpiritual wants at the firft almighty Hand.

1st month 1787—Your joint affectionate salutation came duly to my hands, and with the sympathy expressed in it, afforded me a little of that consolation which the drooping mind sometimes longs to partake of, when meditating on its own weakness and unworthiness of the renewed proofs of friendly regard and christian fellowship. It is pleasant indeed for brethren to dwell together in unity; and O that in order to retain this mark of discipleship, our eye may be single! for this leads to a communion still more excellent and pure, than that which we enjoy with each other in this mixed state of things, even a communion with the light which discovers all things, and is the life of those that believe in it. Yes I do know your path, and that it is a tribulated one: may you run your race therein with patience; for " tribulation worketh patience, patience experience, and experience hope, and hope maketh not ashamed, because the love of God, (and not of ourselves) is shed abroad in our hearts." Here is a foundation, which the gates of hell cannot prevail against, and which, as we keep to it, will preserve us from being soon shaken in mind, or troubled with those changeable things which in the course of our pilgrimage may befal us. I hope you will continue to keep in your remembrance a poor little sister, beset with many discouragements, and sifted with many fears and doubtings, particularly respecting our future movements; for I endeavour what I can to leave the things that are behind.

4th month 1787—Your company was pleasant to us, and the remembrance of you is so, and I trust will continue as long as the sincere engagement of our minds is to be branches in the same Vine.

Though,

Though, separately and unitedly, we may experience the chilling blasts of winter, and feel the dryness and strippedness peculiar to that season; yet learning in the school of Christ, in every state to be content, and perceiving with increasing clearness, where the sap remains, we can rejoice therein, and salute each other in true poverty of spirit.

4th month 1787—I received a kind encouraging letter from thee some months ago, when, with many others, I was about the remains of our dear friend———. We had been paying, for a few days before, the last office of friendship to him, and were witnesses to the awful conflicts of his spirit, in struggling, after many years disobedience to the openings of truth, for that eternal peace for which his soul was poured forth like water, and his bones seemed out of joint; but divine compassion was near, through the efficacy of renewed visitation, to gather into the heavenly garner. The season was altogether so deeply affecting to my mind, which was low and depressed when I went, and I got so involved in the gloomy passages of death through which he had passed, that it seemed as if many circumstances attending my continuance in mutability, were lost in the prospect of that solemn period wherein mortality must be put off. But on reading that part of thy letter wherein thou sayest, that in thy late illness, thy hope was abundantly confirmed in the invisible power of an endless life, I was favoured with a little glimpse of the saints inheritance, which, at times, has revived ever since, as a cordial to my mind; for in the course of divine wisdom, the hand of affliction, and deep spiritual probation, has lain steadily upon me for many months. Thou wouldst

wouldſt hear of an illneſs I had at Sheffield, which occaſioned my dear huſband's haſty return. My dwelling, for ſome time, ſeemed to be at the gates of death both ſpiritually and naturally; being in that ſtate wherein I could ſay with the ſpouſe, that " I ſought him whom my ſoul loveth, yea I ſought him upon my bed, and found him not," yet this inviſible Arm being underneath, was graciouſly revealed in an acceptable time, when, through ſore tribulation, a reſigned frame of mind became more my experience.

5th month 1787—If the right thing does but prevail in the approaching ſolemnity, it may be a time of healing. Thoſe whoſe ſpiritual faculties are alive in the truth, can hardly fail of beginning to feel an exerciſe on that account; and no doubt it is neceſſary that it ſhould be ſo, in order to prepare and reduce the minds of friends to a ſtate of child-like ſimplicity, and that abaſedneſs of ſelf, which endureth all things, hath nothing to loſe, and therefore, with chriſtian firmneſs, rejoiceth in that tribulation, by which the pure lowly feed of the kingdom triumphs in overcoming evil by that which is good. Thou and others have had to drink many bitter cups in that place; and it may be that, through patient perſeverance in well-doing, in ſecret ſuffering with the ſeed, maintaining the faith in that power through which miracles are ſtill wrought, the day is approaching, wherein that life which is the light of men, may become more conſpicuouſly the crown and diadem of our aſſemblies, and of the ſervices performed in the church.

5th month 1787—I received thy letter, and was pleaſed to hear from thee, though the account of thy

thy health, &c. was not fo favourable as might be wifhed; but I hope that after thou got fet off from home, and became refigned to what had fometime appeared right, thou would revive both in body and mind. I have frequently known it to be the cafe with myfelf, having been often worft juft before fetting out, when the mind was depreffed with the weight of future engagemnts, and loaded with the fenfe of its own exceeding great weaknefs, and inability to do any good; and at the fame time, having the comfortable enjoyment of divine help veiled until the needful feafon. This experience was never more confirmed to me than in the prefent journey, nor the fufficiency of that arm, which remains to be mighty to fave, is ftrength in our weaknefs, and a prefent helper in the needful time. If we are but favoured in our future fteppings, to increafe in this experience, our trials which are in the way to it will not be too heavy, in comparifon of that pure confolation which they produce: and as we are endeavouring (all of us I hope) to move forward in a line of fimplicity and faithfulnefs to what we apprehend is right, do not let us add to our difficulties, by admitting carnal reafonings, and taking too much thought for to-morrow; but rather labour after that great attainment of living one day at once.

6th month 1787—You will fee by the foregoing, that we are arrived at the intended place of our abode, and have ventured to afk at laft for a recommendation from our friends of the monthly meeting. I truft it is with diffidence, and the humbling fenfe that we are liable to err, that we take this ftep; and yet, as it appears in the way to peace,

peace, it is no doubt safest to take it, and also most consistent with good order. We wish not to get from under that disposition which, in the feeling of creaturely weakness, "feareth always," lest the subtil, transforming enemy should beguile us, induce to eat of that which is not good, and beget a confidence in our own strength and sufficiency to preserve ourselves. A self-righteous spirit is greatly to be dreaded; and though a state of doubting and discouragement is attended with many more sorrows, yet if the faith remains unshaken, it is at times refreshed with that precious dew, and the springing up of that well of life, which make amends for all, secretly replenish the drooping, yet waiting mind, and encourage it to press forward in the way which the vulture's eye hath not seen, nor any natural fierceness ever trod therein. Well! I trust so much we may say, that our minds, since leaving England, have been bowed in contrition before him who sees in secret, and settled, sometimes, in a quiet dependance upon his almighty Arm, rather desiring to be sustained in obscurity, than to be accounted any thing among men.

8th month 1787—Your joint salutation was truly acceptable; for though our love was not lessened, yet the sensible feeling of it, on reading your letter, was comforting to us, and strengthened the desire, that neither heights nor depths, things present nor things to come, may ever be able to separate us, either from the love of the great Shepherd, or from any of his faithful flock; of which number, may we, beloved friends, approve ourselves in all humility and godly care, enduring hardness as good soldiers of Jesus Christ, and not in our wills entangling

ourselves

ourselves with the affairs of this life; but seeking above all things to please Him who hath mercifully called us into the spiritual warfare. Ah poor—— indeed! any thing that denotes the entrance of the wolf, seems to touch my tenderest feelings; because that little part of the great Shepherd's flock has been peculiarly visited, and their welfare the object of my frequent and fervent solicitude. Oh what need there is of watchfulness! truly the wolf cometh to tear and destroy, though,- in order to deceive, he may put on the sheep's clothing: so that nothing but the true light can discover the hidden things of his dishonesty.——I have had cause to say, since leaving my native country, that the divine hand is full of blessings, and that our real comforts depend not so much upon outward circumstances, as on that holy attractive influence, which at times graciously opens a passage for the humbled mind, out of the cumbers and discouragements of the present time, into a state resembling the green pastures of life, and enables to lie down in quiet resignation as beside the still waters; leaving future events, when we have done our best, to that power which can turn the wilderness into a fruitful field, and cause the fruitful field to be counted for a forest. When this good is mercifully near, and we are favoured with the common comforts of life, there ought to be a grateful acknowledgment thereof, as well as obedient returns.

8th month 1787—Thy brotherly salutation confirmed a hope I had entertained, that there lived in both our minds such a degree of true love, that whether we thus conversed together, or not, we should

nevertheless

nevertheless be favoured to feel one another in our respective lots, and experience the truth of that saying, " deep uttereth unto deep." My dwelling, in general, has seemed so much in twilight, that meditation suited me better than action, and the increase of my acquaintance with the everlasting Friend, whose name is Wonderful, and whose works are inconceivably so to the natural mind, has seemed an enjoyment of the very essence of all friendship. In seasons of awful retirement, since I came this time to this land, my spirit has saluted the few fathers, the brethren and sisters, yea, and the instructors too, whose counsel is the counsel of truth, and whose joy is in its prosperity: and O! that my steppings among you, may be such as to bring no dishonour, nor be the occasion of stumbling to any! I wish to be the companion of such as faithfully and secretly labour for the increasing prevalence of gospel power; that so, through its purifying and sanctifying operations, every work may be wrought, and become an object of the blessing which makes truly rich. Tribulations are undoubtedly the lot of all, who are seeking to follow their Lord and Master in the Regeneration; but He who knows what they stand in need of, in His own due and appointed time, reveals to them His consolations, if they are willing to dive deep enough for them; for thou knowest it is in the deeps that wonders are seen, and pearls procured. If I knew how to put into words, the variety of my sentiments and feelings since coming to Clonmel, the freedom I feel with thee rather urges me to it; but someway or other, they seem enveloped in an undesigned secrecy, and whenever I attempt to unfold, there is

a sudden

a sudden restraint, like the turning of a double lock, and a wise and gracious intimation, to keep in my tent. The Lord is the tent of Jacob. How desirable is it then to be of the wrestling seed, the Jews inward, " of the circumcision that worship God in spirit, rejoice in Christ Jesus, and have no confidence in the flesh:" for these, knowing in whom they have believed, have the refuge of the righteous to flee to; and being thus exercised and favoured, no matter how little and simple such appear, how much they feel their own weakness, nor how prostrate they lie at the feet of their Master, where, with reverent attention His gracious words are heard and received.

I have often feared that, for want of faith enough herein, and a patient waiting in the abasement of self, for the renewed revelation of the divine will, the carrying forward of the Lord's work, both in individuals, in the visible church, and in the earth in general, should be retarded; and those designed to be the instruments thereof should forbear to follow the Lamb through suffering, and to fight under His banner, should lose that hope which maketh not ashamed (because the love of God is shed abroad in the heart) and cast away their shield, as though it had not been anointed. Well! may we profit by these considerations; and looking forward beyond the things that are seen which are temporal, to the things that are not seen which are eternal, hold fast our faith, and the profession of it without wavering, seeing that he is faithful who hath mercifully called us.

I observe thy consignment of a few lovely plants to my care; but hoping and believing that they are
divinely

divinely cared for, and are already taught where to seek their own bread, I feel particularly cautious of being the means of drawing their attention to any source of comfort or instruction, inferior to that which has been opened in the secret of their own souls. I wish them to be more and more acquainted with, and singly to rejoice in, the voice of their beloved; and I know this is all thou covets for them. But we must both allow, that visited minds are sometimes in danger of seizing and resting in secondary consolations, by placing an undue dependance upon the instrument of their good, and being thus prevented from getting down to those nether springs, where, with pure and humble rejoicing, the spirit draweth water, and no flesh glories. I do not mean that these dear girls are in any danger of being too much attached to me: because they have neither occasion to be so, nor are so unwise; but though I love them, and have apprehended myself constrained to demonstrate it, yet my own state generally feels an object of the compassion and sympathy of the feeblest traveller Zion-wards; and this consciousness makes me keep much at home, and mostly in my chamber, where the sweet society of my beloved Robert Grubb, and our truly valuable ———, sends back, now and then, a rising sigh, and urges me to number my blessings; setting before me the comfortable experience of the Apostle, which I am zealously pressing after, that of learning " in all states to be content." We have been favoured with many epistolary visits from our friends in England, which are not unlike little brooks by the way; but ah, we may sit by them until they dry up! however, comforts they are in their proper places.

9th

9th month 1787—Every bleffing is at the difpofal of unerring wifdom; and our true enjoyments are generally proportioned to the refignation our minds attain, to furrender whatever we poffefs to the turnings of the divine hand; counting nothing truly good but what is purified by it. This is a ftate which fweetens the bittereft cups; and fees beyond the tranfient gratifications of a worldly fuperficial fpirit; and is only arrived at by a fingle attention to, and humble waiting and dependance upon, the fecret monitions of the fpirit of truth. —Pleafant profpects, or enjoyments of any kind, are often much veiled from my view, or fhaded with a gloom, which the fallacy of human judgment, and the futility of all natural gratifications, caft upon the moft lively and lawful ideas: having, therefore, fixed our eye upon one glorious object, O may it be preferved fingle to the end of the race! that our running being with patience, and the fteps we take attended with light at the finifhing of the work affigned us, we may then be indifputably convinced, that having had no continuing city here, we have found one which hath foundations.

9th month 1787—As the prefent fcene is, confiftent with the nature of things, chequered with a variety of circumftances and feelings, we muft endeavour after that fortification of fpirit, which fo endures all things as to profit by them, and render ourfelves objects of the care of the great Shepherd. Juft to arrive at an attainment of this kind, is nearly all our drooping minds are led to defire, without any extraordinary exertions for enjoyments out of the line of divine appointment. I feem, at times, more and more encompaffed with doubts and fears; faith

is

is often deeply tried, and such depressions for a little while come over me, that conscious of having ventured, at the call, to walk as on the sea, and the supporting evidence withdrawn, my secret cry resembles poor Peter's when he said, " save Lord or I perish." Nothing short of divine compassion, and the renewed extension of holy help, can strengthen us to press forward with acceptance through the few succeeding probations of our day, and open in us that eye of faith which, looking beyond them all, brightens at the glory that shall be revealed unto those, whose garments have been washed and made white by the spirit and power of the Lamb. There is something in us so prone to settle down at ease in prosperity, that without some fatherly chastisements, we might forget from whom we receive our spiritual and temporal blessings.

10th month 1787—My mind, on returning and since, was favoured with a secret humble trust that I was not out of the way of my duty, in accompanying to Enniscorthy and Carlow, nor in leaving you at the latter place; though my stay afterwards in Waterford was not unaccompanied with that mortification, wherein no flesh can glory, and which was, no doubt, in mercy dispensed to us, to keep the poor vessel in such a degree of sanctification and honour, as to be at all fit for use in the spiritual family. I conclude that I need more of this kind of dispensations than others, because I think more of them falls to my lot, which proves there is more to mortify. But though I often imagine myself ready to faint, yet my fervent prayer is that I may not utterly; but rather be strengthened to endure the cross, and despise the shame of creaturely abasement,

ment, looking to the Author of all true faith, for fuch renewed fupplies as to fteer fafely through this uncertain ftate of being, and for ability, in the due and appointed time, to finifh the wifely allotted portion of work, in reverent dependance that that which is right, and abundantly more than we deferve, will be mercifully recompenfed. In the fervice wherein thou art now engaged, I truft help will not fail of being afforded in the needful time, fo as to give you all abundant caufe humbly to acknowledge, in the winding up of your vifit, that ye have lacked nothing. Perhaps the line of your proceeding, as to paffing from place to place, is right; but fome way my mind follows you with a fort of regret, that more time was not allowed to have vifited, if truth had opened the way, the families of friends in the ftation of minifters and elders. There is much truth in a common faying, that the work which is well done, is twice done; and though this may be found the more mortifying and arduous part of the fervice, yet the neceffity and propriety of it being great, the peace refulting from faithful labour therein, would no doubt have been proportioned. But this feems like an unfeafonable hint, and I do not know any ufe there may be in dropping it, except by way of preface to an obfervation I was about to make, that friends upon religious vifits often appear to be cramped in their paffing along, from a fort of human prudence which dictates their making a long ftring of appointments, perhaps exceeding what is perceived by the eye of faith: thus they may be prevented from approving themfelves thofe fimple, humble followers of the great Mafter, which in the fincerity

rity of their own hearts they have earneftly defired to be. Whether this proceeds from the want of faith in individuals, or the undifcerned influence of general cuftom, I know not, but certainly it is a fafe and hidden path which the chriftian traveller walks in, when, in no refpect, he defires to take the lead, but refignedly gives himfelf up to be led, ftep by ftep, through the difficulties of his allotted line of fervice.

11th month 1787—I received this morning, with comfort, the long retained token of thy affection; and can affure thee I am poor enough to enter with heart-felt fympathy, into the fituation thou defcribes, poffeffing nothing whereon to build hopes of divine acceptance, unlefs renewed by the creative word of Omnipotence, and replenifhed with ftrength to hold on my way. Let us not then caft away our confidence, nor conclude ourfelves unprofitably tried, when we fee ourfelves as we are; but rather rejoice in this tribulation, and temptation to call in queftion all that felfifh propriety, which human nature would fubtilly fuggeft to us as wrought by the heavenly Hand. Count it all joy that thou art fo clothed with a fecret fenfe of corruption, and art fenfible of thy own incapacity to do any good thing; and rather defire to live long under thefe humbling impreffions, than to be taken away from all opportunity of magnifying that " grace, by which thou art what thou art," poor as thou thinkeft thyfelf. Should we be foolifh enough to think we know any thing, the voice of Wifdom would foon inform us, that we know nothing as we ought to know : in patience then poffefs thy foul, and keep in view an increafing refig-

nation

nation to every secret pointing to duty. We are very apt anxiously to look for that good in our own way, and in our own time, which is only to be obtained by doing the divine will, after we have known it: forgetting that they who err herein, are beaten with many stripes : if this is not now thy state, the hint will do thee no harm. He who knows what is best for us, wisely makes us weary of ourselves and all visible objects, in order to beget that hunger and thirst after righteousness, to which the blessings and promise belong : and so to attach us, in sacred union with himself, and love to His cause, as that in these days of lukewarmness in holy zeal, when the pure seed, through desertion, breathes the powerful query, " whom shall we send, and who will go for us ?" we may, in singleness of heart, and living faith in divine sufficiency, answer, " here am I, send me," Though this seems an intercourse superior to what we often think is ever allowed us, yet the gentle movings of the spiritual life, and the subjected disposition of our minds thereto, in my apprehension, strongly resembles it ; and if many visited young people in this land, as well as my own, had placed their dependance upon the sanctifying operation of that sacred fire, which quickens the mind and prepares the sacrifice, rather than consulted vainly with flesh and blood, they would have been stronger in the faith, and more of them righteous contenders for it.

11th month 1787—It is by a single dependance upon that divine and creative power, by which all things were made that are made, that we find hard things made easy, and the mixture of human events so sanctified, as to be rendered salutary portions;

the immortal part in us is strengthened to ascend, as with wings of faith and love, that mountain spoken of by the prophet, where " nothing can hurt or destroy." A true gospel spirit so strongly resembles this desirable habitation, that when, in some degree of its own purity, it breaks in upon our impoverished minds, we are renewedly convinced that flesh and blood hath not revealed it unto us; but humbly submitting to its operations and directions, self becomes of no reputation, " and the Lord alone is exalted in that day." I feel, as I am writing, a secret breathing for thy brother's and thy preservation, and encouragement to pursue invariably the one thing needful, because it is sealed, that *that* shall never be taken away. The purity and permanency of heavenly treasure, are objects of no small magnitude to the enlightened mind, which has seen the fluctuation of visible enjoyments, and the vanity of all its efforts, without divine assistance, to obtain the smallest particle of true spiritual bread, or one drop of that consolation which is only derived from the pure gift, or well in us springing up into life everlasting. But it is not enough to be enlightened; we must also wait, in the abasement of self, for the thing spoken of and desired; and be willing to accept the Apostle's exhortation, not to be conformed to this world, but transformed by the renewing of our minds, so as to prove what is the good and perfect and acceptable will, and then to do it, even at the loss of human approbation, and all the riches of the unregenerate will and wisdom of the creature. Here we learn the mystery of buying the truth, and selling all that we have for it; a mystery which, among many more, is hid from the wise and prudent, and revealed unto

the

the babes in Chrift. I often lament my unfitnefs to receive thefe things, and a difpofition, out of the clearnefs and power of the gofpel, to accommodate myfelf, particularly in company, to a worldly fpirit, rather than fuffer as a fool for the feed's fake; and yet I truft I am making war againft it, and have victory in view.

1ft month 1788—To be furnifhed with that excellent armour thou fpeaks of, is truly defirable, and when without it, the prayer of my heart is, quietly to keep in my tent; and even with it, to make no boaft, nor to ufe it but by renewed commiffion. It is one of the effentials for the poor chriftian traveller in every ftation in life; becaufe of the open attacks, the fide blows, and crafty purfuits of our unwearied adverfary. I feel them daily, and long for an increafe of ftrength to refift him, fteadfaft in the faith. He many times feeks to make our hearts fad, when the Lord has not made them fad, and to perplex and embitter our paffage through life, when he perceives that *that* is the length of his chain. We propofe fetting off for Cork in the morning. Even that is a burden; and I might foon work myfelf up to believe that I am not able to go half way to Clogheen. How admirably wife, and adapted to the weaknefs of our frame, was that exhortation of the great Mafter, " take no thought for to-morrow:" this and fuch like compaffionate counfel, fometimes drops into my mind in the midft of my conflicts, and proves to be words of that kind which both winds and waves obey.

2d month 1788—Though the root of any good affection be alive, yet there is but one right feafon prefcribed in divine œconomy for it to manifeft itfelf in the branches, by caufing them to bud, bloffom, and bear fruit; and that being the fpring-time of divine favour, when the Sun of Righteoufnefs breaks forth upon the Lord's plantation, we muft wait for it in patient, though earneft expectation, that as our abiding is in the allotment of pure wifdom, the winter (however long) will in time be paft, the rains and tempefts will fubfide, the time of the finging of birds come, and the voice of the turtle be heard in our land: then, though we enjoy it in but a fmall degree, we can falute each other in fpirit and word, and hail all thofe who, like Mary, are bearing precious feed, let their ftations in religious or civil fociety be what they may. A falutation of this fort fprings in my heart to my endeared friends; to the parents who have known Him that is from the beginning, and to the younger branches who have meafurably been ftrengthened to overcome the wicked one; fincerely defiring, that as we have, through abundant mercy, been begotten again to a lively hope by the power of the firft refurrection, we may, through our varied exercifes, keep our eye fingle to the preferving power of divine love, and to that inheritance which is incorruptible and fadeth not away, referved in heaven for thofe who are kept by the virtue thereof, and the precious gift of faith unto the laft day. For herein is great joy, when outward circumftances, and the accufer of the brethren fpeak trouble; here the tribulated chriftian traveller finds an undefiled reft, and by the light commits his fpirit in pure refignation to the guiding hand of Omnipotence; feeling to the confolation of his afflicted foul, that for all his omiffions and commiffions, he has an advocate

vocate with the Father, not an High Priest that cannot be touched with a feeling of our infirmities, but one tempted in like manner, and who knows how to succour those that are tried. Well might the Psalmist, who was so largely acquainted with the dealings of infinite wisdom, exclaim, " how excellent is thy loving kindness, O Lord; because thereof, the sons of men put their trust under the shadow of thy wing."

3d month 1788—We were at their week-day meeting here yesterday, and had a large publick meeting in the evening, in both of which, I trust, we were owned by the Master of all rightly gathered assemblies, and might have been more so, if resignation, and a willingness to appear weak and foolish as we are, had been more experienced. I often think that if, in this respect, we were sufficiently humble, we should fare better than we do; and that, while we were preserved from foolish preaching, the foolishness of preaching (as the worldly wise esteem it) when in the demonstration of the spirit, would be blessed beyond our conception, and made something like the barley loaves by which the multitude were fed. We know our own employments; but the mysterious workings of the heavenly hand, in carrying forward the redemption of the nations from the fall, are wisely concealed from us: yet the inquisitiveness and judgments of the creaturely part, often lead us into discouragements when we should, in the simplicity of little children, do as we are bidden, and leave the event to Him who knows best how, and when, to use the weak and foolish things of this world, to confound the wisdom of the wise.

3d month 1788—By way of apology for my silence

silence let me say, that writing, in many respects, less suited the disposition and qualifications of my mind, for many months back, than a silent meditation upon the nothingness of self; which was far from always obstructing the sweet circulation of christian fellowship, and solicitude for the preservation, under the shadow of the Holy Wing, of all those who, by dispensations unerringly wise, are involved in the depths of discouragement and dismay, with respect to their own ability to promote any good word and work, and yet whose diffident minds are often assaulted by the accuser of the brethren. These have, however, no occasion of casting away their confidence, when they reflect upon the many deliverances which they have received through the communication of eternal help, and remember the gracious promise of the great Master, to those who dwell under his righteous government; " lo ! I am with you always, even to the end of the world." —You are as epistles written in my heart, wherein I often meditate with secret comfort, under the belief that you are, in unerring wisdom, designed to be fellow-helpers in promoting the cause of truth and righteousness, and fellow travellers in the way thereof. If you meet with trials and difficulties, you know there is nothing new in that; they have ever attended the footsteps of the flock; and when we are careful not to multiply them by any default of ours, they are so many proofs of our being the followers of a suffering Lord, which are sealed by our extracting benefit from them, and sanctified by obedience. Hold on then as you have begun; " count nothing too near, or too dear to part with for Christ's sake and the gospel's; fear not that

humiliating

humiliating baptifm, which crucifies us to the world, and the world unto us; and may the Shepherd of Ifrael lead you as his own fheep, convey to you the indifputable intelligence of his own will, and fo preferve you in a ftate of fidelity to himfelf, as that none fhall be able to pluck you out of his holy Hand!

————1788—It is a favour that the beft root needs no great profeffion, or fpecious words to nourifh it; it is not ftrengthened by a multitude of luxuriant branches, though, if it be alive, it will difcover itfelf by little buddings, bloffomings, and fruit. While therefore we are not unprofitably anxious, in time of winter, for that which is not to be had, neither let us be too unconcerned, when the full time is come for the manifeftations of the life of the tree, nor count them of little value, but cherifh and protect them, left fome indifcreet hand, or fpirit in ourfelves, fhould rub off that wherein is hiddenly contained the choiceft fruit, and fo render the coming of the fpring, and the genial influence of the Sun of Righteoufnefs, ineffectual to us. Many cautions are neceffary under this fimile, for even when a tree bids fair for profiting and enriching thofe who poffefs it, if that which it is to produce in the fulnefs of time, be gathered before it is ripe, it fets the teeth of the eater on edge, and caufes the tree to be evil fpoken of. Thus, on many hands, dangers occur to us in the conduct of our gifts, in religious and civil departments. How needful is it then, to afk wifdom where it is to be had, and to ufe it when we have it; and alfo to cultivate that prudence which is her fifter in fervice, and which often oppofes plans of our own contriving. Thefe are fentiments which, though thrown out to you, tend to shew me where, and how, I often miss my way; and excite me to review the consideration of that merciful kindness, which is sometimes extended to us in a very low estate; when, in our own eyes, we seem most undeserving of that help which can alone lift up our heads in hope, when the floods of affliction prevail, and the billows pass over us. May we deepen in our experience of the Lord's fatherly dealings with us; that so, approving ourselves more and more babes in Christ, our knowledge of the mysteries of the kingdom may be pure, and of that preserving nature, that never puffeth up.

————1788—It is not because thou and thy dear wife were forgotten by us, that neither my husband nor I have, since our return from England, dropped you a line. Silence, on my part, has chiefly originated in a consciousness that I have not been deep enough in my spirit, so to draw water out of the wells of salvation as to be able, in true religious sympathy, profitably to visit thy often discouraged mind. To feel our incapacity to minister, in a spiritual sense, a cup of cold water to ever so feeble a disciple (unto whom we may nevertheless be bound in a constant friendship) is a merciful impression; because it humbles us, and seals upon our spirits that invariable truth, that " there is none good but one." What is this sense, but the anointing itself, which has holy certainty in it, seeing that it is no lie. Except it abide in us to this effect, our profession of being believers is vain; we shall grow weary in the christian life, and our own righteousness will soon exhaust our strength: for supplies from the eternal Fountain would soon cease were we to appropriate them to the prosecution of ends which

the

the Lord never required at our hands, and neglect that life of faith, of humble dependance upon the pure gift, and thofe precious influences, hope and charity, which conftrain us to render unto the great Law-giver, in His time only, whatfoever he requires at our hands, though incomplete and foolifh to the unfimplified mind. I often wifh, on my own account, to be more in fubftance than I am. That infinite kindnefs has made me a partaker of the common falvation, has fhed abroad in my heart a meafure of his love, and ftrengthened me, at times, to lay hold on eternal life, I truft the deceivablenefs of unrighteoufnefs will never be fuffered to draw me from the belief of: but I look at the office of a gofpel minifter with an awfulnefs which convinces me, that there are baptifms, humiliations, and deaths peculiar to it; and that, except thefe are often renewed, in order to ftrip off the plumage of paft experience, and of that knowledge of heavenly things, which, being like yefterday's manna, cannot fuftain, but fubtilly puffs up the mind, that babe's ftate, unto which the myfteries of the kingdom are unfolded, is unattainable, and the infcription of holinefs unto the Lord is withheld, becaufe they are not cleanfed through the word fpoken unto them. What will it do for us, even to be called to the work of the miniftry, if we fubmit not to thofe purgations which unerring Wifdom appoints? We may become veffels marred on the wheel; or, to ufe another fimile, if we fuffer not ourfelves, in chriftian patience, to be bundled up as with the dry rods, and to be as deftitute of verdure as they, we may, for want of complying with the appointed means of fruitfulnefs, fruftrate the divine purpofe to

Q 5 d·ftinguifh

diftinguifh thofe who are invifibly preferved by the hidden life. Perhaps it may not be unfafe to conclude, that in our fociety there are fuch defects ; but, as an individual, I find it fafeft, in conformity to the great Mafter's command, to judge not, except, through the fpirit of the Son, the judgment of the everlafting Father is known: and at fuch feafons, the mind is too much humbled vainly to feed on this revealed knowledge.

9th month 1788—Thy letter faluted us two days after our arrival at home, and was truly cordial, reviving with great fweetnefs our love and friendfhip with thee and thy dear wife, and alfo ftrengthening our hope, that He who, we truft, directed our fteps to your parts, and mercifully preferved us through many jeopardies, will, as you and we furrender ourfelves to His all-wife difpofal, fo carry on the eternal purpofe of his will as to increafe our fruitfulnefs to His glory; and though very remotely fituated one from another, make us partakers of the fame living fountain, whofe waters purify and gladden the baptized members of the church of Chrift where-ever fcattered, or however obfcured by the general cloud of darknefs which the profeffors of chriftianity are too apt to content themfelves in. But as the eternal purpofes of God are, the election of His own precious feed in us, (the Lamb that was flain) and the reprobation of that fpirit or feed of the ferpent, which with all the wrath and artifice of a fallen fon of the morning, is ever feeking to oppofe the coming of the kingdom of the Meffiah, how ought we to watch and be fober; confidering ourfelves no longer fafe, nor objects of divine favour, than while our fpirits and affections

are

are dedicated to his righteous control, cleanfing and fanctifying by the converting influence of His own power. The feed of the kingdom, through divine mercy remaining in us, and a difpofition to cherifh and embrace it, preferves from the fin which grieves the Spirit, and leads into death. Wherefore, to ftand in that which is elect, and to experience redemption from that fpirit which wars with it, ought invariably to be our aim; and if, in a purfuit fo effentially neceffary, we meet with fuffering and deep fpiritual conflict, yet remembering how inferior it all is to what He met with, who being truly the good Shepherd, laid down His life for the fheep; and experiencing Him to be in us the hope of glory, the afflictions of the prefent time are counted light, and the omnipotence of the Lord's everlafting arm (as we fingly depend upon it) found to give victory over the enemies of our own hearts; to lead, in the meeknefs of wifdom, through perfecutions from without, and to build up in the true faith and fteadfaftnefs of the great Captain, who goes forth conquering and to conquer. I know that religion is in a ftate with you, as well as with us, which requires a patient waiting and quiet hoping for the falvation of God; which is often near to be revealed when we faint in our minds, and therefore fail of inheriting that blefling the patriarch Jacob wreftled for, through a night of faithful and fuccefsful exercife. Thy increafe in heavenly treafure, my beloved friend and brother in the truth, is fecretly and ftrongly coveted by me; my heart often meditates upon thy folitary fituation; and, in the renewings of gofpel love, thou and thy valuable wife are made like bone of my

bon.

bone, and flesh of my flesh. May the God of all grace and confolation ftrengthen and fuccour you ! and I moft affuredly believe he will, as your love of his inward and fpiritual appearance, and glorious work among men, grows as a tree of righteoufnefs, bringing forth fruit in its feafon, and enduring with humble fubmiffion, every wintry and pruning difpenfation. We have heard fomething of thy profpect of devoting thyfelf to the education of children; a work peculiarly wanted in your fociety, and which, if thou enters into, in the fimplicity and fincerity which truth gives, will, there is no doubt, be a bleffing to many, and thou thereby rendered a feeling fubfcriber to that truth, " he that watereth, is watered himfelf." Thou mayeft find it an arduous undertaking, and attended with mortifying circumftances; but the liberal foul (though it may fuffer) knows beft how to travel profitably through them all. It is not human approbation that we ought to depend upon, or have fingly in view; but our ftudy fhould be to fhew ourfelves approved unto God; and then, whatever vocation in His wifdom we are placed in, or however weak we may feel ourfelves, we fhall have no juft caufe to be afhamed.

11th month 1788—I can feelingly fubfcribe to the truth of what thou fayeft, that it is good to fpend one's days in the bands of a free and fincere friendfhip, and in the unity of a folid and conftant faith. We are favoured with many in thefe parts, who have been mercifully gathered to the pure fpring of eternal life, where true love and unity originate, and from whence they bring forth acceptable fruits; but, as thofe confolations fometimes abound, fo do tribulations, on account of the fpirit

of

of the world, and many other fnares, by which the
enemy of all good is daily feeking to draw afide;
and for want of watchfulnefs and care, he prevails
to the great hurt of fome, and cafting a fhade over
the purity and fimplicity that there is in the gofpel
of Chrift. So that, notwithftanding we are encompaffed with many bleffings and advantages, we
are not without our portion of trials; and can therefore, in much fympathy and love, dip in fpirit
with thee, and feel thee as a fellow traveller in that
path of fuffering and probation which, in infinite
Wifdom, is caft up for the regeneration and eftablifhment of all thofe who walk in it, and hold out
unto the end. Fear not, neither be difmayed,
though thou feel thyfelf as a folitary bird, as a pelican in the wildernefs, or a fparrow upon the houfe
top; He that is in thee, is greater than he that is
in the world; His wifdom will direct thee, His
counfel guide thee, and His everlafting omnipotent
arm fuftain thee, as thy faith is fteadfaft therein, and
thy patience maintained in travelling through the
abafing difpenfations which may fall to thy lot: for
I do believe thou art intended to be a man for God,
and no wonder then, if thou fuffer perfecution and
affliction: remember they are but for a moment,
and light, compared with that exceeding and eternal weight of glory, which is revealed to the poor
diftreffed mind, when it looks beyond the " things
which are feen, to the things which are not feen."
I feel much love to the dear young people among
you, and fhall be glad for them to be told fo; and
that the good account thou fent refpecting them has
rejoiced the hearts of many. If they follow on to
know the Lord, their minds will increafe in holy
ftability;

stability; the enjoyments of this world will fade in their view ; and an inward acquaintance with the Spirit of Truth will become moſt precious to them ; they will not do their works (like the Phariſees) to be ſeen of men, but the ſolidity and weightineſs of their ſpirits, will demonſtrate that they have been with Jeſus, from whom they receive all their qualifications to perform true worſhip, or to do any thing that is good.

10th month 1788—Thy letter, which arrived about a week ago, was ſweetly refreſhing and truly ſalutary to us ; and I may now tell thee, that though acceptable, as an individual I needed it not to revive the ſtrength of affectionate attachment ; for my ſpirit often embraces thee in the flowings of increaſing love and fellowſhip, and feels thee, according to my ſmall meaſure of true knowledge, in that precious unity which is better than all words (though ever ſo frequently and finely expreſſed) without it. Were it not for this cordial drop, which, like oil, ſometimes ſwims on the top of our bittereſt cups, our faith would hardly be ſtrong enough to make us victorious over even the little perplexities attendant upon this pilgrimage and ſtate of probation ; but He who knows that we are " feeble folk," and gracioufly compaſſionates our caſe, becomes to us not only the ſhadow of a mighty rock in a weary land, but teaches us ſo to build our neſt therein, that, in times of ſtorm and trial, his holy encloſure preſerves us, his faith ſtays us, and this rock pours out precious oil. May our dwelling ever be here, and our inheritance be enlarged in that which is pure ! then, let our allotments be what they may, whether our bodies inhabit the dark, or the more illuminated parts of the

earth ;

earth; whether we are encompaffed with forrow and travail, or have to rejoice more fenfibly in the revealed falvation of the Almighty Arm; all will work together for good, and we grow in qualification to worfhip and magnify that great and excellent Name, which only is worthy of the incenfe that in every place and fituation is to be offered.

11th month 1788—If I know my own heart, it is my defire to know my bufinefs, and fimply to do it, whether it is taken cognizance of, or not, by the truly wife and honourable; whofe friendfhip, though ftrengthening, confoling, and therefore acceptable, may (if the heart be not in fome degree redeemed and redeeming from the myfterious workings of felflove) be perverted, and inftead of nourifhing the pure immortal part, build us up in an airy notion of our own merits and attainments, and prove a fnare inftead of a bleffing. A little acquaintance with one's own human nature, a frequent detection of its corruption, and the perplexities into which it introduces us when its fubtil arguments prevail, are enough to weary out a mind bleffed with the leaft fincere afpiration after permanent good, durable riches and righteoufnefs; and to content us in the moft obfcure fituation, if, through unmerited mercy, it may but be in the courts of the Lord; with the coarfeft food, if but miniftered to us from the hand which is full of bleffings; and under the moft unpleafant work, if faith is vouchfafed, that in love and pity it will be accepted. Some of us here feel it to be a low time; my knees often are ready to fmite together, and my foul is exceeding forrowful. That there are caufes in myfelf, and circumftances attending our prefent fituation, I doubt not; " give me me wifdom, and reject me not from among thy children," is my fecret petition.

11th month 1788—We have twelve girls, and expect more foon; fo that thou wilt believe cares multiply upon us: but, all our endeavours will be ineffectual, both in this, and all other undertakings, except the bleffing which makes truly rich, in unmerited mercy, refts upon them. Did the world know, how dependant all fubftantial comfort and permanent joy are upon this heavenly gift, people in general would toil lefs, think lefs of their own wifdom, and more fimply follow that day-ftar which arifeth in the heart, and directeth to the pure life, in which the Father is well pleafed. It is a comfortable belief to my mind, that thou art arrefted by this precious principle of divine light, which difcovers things as they really are. Be not afraid to be led by it, into ways thou knoweft not, and into paths thou haft not feen; for, in due time, it will difpel the darknefs before thee, and make crooked things ftraight. One of the moft beautiful, though moft abafing difpenfations, in the true chriftian progrefs, is that of becoming as a little child; the judgment is here taken away for purification, and to be made truly ufeful in the Lord's work, the foul breathes only to the parent for food, and depends upon no other for counfel. It is generally weak, but knowing itfelf fo, it is fafe: O happy ftate to be rightly brought into! May we never be afhamed of it, but for our encouragement remember, that of fuch is the kingdom of heaven.

————1788—Self gratification in our own way and time, has not been allotted us for the path to folid peace; and if increafing humiliation fhould prove the food moft convenient for us, we wifh to accept

accept it from that hand, which has an indifputable right to do with us as feemeth good in the fight of infinite wifdom, and which has power to convert the greateft trials into true fpiritual refrefhment.

—The ways of infinite Wifdom with thofe He choofes to bring through, and redeem from the fallacy of human underftanding, and corrupt nature, are fo incomprehenfible and humiliating as indeed puts us out of the capacity of faying, " what doeft thou ?" for who hath been his counfellor ? feeing he giveth not account to any of his matters, until the fimplicity of a babe in Chrift is attained unto, when he reveals, according to his purpofes, thofe myfteries unto them, which are hid from the wife and prudent.

—That junction between the monthly meetings is comforting, if only from the ftrength which the few living members may be fuffered to feel in the unity of one another's fpirits, and the bleffing which may be upon their endeavours to wafh one another's feet, and to bear up one another's hands. That love which has heretofore flowed in my heart as a river, to the poor in fpirit on that fide the county, fweetly revives as I am writing, under a renewed hope, that the eternal fountain of life will not be clofed among them, however low and unworthy they may fometimes feel themfelves to be of its pure refrefhment. And if it be in abundant mercy kept open, and they that are acquainted with it gather to it, having their qualifications from it, and ufe them under its influence, they will be a bleffing one to another, and more may be gathered to an inward experience of the fame purifying unction, than, in fome feafons of difcouragement, they have an idea of.

12th

12th month 1788—We have been fitting in a friend's family, where————demonftrated that her mind, through all thefe ftorms and tempefts, has found where to anchor and unload her veffel, with an increafe of fimplicity and obedience. I wifh fhe may now leave the things that are behind; and that we may all become more and more, not only as children, but as weaned children. To be reduced to this humbled ftate, has not only its mortifications, but its joys. The chriftian's life confifteth not in the abundance of the apparent confolations and gratifications he poffeffes; but in the renewal from time to time, of the hidden manna which the golden pot contains, within the veil of perifhing things. Thou knoweft enough of fuch fituations as ours, to make thee believe we are not without a portion of trials, (no doubt wifely proportioned to us;) yet I dare not complain, having thus far, as we have paffed along, found Him whom my foul loveth, in whofe prefence no murmuring has a right to appear. Childlike fimplicity is an experience which every chofen fervant, however feeble, ought to endeavour for. We get nothing by the contrary; for by ever fo much taking thought, we cannot add one cubit to our ftature, or make one hair of our head white or black. May you proceed on this family vifit, in the faith, nothing doubting. It was not the abundance of bread, nor yet the finenefs of it, which fed the multitude formerly. For want of faith, we lofe many miracles which the bleffing would ftill effect. Remember poor David's fling and ftone, and out of whofe mouths, ftrength and praife are ordained.

12th month 1788—I received thy affectionate fifterly

sifterly falutation, which, like a little help to the weak and feeble, was falutary and acceptable. Be affured I am one of the weak and feeble; may I therefore be wife enough, like thofe little creatures fpoken of in fcripture, which being feeble folk, build their neft in a rock ! and truly, dear friend, were it not for the fhadow at leaft, of this Rock, amidft the conflicts between nature and grace, the mind would often be overwhelmed, and make the forrowful conclufion, " there is no hope." Ah this Rock ! how fafe a refidence is it ! and methinks its obfcurity from the worldly wife, and the felfifh mind, adds greatly to its fafety. I feldom get to it but by combat, which fhews that my enemies are lively; and though it is fometimes my lot, in the crofs, to fet before others their inherent infirmities, and transformed adverfary, yet I humbly truft I fhall not, and pray that I never may, forget mine own.

12th month 1788—My heart was favoured to enter a little into thy affecting account of dear M. G's. deceafe, and your united vifit previous thereto. That valuable woman's laft days being fo memorably employed in her Mafter's fervice, (after a life of diffidence and obfcurity, compared with her religious qualifications, and attachment to the caufe of truth) was a diftinguifhing mark of everlafting love and favour to her. Her clofe feems fo lively, and her fun fet in fuch brightnefs and ferenity, that it conveys fomething animating to thofe who are far behind in fitnefs, like myfelf, to count not their lives dear unto themfelves, if they alfo may fo finifh their courfe with joy. And that humble tribulated difciple L. H. appears alfo ready to rife triumphant above

above death, hell, and the grave: all that is covetous within me exerts itſelf in the proſpect of the joyous ſettlements of ſuch travailing ſouls, in undefiled manſions where there is no more change. Oh that I were but as willing to commit my ſpirit into the divine hand, during my reſidence in this poor frail tabernacle, (where there is moſt need of help) as to inherit the rewards of thoſe who, through more tribulations, more effectual waſhing, and better occupation of their gifts, enter into the joy of their Lord! Well! dear friend, fear not though thou haſt made an exchange ſo unſuited to thy natural diſpoſition in thy preſent ſtation, He who knows the ſacrifice, becauſe Himſelf prepared it, (how little ſoever thou mayeſt think due to thyſelf) will proportionably enrich thee, and preſent thee with the bleſſings of his goodneſs, and crown thee the more with that humility and ſelf-abaſedneſs which are ſo precious in His ſight. Were it not that He loved us before we loved Him, peradventure we might ſometimes think our lot a hard one, and find ſome cauſe to deſpair of His mercy, or conclude that His holy eye penetrates not into our loneſome and obſcure dwellings (however raiſed up as ſpectacles to angels and to men) neither marks the way that we take. That ſacred prerogative of the everlaſting Father, of attracting and quickening the ſoul, opening and ſhutting the heavenly treaſury, is, I do believe, the very thing which diſtracts that mind wherein patience has not had its perfect work, though it is the very thing wherein it ought to glory.

————1788—My huſband and I received thy letter of affection for us, and lamentation over thyſelf.

felf. Our minds are drawn into near fympathy with thee, and we believe that this afflictive difpenfation, is defigned for thy increafing acceptance with the Father of fpirits, who knows beft how to purify the veffels of His own houfe. Thefe, thou knoweft, are not only to be of gold, but of beaten gold, in order to fafhion them according to His good pleafure, and render them fit for the infcription of holinefs. Now, my dear friend, as thy heart's defire is to repofe thyfelf in the joys of God's falvation, endeavour to attain that holy quietude, wherein the delufions of the grand enemy are baffled, and the tribulated fpirit is ftrengthened to receive the bittereft cup with thankfgiving. We are of ourfelves very weak, and it is fometimes confiftent with infinite Wifdom, that we fhould be left to a deep fenfe thereof, that no flefh may glory in His prefence; but that the hunger, the thirft, and the humiliation of the foul, may be fully proved. Therefore marvel not, as though fome new thing had happened unto thee. It was the path which the holy Apoftle was led in, when he declared on his own, and his brethren's behalf, that they had the fentence of death in themfelves, that they fhould not truft in themfelves, but in God who raifeth the dead: and we have many inftances in our fociety in thefe parts, of upright-hearted advocates of the chriftian religion being tried with deep poverty of fpirit, and difcouragement in the profpect of the Lord's work, and of their own incapacity to perform it. We have alfo inftances of thefe humiliations tending to root them deeper in the experience of that fundamental truth, that the true believers in Chrift have received an anointing which abideth

in

in them, and need not that another ſhould teach them, but as this ſame anointing teacheth them, which is truth, and is no lie. And being thus led on to a higher degree of union and fellowſhip with the Father, and with the Son, their qualifications have increaſed to endure, for the precious feed's ſake, the watchings, the faſtings, and the deaths many, unto which, according to our meaſure, we are all, in this mixed ſtate of things, called. And when their mouths have been opened again in the congregation of the people, they have depended the more ſingly and ſimply upon divine impulſe, and the puttings forth, and ſtrengthening virtue of the Shepherd of Iſrael. Thus the exerciſed have been benefitted, and the Lord's heritage comforted. I humbly truſt, that theſe bleſſings will reſult from thy late tribulations; and that thou wilt have to ſay, hitherto the Lord (and not man) hath helped me. It is to be lamented when, for want of theſe baptiſms of ſpirit, a ſuperficial miniſtry, and activity in the church prevail; for theſe are like blaſts from the wildernefs, which, inſtead of cheriſhing, chill the hidden life, and build up in the notion, rather than in the humbling experience of true religion. It is much better to appear nothing when we are nothing; that we may be emptied and cleanſed from all ſelf-love, and learn patience and contentedneſs therewith. I ſalute thee in chriſtian love and ſympathy, and as a tribulated fellow-traveller encompaſſed with manifold infirmities, remain thy friend and ſiſter in the truth.

1ſt month 1789—My mind has often ſecretly viſited and ſympathized with thee, under the various and deep exerciſes which I do believe have fallen to thy lot, in the courſe of unerring wiſdom; but it has

has as often seemed more my busines, thus silently to feel thee under the precious influence of that love which the children of the one Almighty Father feel towards each other, than to be forward in expressing it. He who has graciously called thee out of darkness into his marvellous light, turned his hand upon thee for good, and thus far, sustained thee through many refining dispensations, will not now leave thee, when Jordan may rise high, and seem to overflow its banks; but in his own due and appointed time, which must be waited for, he will divide the waters, and discover to thee, with indisputable clearness, a way where thou hast seen none; yea, according to His promise to His own seed, He will make darkness light before thee, and crooked things straight; these things will he do unto thee, and will not forsake thee. I think I know, (if I am dipped into a right sense of thy state) that the enemy of all good is exceedingly envious against the precious life, or seed of the kingdom, which is divinely intended, through suffering, to be so brought into dominion, as to establish thee in the liberty of the children of God, whereby thy usefulness in the church, in this dark and cloudy day, will increase. Like the woman that brought forth the man-child, seen by John in the vision of light and life, thou mayst have to flee into the wilderness for preservation, because of the persecutions of the dragon, and the floods he may be permitted to pour out of his mouth. His enmity remains to be with the pure seed; and they who desire to cherish this excellent treasure, in their earthen vessels, and to live godly in Christ Jesus, must expect many of his cruel assaults, in temptations, provocations, and insinuations: but the Rock of ages

remains

remains to be their refuge, and as their tribulated fpirits endeavour to retire here, and place no confidence in the flefh, notwithftanding it may be with fore conflict they gain this fure dwelling place, they will be amply rewarded, and have, in humility of foul, to rejoice in the impregnablenefs of the defence, and to magnify the power through which all things are poffible. Whatever has a tendency to fubject and reduce the creaturely part in us, however bitter its operations may be, is gratefully to be received by the upright foul, as one of the means whereby the adoption, and inheritance of the glorious promifes of the gofpel, is attained; and one of thofe bitter things which to the truly hungry foul is fweet. Therefore, let me fay unto thee, fear not, thy God is with thee, and will work for thee, as thou art willing to have all the refiftance of thy nature to every of his holy requifitions, wrought upon and fubdued, in the day of his power. The juft are to live by faith, that faith which gives the victory, and triumphs over death, hell, and the grave. Mayft thou fight the good fight thereof; and may I be thy companion in this neceffary warfare; that fo the attacks of our grand adverfary upon fuch chriftian virtues as have been mercifully conceived in our fouls, may all be rendered fruftrate; and we abiding under the facred influence of the powerful word of patience, may often have our fpiritual eye opened to look beyond the things which are feen, to the things which are not feen; and for this joy fet before us, count not our lives dear unto ourfelves, neither love them unto death! Though my heart, as I faid in the beginning, has fecretly vifited and faluted thee, yet I had no thought of expreffing pressing so much on these solemn subjects, when I took up my pen; but only just to convince thee that thou hast in me (though I acknowledge I was restrained in thy company lately from shewing it) a sympathizing friend and sister, according to my measure. Though, dear friend, we may be led in silent travail, and as by the gates of hell and death, yet let us remember, that this is the way in which inscrutable wisdom has ever led his redeemed children in all ages.

1st month 1789—There are seasons wherein the Bridegroom of souls withdraws himself, or, as to the sensible enjoyment of his sacred soul-enriching presence, is taken away, and then the children of the bride-chamber cannot but fast and mourn; and as I do believe thou art one of these, thou must learn more and more to endure hardness, and to bear such dispensations with christian fortitude, in that hope which anchors the soul on the invisible Rock of ages. That which is seen is not hope, and therefore, remember that this is the season wherein thy confidence in almighty help, thy faith, patience, and fervent charity, are to be tried, rather than when the bridegroom is obviously with thee, when thou canst not fail to rejoice.

2d month 1789—Thy letter addressed to my husband, M. D. and myself, was very satisfactory to us; as we found thereby that the precious unity of the spirit was mercifully preserved in thy mind and ours, notwithstanding our remote situation, and our own peculiar impediments to the growth of this immortal plant. We all feel, at times, our faith to be closely tried, and this hath been the experience of those in all ages who were pressing after a city which hath foundations; the spirit of this world, and the corruptions of our own nature, with great subtilty, oppose the government of the Son of Peace in the heart, wherein the unity of the one spirit consists. These enemies of our own houses, are the great objects of the spiritual war; and as we maintain that by the aid of spiritual weapons, our faith will grow stronger by its manifold provings, and a victorious fight will at last abundantly compensate for every afflictive dispensation, and conflict of soul. Let patience then have its perfect work, that thou mayst " be perfect and entire, (as faith the Apostle) lacking nothing." Many friends here, who love you in the truth, have sympathized with you on account of your late prospect of suffering, concerning what some of you apprehend to be the law of your God; and your relief therefrom is equally rejoicing. Is it not cause of humble thankfulness, that some weak minds are spared from giving publick demonstration of their fidelity to the christian religion, at a time when, peradventure, their faith therein was not strong enough to be accompanied by such works? A query of this sort to themselves ought deeply to convince them of this renewed obligation they are under to their heavenly father, " whose eyes run to and fro in the earth, beholding the evil and the good; and that nothing short of increasing faithfulness to known duty, and watchfulness thereunto in spirit, can render them approved in the fight of so gracious a Being. We are glad to believe there are sincere-hearted men and women among you; may these be of one heart and one mind, walking " by the same rule, and minding the same thing," gathering together in the sacred Name, and

diligently

diligently waiting therein the time which infinite wifdom prefcribes, (though in ever fuch humiliation to the creature) before the people's minds are drawn to outward teftimonies. Oh ftrengthen one another in this holy exercife! It is effential for gofpel minifters to experience; that therein the fpirits may be tried, every transformation of the enemy judged down, and the fuffering feed of the kingdom only exalted. If this reduction of felf, and all felfifh working, were the object of your ftrong and feeble members, your affemblies would be folemn, your feeding would be upon the bread of life, and your fouls would worfhip and adore the divine Prefence, which delights to dwell in you, and among you. Thy account of the young people's faithfulnefs was acceptable; and, with thee, " I wifh it may be a fincere ftep towards virtue." Hearing of the two marriages likely to be fo agreeably accomplifhed, is alfo pleafant; and I hope that the reflection will be laftingly comfortable to the parties when their minds are growing under the influence of heavenly dew, and in obedience to the crofs of Chrift.

2d month 1789—If you fully knew the ftate of our minds, and how clofely they have been occupied fince our parting from you, I am ready to conclude, that fometimes you could hardly have refrained from dropping us a word in feafon. Perhaps it is felf-love which directs to this vein of confolation; an hunger after fenfible enjoyments, which generally manifefts itfelf to be infatiable, and the feeding of which feldom ftrengthens the root and ground of true chriftian fellowfhip. It has been our lot, and I doubt not but it has been yours, fince we faw each other, to pafs through trials inward and outward; wherein nothing short of the Arm of Omnipotence could profitably sustain and bring through: O! that our faith may be strengthened in it; that as our race will soon be run, we may, during its humiliating course, invariably pursue the one thing needful. Then will our steps, amidst the briers and thorns of this world, and all the chilling blasts of its spirit, be rewarded in the riches of the mercy of Him who trod the path before us. I remember the unity we were favoured to feel in our little services, and the uninterrupted harmony of our connection as companions; and these things have left upon my mind impressions too sacred to be lost in forgetfulness. Instead of their dying, I think of late they have been replenished with a degree of the best life: and as we endeavour simply to move in the lots assigned us by our all-wise Creator, however distant our outward dwellings may be, the immortal part will not fail to assimilate us in the precious covenant of love and life. It is a wonderful union which christian travellers enjoy, when they meet one another in spirit. Though their communications be mournful, yet understanding each other's language, and being companions, they are encouraged and strengthened thereby, to proceed on their journey towards a city which hath foundations, whose peace is everlasting.

3d month 1789—The precious evidence of peace, is one of those rare and valuable flowers, that seem in danger of withering with too much display in the open air. The shade, we are sometimes favoured to retire to, when the world may judge us in its own fluctuating spirit: " when thou prayest, enter into the closet and shut the door," &c.

3d

3d month 1789—It is a very low time with me. There are few I believe that need such baptisms as myself, and therefore it is, no doubt, best for me to bear them as quietly and profitably as I can. He with whom we have to do, afflicts not willingly the children of men, and therefore, if our afflictions are not of our own bringing on, they are a part of the work of that righteousness which produces quietness and assurance for ever. We must not expect to pass through the present vale of tears, without bearing our proportion of suffering, for the body's sake, and those abasements which are so necessary for our own preservation in the truth. Wherefore let us be patient, and establish our hearts, that so we may not be moved or turned away from the hope of the gospel, but through all, stand in the faith that the day of the Lord draweth nigh.——— We often find, to the mortification of the creature, that times and seasons are not at our command, nor even for us always to know : it is the divine prerogative to dispose of them ; and the human mind is taught thereby its own dependancy, and driven in quest of that faith by which the just live. Faith removes our doubts, anchors the soul when upon the fluctuating waters of uncertainty, " is the very substance of things hoped for, and the evidence of things not seen." Fight, my beloved friend, the good fight thereof, and give no place to the accuser ; so will thy possession of this heavenly gift increase, thy offerings will continue to be acceptable, and victory become sealed to thee when the combat is over.

3d month 1789—If thou and I are really favoured with the precious evidence of gospel union, let us be tenacious of its purity. On thy part, do not fail to " exhort and reprove with all authority," even when the deceitfulnefs of my heart judges itfelf better than it is. What fignifies that part in us which cannot inherit the kingdom ? I cannot fay that I am light hearted, though it is comfortable to believe thy burdens decreafe ; nor do I wifh to caft a gloom upon, and cloud that fky, which, after much tempeftuous weather, and a frequent oppreffive atmofphere, may attract the ftrengthened fight to greater heights of clearnefs and purity, than, in fome paft feafons, the nature of things would allow. I congratulate thee as one, not only beholding the vifion, but gradually and effectually afcending the ladder which reaches from earth to heaven ; on which, methinks, the defcending angels are fent to ftrengthen poor weary pilgrims. May I be thy companion ; not fo much for the fake of thy company, though that is truly pleafant, as for the glorious reft within the pearl gates, when the tribulated fteps to it fhall for ever ceafe. I believe I do not fo frequently write to any one on this fubject as to thyfelf; and I would not have thee think that my converfation is proportionably in heaven. Thefe profpects animate the foul ; but the difcouragements and perfecutions from that which is born of the flefh, feem as if they would drag every holy afpiration into the mire and the clay of the horrible pit.

5th month 1789—It juft occurred to me as I took up the pen, that probably there is a greater fimilarity in our exercifes, than we are generally aware of, and perhaps we are oftener dipped into fympathy one with another than we are capable of perceiving.

perceiving. Religious sympathy is I am persuaded a great mystery. The apostle sought to fill up that which remained (of his portion) of the sufferings of Christ, for the church's sake ; and may we be like minded respecting those baptisms, which introduce into a fellowship with the effectual sufferings of the Lamb, and work in us a conformity to His death ; thereby qualifying, through the power of His resurrection, to demonstrate, that they are not only for our own, but also for the church's sake. Under these dispensations, can we fail, at times, of feeling ourselves alone ? We should not be exercised according to our measures, in his tribulated path, if, in the awful moment when the crucifixion of our wills is approaching, our associates and friends stood around us with the cup of consolation ; no ! it were his enemies then who, hastening their own destruction, pierced him, and ministered the vinegar and the gall. Let us then seize the comparison for our humiliation. Christ in us can unseal the mystery, and amidst His holy leadings in the regeneration, can renew the drooping mind with the consoling language of, " fear not, greater is He that is in you, than he that is in the world." I wish that thy mind may be encouraged, without unprofitable reasoning, to labour onward in the hidden paths and pilgrimage of the Jew inward. Thou hast put thy hand to a good work, for which I do believe thou art chosen. The enemy of all good, will, as formerly, seek to destroy the immortal birth, and not fail to cast forth floods out of his mouth, and represent them to be the ministration of just condemnation. To be preserved from this attack upon thy best life, peradventure thou

thou mayeft be induced to flee into the wildernefs, where methinks I now vifit thee, and where thou wilt not be fuffered to fall; but thou wilt be fuftained with the bread which the world knows not of, and come forth in the appointed time, more and more weaned from all human dependancies.

5th month 1789—Few fources of comfort prefented at the opening of thefe mixed affemblies, and unlefs the one great fource of light and purity produces to the believers the newnefs of the fpirit, they cannot but faft; and well is it for them, when, to their fafting, they can acceptably add mourning. For my part, I have in general through the courfe of the fittings of this meeting (which are moftly gone through) felt myfelf fomething like Mary, who fat at the bleffed Mafter's fepulchre, with a language fimilar to that of " they have taken away my Lord, and I know not where they have laid Him." To thy fympathetic mind, this may be a fufficient defcription how things have gone with thy Sarah Grubb. Perhaps in the laft moment of extremity (for fometimes we are wifely tried to the laft) the joyful tidings may falute the fpiritual ear, " thy Lord is rifen, and behold he goeth before thee;" this is the crown of all true rejoicing; this is the bleffing of which the creature muft ever acknowledge itfelf unworthy. It is a knowledge which indeed puffeth not up; and were it not that Lucifer, that fallen fon of the morning, is feeking to intrude, and fometimes does intrude himfelf, and attracts the unwary mind to fome mountain of felf exaltation, peradventure the manifeftations and confolations of the Spirit, would more often, and more eminently abound among the

Lord's

Lord's visited and adopted children. " Feed me
then with food convenient for me, left I be full
and deny thee :" O desirable resignation !

5th month 1789—I was sorry to hear that thy
mind was still in so dejected a state. Causes for situations of this sort cannot always be comprehended
by us, and therefore we ought to be careful how we
conclude that they either are, or are not, in the
ordering of best Wisdom. One thing however
affords consolation to the truly contrite mind; that
all things shall work together for good to those
who love and fear God. As I do believe, thou art
one of those, and that thou sincerely desirest also to
walk acceptably before Him, learn more and more,
patiently and thankfully, to receive from His holy
hand, whatsoever He appoints or permits, as dispensations which he only can sanctify. It is a sort
of school the mind has to enter into, when sensible
of its own infirmities, it pursues the things of the
kingdom, and the knowledge how to discern them
from the mysterious workings and cogitations of
corrupt self. It has many lessons to learn, hard to
flesh and blood; and perhaps one of the most
difficult is, to think nothing too hard, nothing too
near or dear to part with, for the sake of the prize
in view. And were we thoroughly to learn it, I
believe it would clothe us with many amiable and
profitable dispositions, which murmuring Israelites
have seldom time to discover.

6th month 1789—Thou art often very near
and dear to me; and I have felt it renewedly
during the course of the exercising meetings we
have had here: for true love sometimes springs up,
and attracts our attention to some suffering object,

when we are ready to think ourselves destitute of its sacred virtue, and too much scattered in mind from its hidden track livingly to converse with it. So, my dear friend, it has often been with me since we saw each other; believing that thou hast trials peculiar to thyself, and peradventure, art too much depressed therewith. Let not any discouragement sink thee below an holy confidence, that the everlasting Arm is underneath; and that, if thou " deal thy bread to the hungry, and thy water to the thirsty soul, thy light shall break forth out of obscurity, and thy darkness become as the noon-day." Believe not the most subtil insinuation, that thy passage through life will continue thorny as it is; for it is in the deceivableness of unrighteousness that these things are suggested to us, in order to remove us from that steadfastness and hope of the gospel, in which visited minds are designed to be established.

7th month 1789—My heart and eyes have been afresh affected by a lively revival of days that are past: days of sore tribulation, when the old heavens and old earth were passing away, and a capacity unbegotten to rejoice in the discovery of the new. Yea, they were days when the battle was hot between flesh and spirit; and for want of being accustomed to the weapons of warfare, mind and body were wearied, and the vitals of both nearly overcome. When I reflect upon the kindness of infinite goodness many ways manifested to my weak state, and the ingratitude of my heart, I wonder at the long forbearance, and continued effusions of the quickening and purifying virtue of the immortal Word: I wonder at my present
back-

backwardness in the christian life; and my want of zeal in the pursuit of the one thing needful. May thy bosom friend and thyself, be so helpful and blessed to each other, as, in the sacred covenant wherein ye are bound, unitedly to stretch forth your hands, unfettered by any thing of your own, and let another bind, or gird you, even though you may be carried thereby whither ye would not. The inexpressibly near unity and affection which I felt with, and for your spirits, in our late and short junction, has left a sweet and consoling savour behind; which now, and sometimes, when a different influence would prevail, springs up as under the threshold of the door, and rises until it becomes a river, which my often tried mind measurably rejoices and swims in. Count not your lives dear unto yourselves, when called for at your hands; and when not, labour after tranquillity of soul; remembering, that, however little and poor ye may be, ye cannot, by taking ever so much thought, add one cubit to your stature. But resignation itself is a gift. Oh that ye may covet the best gifts! for it is as we have them in view, and pray for them, according to the mind of the spirit, that we receive.

8th month 1789—Thou art, dear friend, an epistle written in my heart, where I sometimes read thee, and thy mournful, humble steppings with joy; consistent with the divine command, to rejoice in his new creation, of which, in infinite mercy, thou art happily a part; having known old things to pass away, and new ones to be brought in, where the righteousness of the creature is beheld to be as filthy rags; and where the

righteousness

righteoufnefs of God, the obedience of faith, dwells. Let it dwell, and more and more abound in thy experience; for thereby thy ftrength will increafe, and nothing, in divine appointment, will be found too hard for thee to perform. In true fimplicity, to lean upon and follow the Beloved of fouls, is a wonderful prefervation from that reafoning, and vain confultation with flefh and blood, which diftracts the mind, and often caufes it to err from the faith. It is true our fpiritual guide, for wife purpofes, conceals himfelf from us, the bridegroom is taken away, and then the difciples cannot but mourn; and better it is for them that they fhould mourn, than enter into the remoteft confederacy with his enemy againft him, call in queftion His manifeftations, and doubt whether He is to us that friend, of whom He has given us in broad day light, living proofs. An unbelieving heart is a temptation moft fubtil, and often very plaufibly prefented. Beware of it, dear friend! Be not afraid to have thy foolifhnefs for Chrift's fake perfected; for his gofpel, which is the power of God unto falvation to all them that believe, is a fund of requifites for the chriftian traveller; from the babe's to the ftrong man's food, the clothing of the lilies in the heavenly garden, to the accoutrements and victorious armour of the Lamb's foldiers. Fear not therefore, though thou be a child, and feem to thyfelf that thou canft not go; for the Lord hath anointed thee, and will therefore ftrengthen thee for His work, and feed thee with food convenient for thee.

8th month 1789—You are very often remembered by me in fifterly fympathy and affection, though feldom told of it; and I truft that nothing relating

relating to my filence will be able to make different impreffions. I find it very difficult in our large family, and amidft other duties than thofe which relate to it (though but few of them comparatively fall to my lot,) to fit down and quietly converfe with my friends; and yet they come upon, or rather arreft, my mental attention, when in the very thick of cares and anxieties; fo that I hope the invifible intercourfe of kindred fpirits, is lefs dependant upon outward and vifible figns, than we fometimes imagine; and peradventure, the more we look beyond the things that are feen, to the things that are not feen, the more we then poffefs the very thing which our natures prompt us to toil for. Neverthelefs, as a fecondary confolation, it is lawful thus to commune. Your laft joint epiftle was to me a pleafant repaft, though fome of its ingredients were bitter herbs: you know fo well how, in every new difpenfation, to look to " the great firft caufe," and to wait for that fanctification of the Spirit, which caufeth all things to work together for good to them that love Him, that it feems unneceffary for me to remark upon it; an entire freedom clothes my mind refpecting you; yea, and l may add, a belief that your bittereft cups will be fweetened in the due and appointed time. To wait for that, has often been hard duty to the haftinefs of my defires. But were we not to be fo exercifed; where or how could we obtain profitable experience in the chriftian's path? how could we live by faith, when all things were accountable to us? or when arrive at the quiet and fafe harbour of pure refignation, if the ftorms of carnal reafoning were never to rife? There is a great and an

attainable

attainable purity in that ſtate of mind, which forbears to judge even in its own cauſe; which, in ſingleneſs, caſts its burden upon the Lord, and accepts every permitted tribulation and chaſtiſement, as a renewed ſeal of adoption, and evidence of our being intended to be joint heirs with Chriſt; and therefore bound and induced, by the unfailing mercies of God, to follow through all, our holy Head; and by the increaſe of his ſpirit, not to fear humbly to breathe the language of Abba Father. I look up with an emulous eye, to an experience which I generally live far ſhort of: but let us preſs forward, for we ſhall reap if we faint not.

―――You are a collection of choſen veſſels at that place. Oh ſuffer not the enemy to put in his cloven foot among you, for he mars the pureſt deſigns; and to fruſtrate the gracious intention, of the Lord's children being helpmeets to each other, is one of his moſt ſubtil attempts. When there are ſtorms at ſea, veſſels are often ſcattered, and hid one from another; perhaps all equally toſſed: but there is a voice which both winds and waves obey, and which unites them again. Have faith in it, and wait for it, and ye ſhall do well.

8th month 1789—As children of the ſame family, I believe it allowable for us to commune together at times, as we walk in the way and are ſad; for, methinks, the maſter has herein joined himſelf to us, and I truſt will gracioufly continue to do ſo, as we hold faſt our integrity, and become more and more ſkilful in lamentation. Elijah, in a time of deep revolt, thought himſelf alone, and ſaw Iſrael with an eye clouded by diſcouragement, until He who knows all things revealed to him his own

own preserved feed. In the word of eternal life only, is certainty. Well! they that feared the Lord spake often one to another: I look at thee, dear friend, as having very few to speak to who understand the Hebrew tongue; one of the characteristicks of many in this day who are called Christians is, that they are half Jew and half Ashdod; but even at this be not too sorrowful: "when father and mother forsake thee, the Lord will take thee up," and become Himself the supplier of all thy wants. Who knows but He may make thee an instrument for the turning of many to a pure language, and inducing them to call upon the sacred name, the refuge and sanctuary of the righteous; that so they may be preserved in the secret places of the Almighty, until His indignation be overpast. Be a faithful watchman; yea be willing and thankful to become the most menial in the spiritual family. This humility will, with the blessing, insure thy preservation, and at times furnish thee with that bread of eternal life, which the world knows not of.

9th month 1789—I wish we could more frequently converse upon our various concerns, believing that each of us finds them at times awfully important, and attended with their peculiar perplexities. A little company in such paths has a cheering effect, as it seldom happens, in the right ordering of things, that all are sinking under discouragements together; and therefore they can the better speak comfortably when some one or other sensibly possesses the precious gift of faith, which peradventure all are neverthelefs living by.

My head often seems dropping below water; yea,

yea, there are seasons when the billows actually pass over; and, through unutterable mercy, they do pass over, and beyond the present trials. Sowing as in tears, in the variety of ground which we find among the children, my strength gets renewed; and my soul begotten again to a lively hope, that infinite kindness will, in His own time and way, bless our feeble endeavours to prepare subjects for the kingdom of the Prince of peace. It is little we can do; but that little let us labour to perform acceptably to the Almighty Father, and leave the world to gaze upon us, and judge of us as it may: for when we take its sentiments into consideration, or put them in competition with our soul's peace, it is like that false balance which is an abomination to the Lord; whereas the just weight (an implicit attention and obedience to divine requisition) is His delight. I wish, dear friends, that your hands may be strengthened, in the faithful discharge of your duty towards the numerous family you preside in: for the more you erect the standard of truth there, the more your services in society will increase; and what is still better, the deeper your spirits will get in the undefiled consolations of the humble followers of Jesus. These are worth suffering for, and they abound in proportion to our tribulations for His sake.

9th month 1789—I am truly glad thou stands so dedicated to pour water on the hands of this sweet spirited friend; believing such a disposition, conceived in the integrity of the heart, is often acceptable to, and blessed by, the good Spirit which renews the hope of the humble, and revives the minds of the contrite ones. Let not the usual discouragements

couragements to thefe little furrenders, fo prevent thee from following on to the full performance, as to rob thee of the reward of enriching peace, and the increafe of thy experience in the work wherein thou art, beyond all doubt to my mind, rightly introduced. Having put thy hand to the plough, it is not now a day for thee to look back. " Remember Lot's wife," has often been an inftructive caution, and leffon of peculiar inftruction to my mind, when in danger of giving up my fpiritual travail, and, rather than diftinguifh myfelf from thofe to whom my fteppings appeared foolifhnefs, tempted in the bitternefs of my fpirit, to fay, " I will fpeak no more in thy name." The old heavens and the old earth will (I truft) yield thee no more of their forbidden delights; and therefore, how unwife would it be, through an imperfect obedience, to deprive thy tribulated fpirit of that undefiled rejoicing, which is peculiar to the new creation of God. I mean not, by this folicitude refpecting thee, to be the means of promoting an activity from under the renewed influence of pure wifdom, or even the premature difclofing of openings into the undoubted myfteries of the kingdom; for it is a great but neceffary attainment, to know how to keep the Lord's fecrets, and when to reveal them. But a truly refigned and humble ftate of mind is a continual facrifice, and will produce the fruit of the Spirit; fo that I wifh for thee and myfelf, that this root of the matter may be found in us; then, as fteady and uniform travellers we fhall gain ground in the new and living way; and leaving the things that are behind, fhall reach forth to thofe that are before, having

our

our eye fingle unto Jefus, who alfo took up the crofs and defpifed the fhame.

10th month 1789—I feel myfelf nearly interefted in thine and thy wife's welfare, and am pleafed with every renewed capacity to fympathize with you in fpirit, knowing, that if you dwell in that faith which overcomes the world, you muft often experience trials of it, and, for its refinement, be baptized into a fenfe of your own weaknefs ; perhaps fo much fo, as to acknowledge, with the holy Apoftle, that we have the fentence of death in ourfelves, that we fhould not truft in ourfelves, " but in God who raifeth the dead." If this is your exercife, be encouraged to faithfulnefs herein. There are many who willingly cry, hofanna to him who cometh in the name of the Lord, but who are not bound enough in heart to the pure feed of divine light, to watch and to fuffer with it, at a time when there is no form nor comelinefs in it ; and when it feems no otherwife to operate in the foul than by making the creature abhor itfelf. Thefe take not that root in religion, and have not that holy communion or fellowfhip with the Father and with the Son, which qualifies the watchful chriftian foul undoubtedly to know when good cometh ; to rejoice in themfelves, and not in another ; yea, and to bear teftimony, in the quickening virtue of truth, that the Lord is rifen. I greatly defire thy prefervation, dear friend, believing that thou art defigned for an inftrument in the Lord's hands, to carry on his work, his great and marvellous work, among a benighted and rebellious people, and to be the means, in the little fociety thou art joined to, of drawing them, by thy example as well as precept, from the " lo here is Chrift, and lo he is there," to

the

the kingdom of heaven in themselves; and of instructing them in patient waiting for its coming. This being a part of thy office, I know thou must endure much hardness, and meet with persecution in thyself, and in others; because the enemy of all good will transform himself as into an angel of light, and try to beguile both the simple, and those who are measurably instructed in the kingdom : but take for thy example a faithful servant * of Jesus Christ, who fled as the dove to the window of the ark, and stood still in that watch. Then wilt thou be rewarded with the fulness of joy, at the coming of thy Lord, without whom thou canst do nothing; strength will be given thee faithfully to bear those christian testimonies, in which thou hast most surely believed, and also to suffer for them, if it be the Master's will. Then will the light in thee be more and more useful in the house, and the weightiness and reverence of thy spirit, excite the beloved youth also to purchase the field where the pearl lies. May I be thy companion in these exercises! my attainment in religious knowledge is small; and without frequent baptisms of spirit, and watchings unto prayer, I find even that little might soon be taken away. Let me have thy prayers and the sympathy of thy spirit, when ever the pure light teaches thee so to do. It is a comfort to us to feel thee, and some others of your little flock, in the precious covenant of love and life, wherein we desire to be remembered by you and by them.

10th month 1789—Thy peaceful return is matter of joy to me. I wonder not at it, because thou wast
strengthened

* See William Leddra's epistle in Piety Promoted.

strengthened to humble thyself as a little child; and therefore, on the wings of faith and love, art thou exalted to behold and aspire after the hope of thy calling, and even to rejoice in the renewed prospect of the land which is very far off. Ah! how often our spiritual eye wants purging and re-anointing, in order to see these things, and in our measure, to " behold the King in his beauty ;" and even when it is so prepared, wisdom, infinite wisdom, presents it at times with objects more conducive to the establishment of the mind upon the Rock alone, by leaving it so destitute of sensible enjoyment, that it loaths itself, feelingly cries out, " without thee I can do nothing," and panteth, like the hart after the water brooks, for Shiloh, the River of life. Here (in another metaphor) is Christ the Rock found, whereon, a truly religious weariness (not impatience) of this world, and the things thereof, tend to build, stablish and strengthen us. We are but sojourners here; let us then, with becoming earnestness of spirit, invariably seek a city which hath foundations; the very knowledge of whose Builder and Maker is life eternal. Thou art right, my dear friend, in believing me to be in a tried low state of mind, though thou art the first that seems to know any thing of it. I mourn over myself, not knowing why it is so with me. As to opening my mouth in our meetings, it seems as far from me as if I had never known such a concern. A painful gloomy exercise, or a wandering imagination, is what I have principally to travail through; and yet, having been acquainted with a situation of mind much more destitute than this, I dare not but consider the invisible support my soul is blessed with, as an object of reverent gratitude.

tude. Well might David (who knew the various difpenfations of the Lord) pray that His holy fpirit might not be taken from him, at the fame time that he craved the reftoration of the joys of His falvation. But let our allotment be what it may, there is fome attention to be paid to that precept of the gofpel, " to wafh and to anoint rather than to appear to men to faft." My fituation in this large family, where many have their own exercifes to pafs through, calls upon me for the practice of every chriftian virtue which I have, through unmerited mercy, been taught in the fchool of Chrift; and much complaint, or converfation about our inward ftate, except truth opens the way for it (which I truft is now the cafe,) rather decreafes than increafes our ftrength. We have a friend, blefled be the great and ever worthy name, that fticks clofer than any brother; may we then cleave to Him with full purpofe of heart ! He can renew our refignation, and abundantly prepare us to fay, " not my will, but Thine be done."

11th month 1789—I am, through infinite kindnefs, convinced that the immortality of the foul is manifeft in the fpiritual communion which, according to our meafures, we experience in thefe mortal bodies, independant of every medium originating in the invention of man; and though a very defective purity occafions with me a very defective enjoyment of it, yet I feel at times a holy refolution to hold faft that which I have of the unfpeakable gift of faith, and to accept it as an earneft of the inheritance, until, by greater degrees of light, love, and life, the redemption of the purchafed poffeflion is obtained. That thou art my companion herein, and

in

in hidden conflict for this glorious prize, I seem assured beyond a doubt; and greatly desire that the present dispensation of unerring Wisdom may, in proportion to the depths of sorrow which thou hast experienced, lead thee up, on consecrated ground, to this dignified attainment. Ah, my friend, these are humble ascendings, because they are the consequence of descending: but they are safe; therefore fear not, O daughter of Zion; lo " I am with thee, saith the Lord; be not dismayed, I am thy God; I will strengthen thee, I will help thee, yea, I will uphold thee with the right hand of my righteousness."

11th month 1789—These are low trying times with us, and particularly to my mind, feeling myself often as one that has abundant need to go down again to the potter's house; and, through divine favour, strength is at times afforded to descend in spirit to where a right and true sense of myself, and the purity of the cause I am sometimes engaged to advocate, is obtained. We often have need of the prayers, and sympathy of each others spirits, and oh! that we may be kept in that faith which gives the victory, so as to wrestle effectually for the renewed supplies of the Spirit, that none of the discouragements of our day may prevail against us. I know thou hast thy secret provings; but fear not, " greater is He that is in thee, than he that is in the world." We have champions in this land, who seem to defy little David's simplicity; but if those who go forth against such in your parts, as well as here, do it in the name of the Lord God of the armies of Israel, and with those weapons which He approves, victory will finally be on their side.

11th month 1789—I have long feen it neceffary to watch my own heart, left while I nourifhed an approved chriftian fympathy with my fellow pilgrims, and manifefted it in the line of apprehended duty, I fhould alfo draw their attention and affections to myfelf, and thereby wound the pure life by ftrengthening the root of felf love in both; and inftead of building up in the moft holy faith, and in a fingle dependance upon the one true and everlafting Lawgiver, make fuch a compofition of nature and grace, as would keep the mind in fermentation, rather than in perfect peace; rob of His honour the Captain of our falvation; and prevent thofe mighty works being done in His name which call for the finglenefs of the believing heart. I have beheld an evil like this in our camp, and its impediment to the growth of vifited minds to that ftature in Chrift, to which their peace affuredly called them. Do not miftake me; I reverence the bond of chriftian fellowfhip, and in a fenfe of the fellowfhip itfelf, with its facred confoling unction, my fpirit has often been diffolved, and fervently craved its increafe in myfelf and others: yea, I have rejoiced in the flowings of that language, which I can now feelingly adopt to thyfelf (not from partiality fo much as from a renewed concern for thy prefervation) " My longed for and joy, ftand faft in the Lord, my dearly beloved." In feafons like this, we perceive where the mixture lies; the natural part (which cannot inherit the kingdom) blending with a rightly begotten exercife and fympathy with each other. If our moft amiable qualifications, and affectionate endearments, are not fubfervient to, and fanctified by,

the

the refiner of hearts, they are encumbrances to the gofpel, and the fervices of it.

12th month 1789—Accept the expreffions of my renewed love and fympathy for, and with thee; the remembrance of thee is precious to my heart, becaufe I comfortably feel thee to be a fellow-traveller towards a city which hath foundations. We muft not expect the weather, the roads, and the difpofition of our minds for profecuting the journey, to be always pleafant; but we muft ever be careful to keep in the way; to travel when light is upon the path; and to reft in the night. We are not to conclude every thing loft which is out of fight; the moft valuable grain the earth yields, paffes through a temporary death. We are moft of us fenfelefs enough, at times, to be objects of the Apoftle's roufing addrefs, "thou fool, that which thou foweft is not quickened except it die." Human nature is fo fubject to deception, that it can fruftrate, by fome pollution or other, almoft every difpenfation, but death: therefore, be thou faithful unto that, remembering the confequent promife; " thou fhalt receive a crown of life."

12th month 1789—I affure thee my heart feels for thee a cordiality, which at times does myfelf good: for in loving thofe who love the truth, (as I believe thou doft) we unite ourfelves to a chain, the end of which, however remote from the perfection of the divine life, happily connects us with all the living, in feeking after thofe things which excel in purity and duration. One comfort that attends thofe who are fimply, and fingly preffing after the hope of their calling is, that they are not bound to tell all they feel, neither with refpect to
themfelves,

themselves, nor others; it is not essential that they should seek eminence, even in the religious world. They are happily spared the trouble of such vain objects, and find that, in solitude of spirit the Beloved of souls speaks most comfortably to them, and enriches them with most spiritual blessings, which he causes them to enjoy in heavenly places. Oh, how often I covet for myself, and my friends, that we may keep sacred to these "heavenly places," the gifts of the spirit! Nature is apt to feed upon them, to bask itself in their influence, and congratulate itself in the possession of such treasure; when alas! the gold, the precious gold, this way becomes dim, and is often unwisely tinseled over by the unsanctified affection of the creature. I wish,—that thou and I may possess that love or charity which boasteth not itself, nor is soon extinguished by the changeableness ever to be found in the face of perishing things; but may cherish in ourselves the root from whence every christian virtue springs. Then we may have rejoicing in ourselves, rather than in another, and our mental salutations herein be more frequent than our expressions of them. Thy account of dear ———is comfortable, she is a truly valuable woman, and will I hope, more and more, shew herself to be what she is. Obscurity is not always granted to those who most seek it, it is sometimes a favourable climate for the fruits of humiliation's valley; but these are in wisdom, and for the good of mankind, often exposed for those that thirst, and have nothing wherewith to buy.

12th month 1789—A week or two after our return from Dublin, A. S. departed this life. We hear

hear she had fore conflict of mind for some days, greatly fearing her future welfare: so pure did that kingdom appear, when her admired livelinefs, and faculty of pleafing ceafed; when pleafant pictures of fpiritual things were torn to pieces, and the day that burns as an oven came upon them. But this heavinefs of fpirit was a merciful difpenfation; the chaftifement yielded peaceable fruit; for before fhe finally took her leave of vifible things, fhe had to acknowledge unfailing mercies.

12th month 1789—I have feen, in my fhort life, fo much fallacy in human wifdom refpecting matrimonial connections, and fo much bleffing fhowered upon an attention to fimple uncorrupted openings, which have not at firft appeared moft plaufible, that I feem to have no faith left in any direction but that which the devoted heart finds to make for peace. In concerns of this fort, it is often very difficult for fuch to judge, becaufe prepofleffion and inclination are apt to influence our beft feelings. Natural affection bears fome refemblance of facred impulfe; and therefore, methinks that this feed, though ever fo right, muft die in the ground before it be quickened and fanctified. In fhort there are few openings, for our and the general good, which have not to pafs through this temporary death, few gifts but what are defigned to be buried in baptifm, and I wifh thee, if ever thou poffefs a female companion, to obtain her as a fruit of the new creation: that fo thou mayft reap thofe fpiritual advantages which thofe enjoy, who, through the effectual working of the grace of God, drink together into one fpirit, whether in fuffering or in rejoicing; for without

this

this experience, Zion's travellers muſt find ſuch
connections to be ſecretly burdenſome and inſipid.

1ſt month 1790—I rejoice that the Keeper of
Iſrael, who ſleeps not by day, nor ſlumbers by night,
hath thee under his providential care. This is a
ſuſtaining perſuaſion, a hope in times of trial,
which ſettles the otherwiſe toſſed mind on the con-
ſecrated ground of pure dependance: mayſt thou
never doubt it, Satan will not fail to aſſault thee,
ſometimes in roaring about thy dwelling, and ſometimes, with the ſubtilty of the prince of the air,
ſeeking to take poſſeſſion of all within thee, which
can poſſibly incline to diſobey the commands of in-
ſcrutable and infinite wiſdom. Remember he was a
liar from the beginning; and invariably oppoſeth
the exaltation of the mountain of the Lord's houſe.
He prefers any hill to this; and had rather we were
gathered to the heights of our own imaginations,
and the feat of judgment, there to condemn ourſelves, and reaſon out of doors the convictions of
truth, than that we ſhould die daily to the will of
the creature, and ſit in reverent dependance at the
feet of Him who bruiſes the ſerpent's head.

1ſt month 1790—I want thee to be encouraged,
and to put all thy confidence in the everlaſting arm.
Leave, as much as poſſible, things that are behind;
be content with the preſent emptineſs (when it is
thy portion) and neither toil nor ſpin for future
ſupplies. He that clothes the lilies and the graſs
of the field, is abundantly able and ready, in his
own time, to reveal his gracious providence, and
miniſter, from the treaſures of wiſdom and knowledge, to his flock and family, even through the
weak and fooliſh things of this world; ſo that

things which are not, (minds reduced to a fenfe of their nothingnefs) may bring to nought things which are. The chriftian's ftrength confifts in the favour and countenance of his Captain; and the obtaining of this leads the mind into that abafednefs where Satan finds himfelf difcomfited, and his head bruifed. " He fhall bruife thy heel." Little indeed is in his power, if we maintain the humility, the fimplicity, and holy dignity of a converted foul. Many words are unneceffary at prefent. The Mafter, who knows what thou canft bear, will I doubt not give thee thy meat in due feafon, waken thee morning by morning, and caufe thine ear to hear as the learned: in all things may he inftruct thee to difcretion, and preferve thee in the way whereinto he hath led thee, even that way which truly no fowl knoweth! I know, from a degree of experience, that the farther we get from a dependance upon inftrumental confolation, the more likely we are, with holy certainty, to difcover (amidft inward conflicts) the indubitable evidence of being upon the true foundation, the feal of adoption, the white ftone with the new name, &c. The very chaftifements which introduce the mind to this humbling knowledge, are (when paffed by) fweet to the new tafte, as the honey and the honey-comb.

1ft month 1790—I did not forget thee: but truly felf was at that time fo much the object and fubject of my cares and exertions, that if I could but any way keep my head above water thereby, it was more than my doubting mind could at times hope for. Ah, my dear friend, I have a heart prone to rebel againft, and live above the pure principle of truth; and becaufe thereof, my fpirit is at times

covered

covered with mourning as with a garment; and more especially, when I confider the greatnefs, and the holinefs of that Name, of which I venture to make mention in the congregation of the Lord's people. It is mercy, nothing fhort of mercy, fo marvelloufly difplayed in the choice of veflels for facred fervices in the church. " He will have mercy on whom he will have mercy:" this truth baffles human reafoning: and therefore, let thee and me covet an increafe of the increafe of God, and afk in faith for the beft gifts. Being afflicted with the impurity of ftruggling nature, let us come boldly to the throne of grace, to help us in the needful time, and to fettle our fpirits in calm acquiefcence with, and refignation to, the difpenfations of infinite wifdom; that fo, from every temptation and tribulation, our fouls may be reftored, with this immortal and unadulterated fong, " thy will be done." If we are but as the ram's horns, through which the Shepherd of Ifrael fpeaks at times to his people, (in concert with his inward and more defpifed teaching) let us be content, and fimply feek an holy conformity to, and adorning of his doctrine.

2d month 1790—It is not by might or by power, but by the fpirit of the Lord, that His work profpers, or his praife is effected; and therefore a little one may be made " a thoufand, and a fmall one a ftrong nation." Under this perfuafion, the faith is ftrengthened in the Omnipotence of the fmalleft revelation of the Lord's Arm in our little fervices, and our truft removed from the appearance of ftrength, to ftrength itfelf. The rich man cannot glory in his riches, nor the ftrong man in his ftrength, but the caufe of glorying is found to be

in.

in the righteous government and difpenfations of our Holy Head. Thy letter brought you all fo much to my mind, that it feemed as if I was with you, fharing in your concerns, and feeling in part that weight of exercife with which dependant fervants are introduced into their field of labour. Now perhaps I may congratulate you on the completion hereof, and participate in that humble rejoicing wherewith Ebenezers are fet up. I fervently defire to poffefs an increafing capacity to feel with the members of the myftical body, where-ever fcattered, or however concealed in the depths of the wildernefs from the human eye; for I am perfuaded that, as our fpirits are regulated by the prefident of this church, they will, at times, be carried beyond the bounds of obfervation, to vifit the feed in prifon.

3d month 1790—Though my heart fympathizes fo nearly and tenderly with thee and thy dear wife, as that I could mingle my tears with yours, yet I dare not utter the language of commiferation, for your late lofs of a lovely plant out of your garden; but rather of congratulation for the bleffed experience, that "the eternal God is your refuge, and that underneath are the everlafting arms." Herein I rejoice, and will rejoice that fuch unadulterated confolation is miniftered to the poor in fpirit. You have a frefh opportunity, my beloved friends, by pure refignation, to commit your fpirits, your children, and your fubftance, into divine keeping. May nothing impede the progrefs and perfection of this work, this glorious work, whereby the fong of the redeemed is learned, and qualification wrought to unite with the heavenly hoft, in proclaiming, that " worthy is the Lord God and the Lamb, to receive
riches,

riches, honour, and power, both now and for ever." A mind centred to the source of instruction, wisdom, and strength, can receive little more by such communications as these, than an outward and visible sign of that inward and spiritual grace, wherewith the soul is replenished, and wherein it finds the substance of all that is truly good. It is nevertheless an allowable accommodation to the weakness of sense, thus to commune; and having, in moments of drooping, been refreshed by thy tender sympathy and salutations, my heart is bound in christian affection to share thy griefs, and hail thee on every renewed accession to the Master's cross, and participation of his crown. Oh my friend, what nailing we take, before we are bound to it! how nature opposes that holy experience of being led as a lamb to the slaughter, and as a sheep that is dumb before its shearers. Hard as the work is, with God all things are possible; and therefore let us watch and be sober, adding to our faith virtue; that when the power is revealed by which we can do all things, we being in readiness, may advance from strength to strength, and finally appear before the Lord in Zion, among those who are fully sanctified. We are now returned from our quarterly meeting, where I trust the gospel cause did not go backward. We ought not to look for great things; we do not deserve them. And I perceive that when we are most dipped into this sense, life and immortality (being graciously in waiting) are the most sure to be brought to light. Therefore let us be humbled under the mighty hand, that we may be thus truly exalted in due time; yea, in all our provings, let us sink down into our own nothingness, and value every dispensation

sation which clothes us with it; for then, methinks, we shall learn in every thing to give thanks.

3d month 1790—Thou hast, my dear friend, of late appeared to me to be preparing to set out, according to the sacred counsel of the great Master to His disciples, without scrip or purse, or two coats, reduced to a simple dependance upon renewed supplies from the holy treasury, and learning, in a new line of service, to live by faith. Mayst thou increase in the certain knowledge, that the Lord is gracious unto such humble faithful walkers before him. I feel a confidence that it will be so, and that thy feet will grow more and more conspicuously beautiful upon the mountains; because they are, beyond all shadow of doubt, shod with the preparation of the gospel of peace, and through adorable kindness, washed for the service on which thou art now set out: therefore gird up the loins of thy mind, and hope to the end. Do not be afraid of the gloomy exercises into which thy mind may often be baptized. Remember that even the great Master, who knew without fear or doubting that he should glorify the Father, groaned in himself before he raised Lazarus from the dead. Do, I entreat thee, offer thyself up freely, and do not seek to cut thy matter shorter than is consistent with thy peace. Look forward and not backward; for if I am not mistaken, thy progress in the work whereunto thou art called, is not designed to be as slow as some thou mayest esteem thy cotemporaries; and it is as great an evil to take from the words of the prophecy of the book, as to add to them.

3d month 1790—Your many testimonies of affection for us, your repeated accounts respecting yourselves,

yourselves, and, above all, your steady increase in saving knowledge, of which we are persuaded, are frequent occasions of humble thankfulness to the Father of mercies, whose blessings, variously showered upon you and us, are worthy of reverent commemoration, and grateful inquiry, what we shall render unto him therefore. It is little, very little, that we can do for so bountiful a Shepherd; nor does He, blessed be His name, require at our hands what He has not furnished us with ability to perform: but that little, let us present at, or cast into the secret treasury, not doubting His compassionate acceptance. An humble resigned spirit is a gift which, I believe, was never refused at the altar. It is, while preserved, a continual offering, a sweet smelling sacrifice, the favour of life unto life in those that believe; it is a bulwark or fortress, where, in times of desertion, temptation and tribulation, the weary soul finds shelter, and all the armour of light against Satan's attacks and fiery darts. Now, my beloved friends, my heart feels you as companions in the christian path; and in your exercises, your discouragements and poverty of spirit, I participate; though distant in the outward, yet as the Apostle said, " present in spirit." —Be assured that the same afflictions are measurably accomplished in every true member of the mystical body. You have companions therein, and need not be told, that all these things are intended for our refinement, and increasing usefulness and service in the church militant here on earth : that when this mortal shall put on immortality, the tribulated spirit may obtain an eternal residence, in the glorious church triumphant, where all tears are wiped away: these are animating considerations, and prompt us to

endure

endure hardnefs like good foldiers of Jefus Chrift, and to receive with thankfgiving every humiliation and fpiritual baptifm. I know, dear friend, that if thou art mercifully kept quick in underftanding in the fear of the Lord, the weak, unconverted ftate of many of your members will occafion thee to go mourning on thy way, at the fame time that thou finds a neceffity to attend to that command of the great Mafter, to wafh and anoint rather than appear unto men to faft. This hidden exercife of fpirit will efpoufe thee more clofely to the heavenly bridegroom, who hath the fpirit of wifdom and underftanding, and who judges not after the fight of the eye, or the hearing of the ear. I do hope, my beloved friends, that your labours will be bleft though yourfelves think them very weak and fmall. If our treafure is but laid up in heaven, no matter how little our corrupt hearts are entrufted with the knowledge of it. Be not afraid of leaving the fheep and lambs, when the good Shepherd calls to any duty; His care is better than ours, and He can fupply all your needs, by the riches of His grace in Chrift Jefus our Lord.

4th month 1790—I am comforted in finding that your hearts are knit together like David and Jonathan's, in oppofition to every ftratagem which Satan may ufe. As I do believe the cement is compofed of materials acceptable to the penetrating eye of the great Preferver of men, fo I truft you will feel your union to be a balm through the future fteppings of chriftian and focial travel, however it may pleafe infinite Wifdom to difpofe of you, as to your outward fettlements, or journeyings in the prefent world.—Settle it in thy heart to expect
a mixture

a mixture of bitternefs in that cup of comfort, which the great Mafter may minifter to thee. No deadly forrow is in the blefling; but evil things, and mutable things, until our purification is complete, have a power over us which keeps our fpirits in a ftate of profitable groaning; and if we do but experience the fulfilling of that gracious promife, that for the cryings of the poor, and for the fighings of the needy, he will arife, let us thank him and take courage.

My beloved———'s letter came at a time more acceptable than would be prudent for me this way to defcribe. It renewed that precious participation of each other's exercifes and confolations, which I do believe originates in the Fountain of everlafting love. I look with humble admiration at that holy hand which is leading thee about, and inftructing thee; and my faith is ftrong that the Lord will keep thee as the apple of his eye, and, in his own time, make all clouds of difcouragement as the duft of his feet. Thou knoweft and thou wilt more and more know, that, for the right performance of any religious fervice, we want emptying from veffel to veffel; and when we confider how many have fuffered by an imperfect experience of this great work, we ought not to lament at any difpenfation, or change of feafons, which brings us, in the leaft degree, nearer to that ftate and ftature, for which infinite kindnefs defigns us.

5th month 1790—That meafure of converfion which is effentially neceffary, rightly to introduce us into every new line of fervice, bears a ftrong refemblance to the firft ftep of the great apoftle into the chriftian religion: a light fhone around him; such

such conviction seized his soul, that whilst he asked, "who art thou," he called him Lord; he consulted not with flesh and blood: happy resignation! which however, did not keep him out of *the street called Strait*, neither for a time were his eyes suffered to be opened.—We have each our peculiar exercises, as we have each our peculiar infirmities; all which, through sanctification and purification of heart, may help us forward to a final settlement in that glorious city, whose inhabitants no more say they are sick.—I hope thou wilt not draw back from any opening to duty, which thou mayest be favoured with. The right time, and our time, do not always agree; but we ought invariably to bear testimony to the first, by the subordination of the latter. "Wisdom is justified of her children;" and therefore do not reason unprofitably upon thy duty.

7th month 1790—It was pleasant to be informed of thy safe landing in Ireland. I hope thy drooping mind has been refreshed, not only by the strengthening sympathy of fellow-travellers, but also by the composing, and yet animating virtue of Shiloh's streams, and that thou hast been enabled to lie down beside these waters which run softly. Thou knowest that when we can get here, it is like getting home, to a joy with which no stranger can intermeddle. The increase of such a capacity is what my soul longs for; that in this exercising journey before us, wherein creaturely efforts can do little for the promotion of the great cause, the pure seed may, from place to place, be at least secretly visited; and that whether effects may be seen or not

not, the work, in divine condefcenfion, may be hid with the Lord.

11th month 1790—The comfortable evidence thou mentions, of there being a power ftrong in proportion to thy weaknefs, ftrengthens my declining faith, and encourages me to lay hold on the fame bleffed hope, becaufe it met the witnefs in my heart that fays it is the truth. A confidence fo precious is not to be caft away; it is defigned for an anchor to the poor veffel, fecretly attaching it to eternal help, when, in divine wifdom, its courfe is reftrained on the waters of affliction and uncertainty. Then let me fay, caft not away thy confidence, for therein is great recompenfe of reward. We are often tempted to do this; fometimes, in the multitude of objects, forgetting the great fource of good, and means of prefervation; and at others, looking fo timidly and doubtfully at them, as to lofe our intereft in both. May thou and I, watch againft thefe and other evils; and pray, according to our meafur of faith, that that fpirit may prefide in us, which can rejoice in God alone, though none elfe regard it, or can own its life.

————1790—I cannot know that thy fufferings and temptations are fo deep, without feeling an affectionate, fifterly folicitude about thee, at the fame time that I perceive with joy thy fteppings are in the footfteps of the flock. But with the greateft cordiality do I find, that thou canft not draw thy confolations from even the fprings of fellow difciples. The well's mouth being clofed in thyfelf, thou fitteft mourning at it, and every drop of water brought thee from thy neighbour's overflowings, ferves but to augment thy lamentation; for thy thirft cannot be fatisfied with that, which is not the " well in thee fpringing up into everlafting life." I am glad thou art refolved to be patient; if thou holdeft thy integrity herein, and letteft patience have its perfect work, thou wilt find more perfection in this difpenfation than is manifeft at prefent, and moreover thou wilt lack nothing. Then be of good cheer, my beloved friend : believe in the fatherly care and compaffion of Him who is the Lord Almighty; and doubt not that all His chaftifements are the more indelibly to fix the feal of adoption upon thy fpirit; whereby thy qualifications may be ftrengthened to cry Abba, Father! in proportion to the increafe of thy fervices in and for His Name. Were not the experiences of the Lord's dealings to us as individuals fomewhat deep, there might be more danger of ftumbling in the paths of judgment, when, for the welfare of others, we may be turned into them; and marvel not if, after this baptifm with which thou art baptized, the Mafter, who is rich in mercy, and infcrutable in wifdom, calls upon thee for fome new act of dedication. Until then, fight the good fight of faith ; now is thy time to prove the fufficiency of thy ever victorious Captain. Refolve if thou perifh, it fhall be at His footftool. Let not out thine ear to the accufer of the brethren, believe him not, even refpecting thyfelf, when he tells thee that thou art not what thy friends take thee to be. But if the Father chaftens, and draws thee from man's judgment, by fhewing thee the fallibility thereof, cleave to him as to thy beft friend. Experience will convince thee, that whoever ftand

through

through the storms attendant on their pilgrimage for the honour of the great Name, must learn to pass through good report, as well as evil report; with an equal neglect of it as such; for the weapons of their warfare being spiritual, they must not fail to apply them to the spiritual wickedness in the high, but secret places of their own hearts. Self is apt to feed upon the manifest unity of our friends, and to draw our attention from the pure and strengthening virtue which supplieth every joint of the mystical body; rendering us less capable, than we otherwise should be, of eating that bread which the world knows not of.

—————— I have a comfortable hope respecting thy prosperity and preservation, and already rejoice in the symptoms thereof. That one especially, of the passing away of the old heavens and the old earth, is so favourable, that I trust thou wilt fully resign thyself thereto, that so they may be remembered no more, nor come into, to way-lay thy mind in any of its preparations for gospel service. Yes, my heart can feel with thee, in thy frequent incapacity to rejoice in even the purest friendship, or to support it by the effusions of natural affection. Oh that all whose hearts and tongues have been animated with the live coal from the sacred Altar, had fully passed through dispensations of this sort; methinks the priesthood, and other living members in the church, would be more burning and shining lights, have more true christian sympathy for each other, and oftener meet one another in the field of spiritual exercise, or, in other words, enjoy the true communion of saints. We miss many of the excellent promises of the gospel, for want of coming to, and dwelling in, that humbled fituation of mind to which they belong. How many fit in judgment, who never fufficiently, by virtue of the meeknefs of their fpirits, were guided in the midft of its paths! How often do we hear attempts to fing the praife of Zion's King, by thofe whofe general conduct bears no teftimony to a fervent travail of their fpirits after deliverance from the enemies of their own houfes, and who confequently cannot ftand upon its banks. Though I often fear it is the cafe, I dread to fettle down (becaufe it fometimes appears to be my duty to fhew unto others their tranfgreffions) as if the work was done at home, and my foul's adverfary overcome; when, peradventure, his force is redoubled, and his artifice herein more than ever effectual. " Watch and pray," fweetly occurs to my mind, and for this good end, " that ye enter not into temptation;" that the veffel may be preferved in fanctification and honour, and that the immortal birth may have its habitation in a purified temple. Then may the new heavens, the new earth, and the holy mountain, in times of refrefhing, break forth into finging, becaufe the Lord comforts his people, and hath, mercy upon his afflicted.

F I N I S.

www.ingramcontent.com/pod-product-compliance
Lightning Source LLC
Chambersburg PA
CBHW030545300426
44111CB00009B/864